Domestic Violence on Trial

Daniel Jay Sonkin, Ph.D., is a psychotherapist, consultant, and author living in Sausalito, California. Since 1977 he has been developing effective treatment approaches that help men stop using physical, sexual, property, and psychological violence in their personal relationships. In 1980 he became the Offender Services Coordinator for the San Francisco Family Violence Project, developing treatment services for abusers. In addition to his private practice, Dr. Sonkin consults with attorneys on criminal and civil cases involving domestic violence, conducts clinical workshops across the country for persons working with male batterers, and consults with criminal justice and community programs developing services for men who batter women. He is the co-author of the book *The Male Batterer: A Treatment Approach*, and co-author of the first book written for men who batter, *Learning to Live without Violence: A Handbook for Men*. He is currently writing a book for men victimized as children and an anger control manual for adolescents.

DOMESTIC VIOLENCE ON TRIAL

PSYCHOLOGICAL AND LEGAL DIMENSIONS OF FAMILY VIOLENCE

Daniel Jay Sonkin, Ph.D.
Editor

SPRINGER PUBLISHING COMPANY
New York

Springer Publishing Company, Inc.
536 Broadway
New York, NY 10012

87 88 89 90 91 / 5 4 3 2 1

Library of Congress Cataloging-in-Publication Data

Domestic violence on trial.

    Includes bibliographies and index.
    1.   Family violence—Law and legislation—
United States.   2.   Psychology, Forensic.
3.   Abused wives—United States—Psychology.
4.   Abused children—United States—Psychology.
I.   Sonkin, Daniel Jay.   [DNLM: 1.   Child Abuse.
2.   Family.   3.   Spouse Abuse.   4.   Violence.
HQ 809.3 D668]
KF9320.D66   1986   345.73'025   86-29841
ISBN 0-8261-5250-3   347.30525

Printed in the United States of America

Contents

Contributors

Cathy E. Bennett, M.A., is a jury and trial consultant in Houston, Texas, and is president of Cathy E. Bennett & Associates, Inc. She was one of the founders of the field of jury and trial consultation and has worked on over 400 trials. She has assisted in some of this country's most highly publicized trials, including *U.S.* v. *John DeLorean*, American Indian movement trials, and many battered women's cases, including *State* v. *Kay Sandiford* in Houston, Texas. She has assisted lawyers in jury selection, surveys, mock trials, case preparation, and other parts of the design and presentation of a case.

Angela Browne, Ph.D., is a research associate at the Family Violence Research Laboratory at the University of New Hampshire in Durham. She received her doctorate in psychology from Union Graduate School. Her dissertation was a study of domestic violence homicide. Her forthcoming book, *When Battered Women Kill,* is a study of women who have killed their abusers. She has spoken extensively on the issue of domestic violence and is currently the editor-in-chief for the journal *Violence and Victims.* This quarterly journal provides a forum for the latest developments in theory, research, policy, clinical practice, and social services in the area of interpersonal violence and victimization.

Mary Ann Douglas, Ph.D., received her doctorate in clinical psychology from the University of Utah. She is currently the chairperson of the Department of Clinical Psychology, Nova University, Ft. Lauderdale, Florida, where she also teaches and is the founder and director of the Family Violence Clinical Research Program. The program provides for clinical training, research, and direct clinical service. Her research interests include woman battering, incest, and power in intimate relationships. Her clinical practice involves the application of feminist principles to work, primarily with women in individual therapy and with couples and families.

Glenace E. Edwall, Ph.D., received her doctorate in learning and cognition from the University of Minnesota and is currently a Psy.D. candidate in clinical psychology at the University of Denver. While in Denver she worked with Lenore Walker at Walker and Associates, as well as in the Developmental Pediatrics Unit at Fitzsimons Army Medical Center. She is presently a clinical psychology intern in the University of Minnesota Hospitals Internship Consortium, working in hospital pediatric psychology and at Human Services, Inc. of Washington County, Minnesota.

William Fazio, J.D., graduated from the University of San Francisco in 1974. He is currently a deputy district attorney for the San Francisco District Attorney's Office. He served for 4 years as a trial attorney for the sexual assault unit and has been a trial attorney for the homicide division since 1980. Dr. Fazio is a member of the American Board of Criminal Trial Attorneys. He is committed to the aggressive prosecution of offenders of domestic violence and sexual assault.

Marie M. Fortune, M. Div., grew up in North Carolina, where she received her undergraduate degree from Duke University. She received her seminary training at Yale Divinity School and was ordained a minister in the United Church of Christ. She is an educator and minister working in a specialized, community-based ministry. She has served in a local parish and is the founding director of the Center for the Prevention of Sexual and Domestic Violence, a national resource for religious communities located in Seattle, Washington. Rev. Fortune is the author of *Sexual Violence: The Unmentionable Sin* (1983) and *Sexual Abuse Prevention: A Study for Teenagers* (1984), and co-author with Denise Hormann of *Family Violence: A Workshop Manual for Clergy and Other Service Providers* (1980).

Anne L. Ganley, Ph.D., is a staff psychologist at American Lake Veterans Administration Medical Center in Tacoma, Washington. She designed and implemented both the residential (1978) and the nonresidential (1978–present) counseling programs for male batterers and battered women through the Department of Psychology and Psychiatry. In addition to her private practice in Seattle, Dr. Ganley is a consultant and trainer in developing intervention programs for domestic violence in both civilian and military communities throughout the U.S. and Canada. She is the author of numerous publications about domestic violence, including the manual *Court Mandated Counseling for Men Who Batter,* available from the Center for Women Policy Studies in Washington, D.C. Dr. Ganley is a member of the National Coalition Against Domestic Violence.

Gail S. Goodman, Ph.D., is assistant professor and director of the Dual Degree Program in Psychology and Law at the University of Denver. Her research interests include children as witnesses and jurors' reactions to children's testimony. She has written extensively on these topics and received an award from the American Bar Association for her work. She frequently serves as a consultant and expert witness in legal cases involving child witnesses. Dr. Goodman received her doctorate from the University of California, Los Angeles, in developmental psychology.

Robert Hirschhorn, J.D., is an attorney-at-law in Houston, Texas. He is a member of the National Association of Criminal Defense Lawyers, the Texas Criminal Defense Lawyers Association, and the First Amendment Lawyers Association. He has been involved in many high-profile cases, such as the *Brilab* case in Texas, and has assisted in many battered women cases. Mr. Hirschhorn has extensive training as a trial lawyer and additionally has focused on the communication elements of a case.

Del Martin is the author of *Battered Wives*, a book that served as a catalyst for feminist organizing. She is the co-founder of La Casa de las Madres, the refuge for battered women and their children in San Francisco. She served on the Coalition for Justice for Battered Women, which was instrumental in developing the written protocol for the San Francisco criminal justice system that was the basis for a 1984 bill making police training on domestic violence uniform throughout the state of California. Ms. Martin was appointed by Govenor Jerry Brown to the California Commission on Crime Control and Violence Prevention, which was mandated by the legislature to conduct a 3-year study of the root causes of violence in our society. Her interest expanded to violence prevention, as she came to believe that the roots of violence are in the home as the basic unit of patriarchy. She is also the co-author of *The Male Batterer: A Treatment Approach* and *Lesbian/Woman*.

Mary McNeill, J.D., is a graduate of Hasting College of Law in San Francisco, California. Her work in the field of domestic violence began as the coordinator of the Victim Services Unit of the Family Violence Project of the San Francisco District Attorney's Office. Following her direct advocacy work on behalf of battering victims, she served as curriculum development specialist for the project, drafting model training courses for use in law enforcement training nationwide. For the past four years she has trained all levels of officers at the San Francisco Police Academy in proper response techniques for domestic violence cases. Ms. McNeill is currently practicing law in San Francisco, and she continues to conduct training on domestic violence intervention for law enforcement and social service personnel.

New Haven Shelter for Battered Women is a private, nonprofit organization that strives to end domestic violence and free all women and children from the threat or reality of abuse. Serving the Greater New Haven, Connecticut, area, this program offers an emergency shelter for battered women and their children; a 24-hour hotline for support, crisis intervention, information, and referral; group and individual counseling for women and children; advocacy through advice on housing, employment, welfare, parenting, and legal matters; a children's advocacy program working with schools and agencies, teaching mothers and children ways to interact nonviolently, and training in assault prevention and assertiveness; and community education through school workshops, training sessions, and group presentations.

Eva Jefferson Paterson, J.D., is an attorney and assistant director of the San Francisco Lawyer's Committee for Urban Affairs. Dr. Paterson was the lead attorney for *Scott* v. *Hart.* This federal litigation challenged the arrest avoidance policy employed by police in Oakland, California, when responding to calls from battered women. Her work set the stage for other cities negotiating new policies regarding police response to family violence. She was a co-founder of A Safe Place, the first shelter for battered women in Oakland, California, and a founding member of the California Coalition Against Domestic Violence. This coalition helped lobby through the state legislature of California legislative changes that benefit battered women and their children.

Mindy S. Rosenberg, Ph.D., is assistant professor of psychology at Yale University. Her research interests include the study of children's socio-emotional development in violent families and its implications for preventive programming and social policy. She has consulted with staff from shelters for battered women and child protective services about establishing programs for children of violent families. Dr. Rosenberg received her Ph.D. in community–clinical psychology from the University of Virginia.

Lynne Bravo Rosewater, Ph.D., is a licensed psychologist in private practice in Cleveland, Ohio. She focuses on reframing roles for women and men in her work with individuals, couples, families, and groups. Dr. Rosewater is one of the founding members and the current chairperson of the National Feminist Therapy Institute. As a national expert on both domestic violence and the Minnesota Multiphasic Personality Inventory (MMPI) profile for battered women, Dr. Rosewater prepares personality assessments for use in court with battered women who have killed their batterers. She is co-editor of the book *Handbook of Feminist Therapy: Women's Issues in*

Psychotherapy and author of numerous chapters on feminist therapy and test interpretation.

Esta Soler, M.A., has been the executive director for the San Francisco Family Violence Project since the inception of the project in March of 1980. Under Ms. Soler's administration, the Family Violence Project has received numerous awards from both the public and private sector, including the John R. May award of the San Francisco Foundation and Governor Deukmejian's Victim Services Award for 1984. In March 1984 Ms. Soler testified as an expert at the Presidential Task Force on Family Violence. Ms. Soler chaired the Domestic Committee of the Mayor's Criminal Justice Council (1981–1984), where model criminal justice policies and procedures were adopted and promulgated. Ms. Soler is also vice-chair of the San Francisco Human Rights Commission.

Roberta K. Thyfault, J.D., graduated from the California Western School of Law in 1984. She is currently licensed to practice law in both California and Colorado. Since 1980 Dr. Thyfault has served as a trial consultant to attorneys who represent battered women involved in criminal and civil litigation, with the emphasis on women charged with homicide. She also worked with Dr. Lenore Walker as a research assistant at the Battered Women Research Center from 1979 through 1981.

Lenore E. Auerbach Walker, Ed. D., A.B.P.P., is a licensed psychologist in independent practice at Walker & Associates in Denver, Colorado. She does psychological assessments and provides psychotherapy in a general practice with a specialization in women and children who have been victims of men's violent behavior. She often testifies in courts around the country, documenting psychological injury and speaking on behalf of battered women who kill their abusers. Dr. Walker previously authored *The Battered Woman* (1979) and *The Battered Woman Syndrome* (1984), co-authored *The Male Batterer: A Treatment Approach* (1985), edited *Women and Mental Health Policy* (1984), and co-edited the *Handbook of Feminist Therapy* (1985). She is a frequent contributor of book chapters and professional journal articles and speaks nationally to groups who work with women victims/survivors of violence. She is presently working on two books, an edited volume on child sexual abuse and one tentatively titled *Getting It All: Women in the Eighties*.

Foreword

Eva Jefferson Paterson

ACT I: THE CRIME

Time: 2 A.M., early Sunday morning, 1975
Place: The home of Manywomen
Participants: Manywomen, Manymen, two police officers

P.O. 1:	Calm down, calm down, tell us what happened.
MANYWOMEN:	We got into a fight and he beat me. Arrest him!
MANYMEN:	I only slapped her.
P.O. 2:	Look, this is a civil matter, we can't help you. You'll have to get a lawyer.
MANYWOMEN:	But he hit me, I'm bleeding!
MANYMEN:	Look, officers, we were arguing about her spending too much money. It got out of hand but everything is under control now.
P.O. 1 (to partner):	Look, we got several calls backed up. Let's go. There's nothing we can do here.
MANYWOMEN:	Can't I make a citizen's arrest?
P.O. 2:	If you do that he will just be released in a few hours. You two are just going have to get along better. Maybe you can go to marriage counseling.
P.O. 1:	If we have to come back here again, we will arrest you both. We have to go.

In 1975 I was a legal services attorney in East Oakland, California. As a child of the 1960s who had just graduated from law school, I was eager to use my legal skills as an attorney through the use of class action litigation aimed at effecting social, political, and economic change for previously under-represented individuals. From literally the first day I began to see clients, I encountered the type of situation described above, whereby women who had been battered by their husbands, former husbands, boyfriends, or former boyfriends were not receiving adequate police assistance. Since all of my clients were black, my initial reaction was that the Oakland Police Department was failing to protect my clients because of their race. I assumed that if my clients were white women they would be protected. I later discovered that the police failed to protect all women, no matter what their race.

This failure to protect seemed to be a clear violation of the constitutionally guaranteed right to equal protection of the laws. Legal research into the possibility of bringing a class action suit on behalf of a class of black women began.

ACT II: THE RESPONSE

At the time the only people interested in such a suit were women law students. Many of those consulted about the litigation were sympathetic to the problem but felt that such an action to ameliorate the failure to protect women would be impossible. I was urged to pursue other litigation. As a black woman who was still awaiting the results of the bar examination and as an affirmative action admittee to Boalt Hall, the School of Law at the University of California–Berkeley, my confidence level was not high and I often had second thoughts about the wisdom of pursuing the lawsuit. Fortunately, as is often the case when one is on to something that is essentially the right course of action, assistance and support were forthcoming from the many dedicated feminist women who were concerned about battered women. This lawsuit coincided with the rebirth of the modern day battered women's movement.

The lawsuit ultimately resulted in a negotiated settlement that committed the Oakland Police Department to treating domestic violence as a crime and required officers to make arrests when probable cause to make such an arrest existed. Although the lawsuit was an exhausting experience, it resulted in the greater solidarity of women advocating for victims of family violence.

This lawsuit taught us much about this issue. Fortunately, what we learned is exactly what this book is all about. Many of the concepts you are about to read about were extremely helpful in convincing the judge and the Oakland Police Department that change was necessary. Many of the contributors to the book encouraged the litigation team to fight on, submitted declarations to the court that helped us win a critical victory, helped us develop the 10 principles that ultimately were our opening proposals to the Oakland Police Department, and helped us monitor the enforcement of the terms of the settlement.

In 1979 a number of the women who were involved with the litigation and others working with the battered women's movement formed the Coalition for Justice for Battered Women. After meeting with the newly elected mayor of San Francisco and the Police Chief, the group began negotiations with the San Francisco Police Department on St. Valentine's Day of 1980. Eight months later the department agreed to change its policy. The group then began to pressure the San Francisco District Attorney's Office for a more aggressive response to domestic violence cases. Through these efforts changes in policy have been effected and today more women are able to find relief through the courts.

Neither I nor the other contributors will be satisfied if you merely view this book as an explanation of the phenomenon of domestic violence. Those working on this issue have learned that society in general is to a large extent responsible for allowing women to be beaten. For as long as we continue to look the other way and to tolerate the type of violence that results in a woman being beaten once every 18 seconds, women will be maimed and critically injured both physically and psychologically. Therefore, we implore you to become actively involved in combating this problem. Your professional expertise and personal compassion are urgently needed if we are to eliminate domestic violence.

Domestic Violence on Trial describes the connection between mental health and the courts. We now know that an aggressive criminal justice response to family violence is a necessary step to solving this problem. The courts have not been effective in protecting battered women in the past because the criminal justice system is totally reflective of society's attitudes as to what constitutes a crime. If society at large does not believe that domestic violence is criminal activity and if we as a group believe that such conduct is private and does not require the intervention of the state, then the criminal justice system will reflect this attitude. Police officers will not arrest; district attorneys will not prosecute; juries will not convict; judges will not sentence batterers. Although I initially believed that the police were the villains, I soon changed that narrow view and have came to the conclusion that when society changes the entire criminal justice system will also change. This view has been reinforced by the enormous changes that I have witnessed over the past 10 years—changes that are in large part a product of the work of the battered women's movement.

Shelters for battered women and counseling for victims, children, and perpetrators are also critical to solving the problem. One way to helping battered women is through empowerment. The battered women's movement and the litigation have empowered women and given them a sense that they can struggle constructively and win. This is a critical aspect of full recovery from victimization. One way of helping perpetrators stop their violence is through accountability. When an individual is unable or chooses not to control his own behavior, the courts can intervene and hold that perpetrator of violence accountable for his actions. This process is further facilitated through mental health service providers working closely with the system and offering effective treatment and education services to men who batter.

We have learned much in the past 5 years about how violence is transmitted from generation to generation. Boys who watch their fathers batter their mothers are more likely to grow up to batter their partners. Girls who grow up in violent families may grow up with a distorted idea of what it is to be a woman, low self-esteem, or a tendency to become a victim of woman battering. In this way children hold a critical key to the solution of this problem. If we can teach them how to solve problems constructively and nonviolently, they are more prepared to permanently break the cycle of family violence.

Domestic violence is a complex phenomenon that requires equally complex solutions. The authors in this book offer both concrete and theoretical perspectives on these solutions. It is our collective hope that these ideas will help you professionally and personally in dealing with the myriad of issues that constitute domestic violence. While the problem has not been solved, we have made great progress.

ACT THREE: A SUCCESS STORY

Time: 2 A.M., early Sunday morning, 1985
Place: The home of Manywomen
Participants: Manywomen, Manymen, two police officers

> P.O. 1: Sir, you are under arrest for assault and battery. We were here last week and gave you a warning. You are under arrest. We are taking you to jail.
>
> P.O. 2: Manywomen, here is a resource card that lists counseling services, legal assistance, and the name of several shelters where you can go with your children.
>
> MANYWOMEN: Thank you so much. You have been very helpful.

The beginning of a much needed change in society.

Acknowledgments

I would like to thank all of the contributors to this book, without whose dedicated efforts to ending violence in the family such a volume would not have been possible. I would also like to acknowledge the work of the San Francisco Family Violence Project for its exemplary work in this field. Through my work with this and the many domestic violence programs in the San Francisco Bay Area, I have developed a better understanding of both my personal and professional relationships to this issue. It was my work with the San Francisco Family Violence Project and Lenore Walker in particular that inspired me to edit this volume.

I would like to take this opportunity to thank Barbara Watkins and Ursula Springer of Springer Publishing Company for their commitment to this important social issue. They have maintained a high standard in their publications on this issue.

I would like to thank all the men and women who have sought my help in ending the violence in their lives. I have developed a better understanding of myself through my work with them. With each client I have learned to better appreciate that each person has a unique and special positive quality that, when nurtured, allows dreams, hopes, and aspirations to be realized. I have grown to realize that the human spirit can be both strong and fragile and, as such, must be treated with respect and caring.

I would like to thank my family and friends for their unending faith and support in who I am as a person; their belief in me has helped me believe in myself. And finally, my thanks to my partner, Mindy Rosenberg, whose love, support, and caring is felt and appreciated always. Our relationship is a daily reminder that men and women can live together in peace and harmony.

Daniel Jay Sonkin, Ph.D.
Sausalito, California

Introduction

When I first entitled this volume *Domestic Violence on Trial* (an idea I borrowed from Thyfault, 1984), I thought, "Surely, this issue is not really on trial." Since that time my optimism has been tempered by reality. Our society has yet to take the plight of battered women seriously. However, it is not only battered women who are victim and witness to this societal neglect. Women who are raped (Brownmiller, 1975; Bochnak, 1981), women who seek divorce or custody of their children (Walker, this volume), children who are physically or sexually abused (Butler, 1978; Russell, 1984), and women who find themselves defendants in criminal trials (Jones, 1980) are likewise unprotected by the laws that are theoretically there to protect every man, woman and child equally.

What is it about society that is on trial? It is the prevailing sexist attitudes that prevent individuals and institutions from effectively responding to battered women and their children (Martin, 1981, 1982). These attitudes include the belief that women's perceptions of their situations are inaccurate or inferior and that women provoke men's anger and their subsequent violence; women who are violent or assertive in other ways (e.g., seeking a divorce and custody) are labeled vindictive and evil. Traditionally defined standards (by men) of male and female "normal" and "abnormal" behaviors (Chesler, 1972) have contributed to the biased treatment women have received in the mental health practitioner's office (Masson, 1984) and in the courtroom (Armstrong, 1982).

Women who have fought back in self-defense have historically been considered "unwomanly" or "malelike." In the past a woman was not given the opportunity to claim self-defense if she killed her abuser. Women were found guilty of more serious offenses as compared to men who killed. Even when a woman was found guilty of the same offense as a man, she was and still is' in many jurisdictions given a harsher jail sentence. Articles that describe women as "getting away with murder," with such titles as "Thirteen Ways to Leave Your Lover" (*New Times,* Feb. 6, 1978) or "A

Killing Excuse" (*Time*, Nov. 28, 1977) suggest that men have a difficult time accepting that some women are venturing outside their traditional passive roles (Schneider & Jordan, 1981).

Has there been change? Yes. Since 1976 over 500 shelters for battered women have opened their doors to women and children needing protection from their assailants (Martin, 1981). The National Coalition for Battered Women, formed in 1978, has provided technical assistance, legislative lobbying, and networking for the hundreds of programs across the country addressing this issue. Federal legislation appropriated $65 million over 3 years to assist states in preventing family violence (Melling, 1984). State legislation has been developed on the response to family violence by criminal and civil courts and the police (Lerman, 1983). As a result family violence is now being addressed by law enforcement agencies as criminal behavior (San Francisco Family Violence Project, 1982) rather than "family disputes." The general public is more aware of the problem as a result of newspaper articles and television programming such as the films *The Burning Bed* and *A Right to Kill*. The increased response by the criminal justice system has also contributed to the proliferation of treatment programs for male batterers (Sonkin, Martin, & Walker, 1985). Likewise, the organizing of men against violence against women has increased the awareness of this issue among men (Adams, 1984).

These changes have all been the direct result of the battered women's movement. Male-dominated institutions, such as the criminal justice system, have been slow to change their attitudes. It has taken lawsuits and legislation to change the prevailing belief that woman victims of violence somehow cause or deserve their abuse. Although testimony regarding battered woman syndrome has been admitted as evidence in homicide and assault trials in at least 22 states, several states have not allowed such testimony (Kinsports, Bersoff, & Ennis, 1983). Laws regarding self-defense do not take sex differences into account (Walker, 1984), and as a result women are often tried on male standards of behavior. Differences in perception, strength, and decision making can significantly mitigate intent in domestic violence homicide cases (Browne, Thyfault, & Walker, this volume; Thyfault, Bennett, & Hischhorn, this volume). *Domestic Violence on Trial* raises these and other issues regarding the battered woman's or child's experience in the court.

Who should read this book? This edited volume is primarily directed toward mental health and legal professionals and paraprofessionals advocating for battered women and their children—advocating in the sense that the protection and safety of women and children from further victimization is the foremost goal in their efforts to conduct their particular business, whether it is law enforcement, psychotherapy, or legal assistance. This book is also for anyone who has contact with battered women and children or male batterers.

Given the prevalence of family violence (Straus, Gelles, & Steinmetz, 1980), any persons who have contact with the public through their particular professions would greatly benefit from reading this text.

The book is divided into four sections. Each section focuses on a particular aspect of this issue. The foreword and the prologue provide an overview and context for the following chapters. Eva Jefferson Paterson, an attorney and assistant director of the San Francisco Lawyer's Committee for Urban Affairs, was the lead attorney for *Scott* v. *Hart*. This federal litigation challenged the arrest avoidance policy employed by police in Oakland, California, when responding to calls from battered women. Her work set the stage for other cities to negotiate new policies regarding police response to family violence. She sets the frame for this book in her foreword by discussing this case and its impact on the battered women's movement and the criminal justice system.

The story of Catherine is a personal account by a victim of domestic violence. Her story describes her subsequent victimization by the criminal justice system. Although her particular story ends in success, her struggles reflect those of many women who attempt to receive a just response from the criminal justice system.

In Part One, Del Martin, who is considered the founder of the modern-day battered women's movement, discusses the historical roots of domestic violence. She explains that battering is not a recent phenomenon, but has its roots in the patriarchal system. Martin discusses this view within the context of women's experiences and vis-à-vis relationships to psychoanalytic fantasy theories as well as civil and criminal law. It is very crucial to a comprehensive understanding of family violence that professionals realize that woman battering is a social problem, not just a personal aberration inherent in a particular couple's relationship.

The San Francisco Family Violence Project has been one of the most successful programs in the country to address the problems of the criminal justice system in responding to battered women. Esta Soler, the project's executive director since its inception in 1980, writes on the elements of its success. She describes in detail how the project addressed inherent problems within the system. In addition to providing an overview of their police training and victim services unit within the district attorney's office, Soler discusses how community agencies can become involved in addressing the needed policy changes within the governmental agencies charged with the responsibility of protecting battered women and their children.

Part Two specifically addresses the battered woman. Mary Ann Douglas writes about the battered woman syndrome. Referring to this syndrome may appear to be clinicalizing the battered women, that is, making her appear to be inherently weak or disturbed. But the syndrome is intended to be a way of describing what happens to a woman who is repeatedly physically, sexually, or psychologically abused by her partner. The response or the characteristics of the syndrome would occur with anyone experiencing such abuse. Thus it is the batterer's behavior that is unusual, not the response of the victim. Women can and do recover once they separate from the abuser and/or he is forced to change his behavior via the courts.

Roberta Thyfault, Cathy Bennett, and Robert Hirschhorn discuss the admissibility of the battered woman syndrome in court and its relationship to the choosing and perceptions of jurors. Biases inherent in the criminal justice process prevent women from receiving equal treatment with men. Attorneys and expert witnesses must address these biases in order to educate effectively jurors and the bench, so that informed decisions can be rendered.

Three women who have done much for battered women accused of murder are Roberta Thyfault, Angela Browne, and Lenore Walker. Their contribution represents a productive collaboration that began long before this book was conceived. The chapter discusses specific issues the expert witness must address in cases where battered women have killed or assaulted their abuser. Also included are issues that need to be addressed by the attorney, evaluation procedures, and testimony issues and techniques. Walker's extensive experience as an expert witness, Browne's experience as a researcher in the area of domestic violence homicide, and Thyfault's experience as an attorney evaluating battered women who have killed their abusers complement each other so that the final product can offer valuable information to persons of various disciplines.

Lynne Bravo Rosewater has written extensively on the feminist interpretation of traditional psychological tests. Her study of the Minnesota Multiphasic Personality Inventory profile and battered women has greatly assisted individuals working with battered women in legal and mental health settings. Her chapter articulates the manner in which professionals may interpret a standard psychological test, such as the MMPI, in ways that help to clarify the battered woman's perception and experience of her situation. Although her evaluations are most frequently utilized by expert witnesses involved in evaluating women who have killed, all mental health professionals may benefit from utilizing such a test to enhance their ability to help the women recover from and appropriately respond to such abuse.

Part Three addresses the issues of children. Gail Goodman and Mindy Rosenberg discuss child witnesses to violence from both a psychological and legal point of view. Children are often the forgotten victims of family violence. Rosenberg, who has researched the effects on children of witnessing violence, proposes that through understanding how children perceive and incorporate their experience we can develop a better understanding of the transmission of violent behaviors. Goodman has studied children's memory regarding their witnessing or being victims of violence. Likewise, her work sheds light on the transmission of violence. Because children are often called upon to testify in criminal or civil cases involving family violence, she proposes specific issues and techniques that need to be addressed by clinicians working with children or attorneys utilizing such testimony in their cases.

Lenore Walker and Glenace Edwall address the area of child custody. While we are beginning to venture out of the Dark Ages in the criminal courts, we are still stumbling in the dark with regard to child custody in the civil courts. Through a review of the current literature on family violence, the authors attempt to redefine child abuse to include psychological abuse and the witnessing of violence. While not attempting to deny fathers the right to parent, the authors suggest that child custody decisions and arrangements must take into consideration spouse abuse and the effects on child development.

Part Four addresses the issues of the offender. Anne Ganley is one of the country's foremost authorities on treatment of the male batterer. Her treatment techniques are being utilized by most programs addressing this issue. Through her work with male offenders she has been able to incorporate feminist principles, social–psychological theory, and legal objectives to develop a treatment approach that directly addresses violent behavior, the etiology of violence, and the legal needs of society and the courts. In her chapter she discusses the rationale for court-mandated treatment, the philosophical basis of treatment and intervention techniques, and the relationship between the counselor who treats the male batterer and the court. This relationship can determine the success or failure of such treatment.

In Chapter 10 I discuss assessment and the prediction of dangerous behavior. It is necessary that all mental health service providers assess for family violence with every client they treat. The problem is too pervasive and the risk is too high for the victim and the children for the clinician not to develop such a policy. In addition, the liability is great for the counselor who either assesses dangerousness and does nothing or does not thoroughly assess for lethality.

Mary McNeill is an attorney and former victim services coordinator for the San Francisco Family Violence Project. Her chapter addresses the important issue of confidentiality and the therapist's duty to protect victims of violence. Her excellent review of the legal literature and cogent argument for the therapist's protecting victims from violence must be read by any person who has contact with battered women or children or offenders. This chapter discusses three California civil cases—*Tarasoff, Jablonski,* and *Hedlund*—in light of the issue of domestic violence. In each case a mental health professional was found liable for not acting to protect a woman from violence perpetrated by a male client. Although the issue of domestic violence was not specifically addressed by these cases, the author shows from the court records that in each case the victim and offender had a personal relationship, in two cases a specific threat was made, and in one case there was an established pattern of violence. These cases have national implications regarding the therapist's duty to protect victims of violence.

In Chapter 12 William Fazio and I discuss how the prosecutor can utilize expert testimony in cases where batterers have assaulted or killed their partners. Historically, the prosecution has been negligent in responding to this problem as a result of sex-biased attitudes and ignorance as to how to respond to this issue effectively. This chapter outlines theory and procedures for both the expert witness and the prosecutor. A case example is presented to illustrate how expert testimony may be effectively incorporated into a homicide case.

In the Epilogue Marie M. Fortune discusses justice-making for battered women. Her perspective incorporates both the philosophical and the practical. As an ordained minister in the United Church of Christ and the executive director and founder of the Center for the Prevention of Sexual and Domestic Violence in Seattle, Washington, she has spoken extensively on the issue of violence against women. Her chapter outlines the process of justice-making derived from truth-telling and holding the offender account-able to penance—the fundamental change within the batterer and society needed to truly stop violence against women and children. She also addresses the issue of responsibility or blame for violence. In the many workshops I have conducted on domestic violence, the issue of blame seems to spark the most heated debate. The person who wants to assist battered women must not adhere to her (or society's) belief that she has caused his violence. Doing so only propagates the very attitudes and myths that support male violence against women.

Domestic violence is on trial each time a battered woman or child reaches out for help to the criminal or civil justice system and has her credibility as a victim of violence questioned. Domestic violence is on trial each time a battered woman or child tries to protect herself from the abuse and is subsequently brought to trial for doing so. The issue is on trial when mental health professionals attribute a woman's staying in a violent relationship to psychopathology or do not attempt to protect victims from danger. It is on trial when medical doctors do not ask women if their injuries were a result of family violence and fail to report incidents to the police. It is on trial when attorneys do not ask a woman about the violence or do not believe her when she does has the courage to say something. Each of us has a responsibility to testify before our profession and society. The battered woman's words are not enough. We need to educate ourselves and our colleagues and present a cogent argument for an effective response to victims of violence.

No matter what your field of expertise, I and the other authors of this book hope that the evidence presented in this volume will help you make an informed decision on how to respond effectively to family violence in your professional and personal lives.

Daniel Jay Sonkin

REFERENCES

Adams, D. (1984, August). *Stages of anti-sexist awareness and change for men who batter.* Paper presented at the meeting of the American Psychological Association, Toronto, Canada.

Armstrong, G. (1982). Females under the law: "Protected" but unequal. In B.R. Price & N.J. Sokoloff (Eds.), *The criminal justice system and women: Women offenders, victims, workers.* New York: Clark Boardman Company.

Bochnak, E. (Ed.). (1981). *Women's self-defense cases: Theory and practice.* Charlottesville, VA: The Michie Company Law Publishers.

Brownmiller, S. (1975). *Against our will: Women, men and rape.* New York: Simon & Schuster.

Butler, S. (1978). *Conspiracy of silence: The trauma of incest.* San Francisco: Volcano Press.

Chesler, P. (1972). *Women and madness.* New York: Avon Books.

Jones, A. (1980). *Women who kill.* New York: Holt, Rinehart & Winston.

Kinsports, K., Bersoff, D., & Ennis, B. (1983). Brief of *Amicus Curiae.* American Psychological Association, *Hawthorne* v. *Florida,* No. AN−635.

Lerman, L.G. (1983). State legislation on domestic violence. *Response to Violence in the Family,* 6(5), 1−28.

Martin, D. (1981). *Battered wives.* San Francisco: Volcano Press.

Martin, D. (1982). Battered women: Society's problem. In B.R. Price and N.J. Sokoloff (Eds.), *The criminal justice system and women: Women offenders, victims, workers.* New York: Clark Boardman Company.

Melling, L. (1984). Federal legislation for abuse victims. *Response to Violence in the Family,* 7(2), 5−14.

Russell, D.E.H. (1984). *Sexual exploitation: Rape, child sexual abuse and workplace harassment.* Beverly Hills: Sage Publications.

San Francisco Family Violence Project. (1982). *Domestic violence is a crime.* San Francisco: Family Violence Project.

Schneider, E.M. & Jordan, S.B. (1981). Representation of women who defend themselves in response to physical or sexual assault. In E. Bochnak (Ed.), *Women's self defense cases: Theory and practice.* Charlottesville, VA: The Michie Company Law Publishers.

Sonkin, D.J., Martin, D., & Walker, L.E.A. (1985). *The male batterer: A treatment approach.* New York: Springer Publishing.

Straus, M.A., Gelles, R.J., & Steinmetz, S. (1980). *Behind closed doors: Violence in the American family.* New York: Anchor/Doubleday.

Thyfault, R. (1984). Self defense: Battered woman syndrome on trial. *California Western Law Review,* 20(3), 485−510.

Walker, L.E.A. (1984). Battered women, psychology and public policy. *American Psychologist,* 39(10), 1178−1182.

Prologue
Catherine's Experience

New Haven Project for Battered Women

My name is Catherine and I was a battered woman during my 15-year marriage. However, the story begins many years before my husband laid a hand on me. As a child, I routinely saw my father beating my mother. I vividly recall him punching her while she held my baby brother. I remember watching both my mother and brother falling onto the floor. At the time I thought he was a very scary person and I really didn't understand why he would hurt her so. I felt badly for my mother, she seemed to try so hard to do the *right* thing. I never really blamed her until I was older because I never saw any reason why he would beat her. I never considered myself abused until I was an adolescent, but I now realize that watching him hurt her as he did profoundly affected me then and still does today.

As a teenager I became the object of my father's physical violence; I was not allowed to have friends, I was physically abused for perceived disrespect, he would hit and choke me. I remember going to my junior prom with a bruise across my cheek. He dragged me down the high-school auditorium following my graduation because he believed I had a date. I once jumped out of the car because my father had told me he was going to drive off a cliff. He then spent the next few minutes trying to run me over as I looked for a place to hide. During those years, I blamed my mother for being weak for putting up with the violence. I believed then that, unlike my mother, I was too smart and too strong to marry someone who would abuse me.

When I decided to get married, I chose someone both physically and tempermentally the opposite of my father. He was tall, blond, blue-eyed, and calm. I discovered that, although he could be very critical at times and somewhat physically abusive (pushing and shoving), he didn't compare to my father. This was true at first; however, later I discovered my husband's true potential for violence.

After our children were all in school, I returned to finish my degree in philosophy. My husband expressed pride in my studies, despite increasingly frequent comments such as, "this house is a mess," and "you should have been with us on Saturday to rake the leaves." In time I realized to my deep sorrow that I had grown beyond the relationship possible in our marriage. After months of self-examination and dialogue with my husband, I filed for divorce. We had, up to this time, been unable to decide upon arrangements for separation. At one moment my husband would say that he would leave, at another that I should leave. When I offered to move, he said that he would be unable to handle the children.

On Good Friday, one month after I had filed for divorce, we got into an argument. He grabbed and threw me against the walls of the kitchen. He pulled my hair and knocked me to the floor. I was shocked. Although he had used physical violence in the past, it was never to this extreme. The next day he again grabbed my hair, choked me, and twisted my arms. I begged him to leave and tried to convince him of the need for counseling. He told me, "this is my house, these are my children, and you are my wife." He tore the divorce papers up and threw them at me.

I called my attorney and she helped me obtain a restraining order. Our case was heard on the first available court date. The judge ordered my husband to leave our house within 20 days. After our separation, my husband would frequently come into the house and on numerous occasions he would barge into the bathroom while I was taking a bath. He would declare, "I can come into the house whenever I wish." He would tell our children that I was a "bitch" and that I wanted to put him in jail. On Labor Day, he came to the house and declared that he was going to kill several of my friends and "smash my face in." I called the police and the young responding officer tried to convince me not to file a report since it would require the superintendent's notarizing it. I insisted and requested that my husband be arrested for violating the restraining order and threatening me. The officer told me that he could do nothing without corroborating witnesses. I also told the officer that my husband had a shotgun in the trunk of his car. Once again the officer told me there was nothing he could do.

At that time my husband was in counseling, and so I decided to call his therapist. I told him that I thought my husband was going to kill me or himself. The therapist said, "What do you expect if you insist on going ahead with this divorce?"

One month later, my husband confronted me in the front yard as I was returning home. I went into the house and locked the door. He kicked out the window and walked through it into the living room. I ran to the back door and attempted to unlock it. He caught up with me and knocked me to the floor and began to punch me in the face and kick me in the stomach and back. My children heard my screams and my 13-year-old came into the doorway and said, "Daddy, stop!" My husband then went into the living room and began to break all of the windows and the furniture. When he left the house I called the police and asked for an ambulance. My children were taken to my sister's house and I was taken to the hospital. At the emergency room it was found that I had a broken nose, a broken jaw, a severely sprained back, internal injuries, and all of my front teeth had been broken.

I later learned that my husband had gone to the police station, told them what he had done, and had been released after 5 minutes on a promise to appear. The next day he was advised to get some counseling and a trial date was set for sometime in the future. At the time, he was living next door to my sister, who was taking care of the children for the week I was in the hospital. I returned home with my teeth wired, my face bandaged, and bruises from my forehead to my knees.

At the trial my husband's attorney tried to get what is known in Connecticut as "accelerated rehabilitation." This would mean that after my husband would receive counseling his record would be cleared and there would be no record of his assault on me in the future. At the hearing the judge asked my husband and me to stand up together and face the bench. He said, "People like you (both of us), who have a violent home, raise children with many problems." He was blaming me for my husband's violence. My husband did receive a suspended sentence with probation.

At the divorce hearing, my husband's attorney suggested that the assault was due to my late arrival at home and that since my father had routinely assaulted my mother, perhaps I had somehow caused my husband's violence. The attorney accused me of "leaving my career as a housewife and returning to school." During the two-year period between filing for divorce and the final decree, my house went into foreclosure and my legal expenses totaled over $15,000.00. I called the welfare agency and asked for assistance but was told that because I earned more than $500.00 per month I was ineligible. Four years after I filed for divorce, I paid the last of my legal fees.

My story is unfortunately routine, not unusual. Most battered women encounter many obstacles in their struggle for safety. The persons who present the greatest barriers to this end, besides their abusers, are the "helpers" in this society. Police, attorneys, judges, and therapists need to educate themselves so as to better understand the battered woman and how their particular profession can effectively protect her from the abuser's violence. Battered women don't like to be abused. Many women, like myself, try to leave only to encounter the possessive rage of their batterers and a system that offers little or no protection. There needs to be a massive education campaign for the general public that helps people learn to disagree and solve problems without physically hurting those around them. However, when violence does erupt, victims need to know that they can take control of their own lives and that there are resources in the community available that will help them find a life outside of violence.

PART I
Women, Violence, and the Courts

The Histori
Domestic

Del M

Domestic violence* is the use of physical force by one adult member of the household against another adult member. However, this term is most frequently used as a euphemism for wife beating. Most crime reports refer to domestic homicides as "spouse killing spouse" or to less serious assaults as "domestic disturbances," focusing on the relationship without specifying the gender of the assailants and victims.

I deliberately called my book *Battered Wives* (1981) because I was convinced that the vast majority of victims of domestic violence were women and I wanted to emphasize the inequality of the marriage relationship (or its quasi-legal variant) as the context in which the violence occurs. Like Dorie Klein I have avoided the term "woman battering" because it stresses biological gender rather than the relationship that exists between victim and assailant (1982, p. 220).

Today it is commonly accepted that the number of battered wives nationwide in any given year reaches into the millions (Straus, 1978, p. 154). The FBI believes that domestic violence is the most unreported crime, probably ten times more unreported than rape (Durbin, 1974, p. 64). "Spouse abuse, woman-beating, wife battering—whatever its name, this privatized violence against women is endemic in all patriarchal cultures. . . . It exists in every class and race, every nation" (Morgan, 1984, p. 23).

---

* Domestic violence in this chapter refers to violence between adult intimates. This term is differentiated from "family violence," which includes child physical, sexual abuse and other forms of violence between family members.

David G. Gil stated:

Personal violence is usually "reactive violence" rooted in structural violence
[reflecting socially sanctioned practices] rather then initiating violence, since
experiences which inhibit a person's development will often result in stress and
frustration, and in an urge to retaliate by inflicting violence on others. . . .
Chains of violent behavior and attitudes on the personal level will, in turn, feed
back into collective attitudes which reinforce structural violence. (1978, p. 15)

Gil believes that to understand personal violence it is necessary to
"examine social policies that regulate the key-processes of human existence"
(p. 16), including the nature of dominant social values, management of
resources, the organization and distribution of work and production, and
human rights in all their existential spheres.

In placing "domestic violence on trial" we will examine the evidence in
the context Gil describes. Wife beating is a personal violence, but it is also
structural violence that has its roots in historical attitudes toward women and
in the institution of marriage. It involves the control of women by men who
have defined the parameters of women's activities and enforced a male
standard of accepted "feminine" behavior. It is the product of the patriarchal
system—of religious dogma, law, and behavioral science—that makes male
supremacy seem sacred, just, and natural. These institutions have not only
endorsed the husband's authority in the home, but also his use of physical
force to punish a disobedient wife. Furthermore, social institutions have
systematically regulated relations between the sexes to maintain a double
standard that has effectively kept wives legally, socially, emotionally, and
economically dependent on their husbands. Any solution to domestic violence requires an understanding of the social forces that have shaped the disease and polarization of the human race into the proverbial battle of the sexes.

HISTORICAL ORIGINS OF WIFE BEATING

Men have beaten their wives with impunity for centuries. The practice began
with the emergence of the first monogamous pairing relationships, according
to Frederick Engels (1884/1948). In primitive societies prior to that time,
women, as the bearers of children, were the only discernible parents and were
held in high esteem; they had great power in the clans. With the transition
to the pairing relationship, however, the "mother right" was overthrown and
replaced by the "father right." Polygamy and infidelity remained men's
privileges, but the strictest fidelity was demanded of the wife in order to
guarantee and authenticate the husband's fatherhood. The wife was relegated
to certain parts of the home, isolated, guarded, and her activities carefully
monitored to protect her husband's "honor."

Engels called this turning point in human history "the proclamation of a conflict between the sexes entirely unknown hitherto in prehistoric times" (p. 65) and *"the world-historic defeat of the female sex"* (his emphasis, p. 57). In speculating why women allowed this to happen, Engels discarded the idea of "individual sex love" and wondered if women had longed for the right to chastity or marriage with one man only as deliverance from the growing complexity of life.

Susan Brownmiller's explanation seems more likely: "Female fear of an open season on rape, and not a natural inclination toward monogamy, motherhood, and love, was probably the single causative factor in the original subjugation of women by men, the most important key to her historic dependence, her domestication by protective mating." (1975, p. 16)

Thus began the "protection racket," the greatest hoax to be perpetrated on women. They have paid—and continue to pay—dearly for the personal protection they had sought. The word family comes from the Latin word *familia*, signifying the totality of slaves belonging to a man. The slaveowner had absolute power of life and death over his wife and serfs, who *belonged* to him.

It should be noted here that "African women brought to this country in slavery and their Afro-American descendants have been subjected to premeditated sexual abuse unequal to that of any other ethnic minority group" (Wyatt, 1982, p. 20). As slaves they were part of the white man's "family." In marriage between slaves the master could separate the wife from her husband or the children from their parents; he could sell them as individuals or as a family (DeCrow, 1974, p. 411).

THE INFLUENCE OF RELIGION

Christianity and other patriarchal religions affirmed the male-dominating family structure. The husband was held responsible for his wife's behavior and was admonished to beat her when she committed a serious wrong or mortal sin, "not in rage but out of charity and concern for her soul" (Dobash & Dobash, 1979, p. 47). The beatings then were for the "protection" of the woman's soul.

A few clerics were moved to take pity and to protest the harsh cruelty inflicted upon "errant" wives. Bernard of Siena in 1427 suggested that his male parishioners treat their wives with as much mercy as they would their hens or pigs (Davis, 1971, p. 253). Abbé de Brantôme, though reluctant to argue against church doctrine, felt compelled to ask, "But however great the authority of the husband may be, what *sense* is there for him to be allowed to kill his wife?" (p. 261). A good question, since marriage had been sanctified by the church to "protect" women's sexuality and to channel it for the sole purpose of procreation.

Throughout the early writings of Christian theologians are references that denigrate women. They were not to be listened to or trusted. Women were deceptive and seductive and might lure men into committing transgressions. Because of Eve's wrongdoing they were to be eternally punished and to suffer the pain of childbirth. Women were inferior, childlike, and mindless. God endowed men with intelligence, but created women with bodies (broad hips) that made them suitable only for conjugal duties, the bearing and raising of children, and keeping house.

LEGAL RIGHTS OF HUSBANDS

The first law of marriage was proclaimed by Romulus in Rome in the 8th century B. C. (O'Faolain and Martines, 1974). The law "obliged married women, as having no other refuge, to conform themselves entirely to the temper of their husbands and the husbands to rule their wives as necessary and inseparable possessions." (p. 53) Under English common law, upon which American jurisprudence is based, William Blackstone (1765; 1966) confirmed, "By marriage the husband and wife are one person in law; that is, the very being or legal existence of the woman is suspended in marriage" (p. 442). Under the husband's "wing, protection and cover" the wife performed everything.

R. Emerson Dobash and Russell Dobash (1979) observed, "To become a wife meant to take on a special legal status that excluded the woman from the legal process . . . and elevated her husband to the position of lawmaker, judge, jury, and executioner" (p. 61).

The practice of wife beating no doubt flourished in the colonies as it had in England, but it was not legalized until 1824 when the Mississippi Supreme Court ruled that the husband could administer "moderate chastisement in cases of emergency" (Calvert, 1975, p. 88). Most states adopted laws that limited the husband's right to whip his wife to the use of a switch no bigger around than his thumb. In 1874, the North Carolina Supreme Court disavowed the husband's right to chastise his wife "under any circumstances," but went on to say, "If no permanent injury has been inflicted, nor malice, cruelty nor dangerous violence shown by the husband, it is better to draw the curtain, shut out the public gaze, and leave the parties to forget and forgive" (p. 89).

Unfortunately, it was the latter clause that became American law enforcement policy for the century that followed. Police departments across the country routinely adopted a hands-off policy, called incidents of violence domestic "spats" or "quarrels," gave such calls low priority, and discouraged arrests. Police manuals stated that an arrest might aggravate the situation or create danger to the officer due to efforts to resist arrest, that it was better to calm down the parties and mediate their "dispute." When one of the parties demanded an arrest, officers were told to explain the ramifications—loss of wages, bail procedures, court appearances, and so forth. The nonarrest policy conveys tacit approval of the husband's right to beat his wife—a right that no longer exists legally.

The most blatantly sexist police manual, issued by the training division of the Los Angeles Police Academy (still in use in 1982), while admitting in the text that it is *usually* the wife who is mistreated in family disputes, carried a series of cartoons in which the wife was the assailant. One showed her with the proverbial rolling pin poised for action; in another she held a vase with both hands over her husband, who was in a kneeling position with his hands protecting his head; a third cartoon showed the husband's face with one eye closed, a big bump on his forehead, scratches and band-aids on his cheeks and chin, saying, "Yeah; I'll sign." This police training manual makes a mockery of the entirely serious phenomenon of wife beating, which is a crime like any other crime of assault, battery, assault with a deadly weapon, attempted murder, and so forth.

In some states the family court rather than the criminal court has jurisdiction over domestic violence cases, except those that are clearly felonies involving severe injury or murder. From 1972 to 1975 the Rapid Intervention Program, a team of community health workers, acted as the "emergency room" of the New York family court to evaluate such cases and advise the court on disposition (Schlachet, 1978). RIP's orientation was geared to view the family as a unit rather than petitioner-respondent adversaries and to keep the family intact. The staff was sensitized to cultural values of various ethnic groups and "what they considered to be 'appropriate' violence or the socially accepted norm" (p. 226). At best, the family court could issue an order of protection, but police were reluctant to act upon them.

Family court, where "reconciliation" is the primary concern, serves the husband's interest by decriminalizing his behavior (Martin, 1981). Coercing a victim into reconciling and living with her batterer is not only a miscarriage of justice, but highly dangerous. Violence unchecked escalates and increases in frequency and severity. Kansas City police found that 40% of all their homicides in 1971 were due to domestic violence. "In almost 50 percent of these cases police had been summoned five or more times within a two-year period before the murder occurred" (p. 14).

THE LEGAL "STATUS" OF WIVES

For women, marriage and motherhood has been a social imperative. Unmarried or divorced women have traditionally been regarded as failures. When a woman assumed the role of wife, however, she lost her identity and status as a person. She took her husband's domicile and his name and conformed to his demands as the legal head of the household.

In an essay on "Marriage and Love" Emma Goldman (1917; 1970) wrote: "The institution of marriage makes a parasite of woman, an absolute dependent. It incapacitates her for life's struggle, annihilates her social consciousness, paralyzes her imagination, and then imposes its gracious protection, which in reality is a snare, a travesty on human character."

Although some statutory remedies have been enacted in some states during the last decade, the nonstatus of women in marriage described by Blackstone existed well into the twentieth century. A 1944 Florida Supreme Court decision (DeCrow, 1974) candidly gave substance to Goldman's assertion: "A woman's responsibilities and faculties remain intact from age of maturity until she finds her mate; whereupon incompetency seizes her and she needs protection in an extreme degree. Upon the advent of widowhood she is reinvested with all her capabilities which were dormant during marriage, only to lose them again upon remarriage" (p. 169).

Marriage is the basic mechanism by which patriarchy is maintained. The law requires the husband to support the family and holds the wife responsible for maintaining the household and caring for the children. The marriage contract is unwritten, but case law has reinforced the husband's authority and has imposed many restrictions on the wife's activities—which makes it apparent the state's overriding interest is in protecting the patriarchal family structure.

In her review of court decisions, Karen DeCrow (1974) found that many wives have been falsely led to believe that they are protected by community property laws. In common-law states the husband's earnings and investments belong solely to him and are under his control. However, in community-property states, with the notable exception of a few states that have only recently given wives rights to joint management, the husband also has sole authority over "community" property, including all of the wife's earnings. A man need not pay his wife wages when she works in his business. Legally she owes him her industry and economy without compensation. Even if the wife is the sole breadwinner, the husband still has legal control and can dissipate the family assets without her knowledge or consent. The standard of living of the family is determined by the husband, and that standard need not be commensurate to his wealth or circumstances. The wife is totally dependent upon his whim or generosity.

By early common law a husband had "sexual title" to his wife, the absolute right to have sexual intercourse with her on demand (Martin, 1982). Marriage vows were legally interpreted as the wife's continuing consent to be sexually available to her husband. If she refused him, he was within his rights to force her to submit. Laws against rape were originally conceived as property laws to protect the virginity of marriageable daughters and the sexual exclusivity of wives.

Rape statutes specifically exempted husbands. In some states, even though the woman had established her own domicile and filed for divorce, the husband was still entitled access to her home and to her person. Technically, until the final divorce decree was granted, she was still his wife. Male legislators who persistently oppose recognizing rape in marriage as a crime argue that vindictive wives may bring false charges against their husbands. The assumption is that women lie, are ruled by emotion, and are prone to exaggeration. The poor husband, after all, was "only looking for a little satisfaction."

THE "PROTECTION" OF DIVORCE AND LABOR LAWS

In the premodern world divorce from even the most tyrranical and cruel husband was not an option. Women received little education or training—nothing that would prepare them to earn a living or be independent.

During the legal reform movement of the 1880s in England (Davis, 1971), the law was changed to permit a wife who had been habitually beaten by her husband to the point of endangering her life to separate from him, but not to divorce him. Also, a law was enacted to prohibit a husband from selling his wife or daughter into prostitution, but only if she was under 16 years of age.

Until 1949 a divorce was not obtainable in South Carolina under any circumstances. Adultery was the only ground for divorce in New York until 1967. A 1963 Kentucky law granted a husband a divorce for "adultery by the wife or such lewd, lascivious behavior on her part as proves her to be unchaste, without actual proof of an act of adultery" (Kanowitz, 1969, p. 276). Also, Kentucky provided that a husband may divorce his wife for mere drunkenness alone. She, on the other hand, could only divorce him for drunkenness if he neglected his family support obligation, or if he was "*living in adultery.*" At least 14 states permitted a husband, but not a wife, a divorce upon proof of the other's "unchaste condition at the time of the marriage" (p. 96).

Though most states had laws recognizing physical cruelty as a ground for divorce, one or two beatings did not automatically qualify. The husband's violent behavior had to be a continued course of conduct over a period of time, not just an occasional incident due to the "normal stress" of marriage. In states where physical cruelty was not a ground for divorce, the wife who fled for her life could be divorced by her husband for abandonment or desertion. The same system that refused to prosecute the wife batterer also had the power to keep his marriage intact if he so desired or to grant him a divorce (and an advantageous financial settlement) if his wife dared to leave him.

Although women can obtain divorces more easily today, it usually means a substantial reduction in their standard of living or instant poverty. Alimony is rarely awarded unless the couple has been married for a long time, the woman has no means of support, and the husband can afford it. The U.S. Census Bureau reported that, of the more than 4 million women who had been awarded child support in 1981, only 46.7 percent received the full amount, 25.1 percent received partial payment, and 28.4 percent got nothing. Even when the payments are made, they are usually minimal; they rarely begin to meet expenses.

Some wives agree to unfair settlements of community property under duress or fear they will lose custody of the children. They are more concerned with getting away from the violence and terminating the marriage than haggling over financial details.

Once a divorce is granted and custody awarded, however, the battered wife often learns that she has traded one set of impossible circumstances for another. She may be restricted in where she may live to ensure the availability of the children for the father's visitations. Motions to prohibit visitation by violent fathers were denied by judges who felt that payment of child support entitled the father to see his children. However, these visits can, and often do, precipitate further violence. Some ex-husbands also harass and threaten their former wives at work, where in some instances shootings have occurred. The batterer's extreme possessiveness and violent response patterns do not cease abruptly just because a divorce has been granted.

Women who are single heads of households are disadvantaged in the job market. Women's work has been clustered in low-paying jobs. Labor laws, designed to "protect" women, limited the hours they could work or the weight they could lift, effectively denying them eligibility for overtime pay, promotions, and raises. The cost of child care did not leave enough money to cover other basic expenses. Many fared better financially by joining the welfare rolls.

The U.S. Commission on Civil Rights report released in 1983 revealed that female-headed households in 1981 had a poverty rate of 68 percent for blacks, 67 percent for Hispanics, and 43 percent for white women. Of those with preschool children, 84 percent were on welfare. Up to one-third of the women on welfare did work, but were unable to earn enough to support their families. Working women on the average earned 59 cents to a man's dollar. For women of color the average was considerably lower: 55 cents for black women and 50 cents for Hispanic women. The median income for mother-only families was $8,653; for black mothers it was $6,565, and for Hispanic mothers only $5,934. Women of color are at the bottom of the wage scale because they are subject to racial discrimination *and* sex discrimination.

The economic subordination of women in our society is a strong factor in keeping battered wives trapped in violent homes. Without employment training or experience, without pay equity for people of all races, without affordable housing and child care, many will continue to be victimized.

"SCIENCE" AND FEMALE MASOCHISM

At the turn of the century, when husbands lost the legal right to chastise their wives, a new "science" came along to fill the void. The cultural bias of masculine supremacy was reinforced by psychoanalytic theories that reflect historical attitudes of women's anatomical and psychological inferiority. Of particular significance is Sigmund Freud's "seduction" theory, his conclusion that masochism is uniquely "feminine," and the ways in which these theories became imperatives in the psychology of women.

In 1896 Freud presented a paper on "The Etiology of Hysteria" in which he stated that accounts of sexual abuse by fathers appeared frequently among his female patients. He suggested that childhood sexual trauma had a damaging effect on the later lives of its victims. He spoke of the balance of power between the adult's authority and the right to punish and the child's helplessness and lack of control when prematurely aroused sexually. The genuineness of the distress his patients felt and the great reluctance they exhibited in recalling childhood sexual scenes convinced Freud of their reality (Masson, 1984). His paper, however, received an icy reception from his male colleagues. In a letter to his friend Wilhelm Fleiss, Freud complained that "the word has been given out to abandon me, and a void is forming around me." (p. 36). In 1905 he made a public retraction: "I was at last obliged to recognize that these scenes of seduction had never taken place, and that they were only fantasies which my patients made up."

The abandonment of the seduction theory paved the way for the birth of psychoanalysis, based on the discovery of infantile sexual fantasies and the Oedipal period in psychosexual development. Freud later determined that the mother institutes a young girl's first genital sensations when she bathes and attends to her toilet training. "The fact that the mother thus unavoidably initiates the child into the phallic phase is, I think, the reason why, in phantasies of later years, the father so regularly appears as the sexual seducer. When the girl turns away from her mother, she also makes over to her father her introduction into sexual life" (Strouse, 1974, pp. 50–51).

Freud's abandonment of the seduction theory was "not for theoretical or clinical reasons but for complex ones that had nothing to do with science" (Masson, p. 59). What it did, however, was to trivialize accounts of childhood beatings and sexual seductions as figments of imagination in which the child expresses her hostility toward parental authority. Oedipal fathers were thus vindicated. In later psychoanalytic theory the "seduced" child became the seducer, and victims of wife abuse were seen as partners in provocation and punishment to gratify their masochistic needs.

In a lecture on "Femininity" Freud stated: "The suppression of women's aggressiveness which is prescribed for them constitutionally and imposed on them socially favours the development of masochistic impulses, which succeed, as we know, in binding erotically the destructive trends which have been diverted inwards. Thus, masochism, as people say, is truly feminine" (Strouse, p. 76).

Psychological concepts of femininity stem from culturally prescribed gender roles and male values that are based on the view that women are inferior opposites of men. To be feminine was to be submissive, passive, dependent, nonrational, emotional, impulsive, frivolous, sentimental, tender, gentle, home-loving, self-sacrificing, and, of course, masochistic. The woman who adopted these characteristics as her own was considered "normal." If she had difficulty in accepting her "femininity" and showed signs of discontent with her role, she suffered "penis-envy" and a "masculine complex" that could be overcome by having a boy child.

Karen Horney, in 1926, first raised the question of "how far has the evolution of women, as depicted by us today in analysis, been measured by masculine standards and how therefore does this picture fail to present quite accurately the real nature of woman" (Strouse, p. 173). She observed that analysts explain penis-envy "by its biological relations and not by social factors" and "the woman's sense of being at a disadvantage socially as the rationalization of her penis-envy" (p. 176). She also pointed out, "In actual fact a girl is exposed from birth onward to the suggestion—inevitable, whether conveyed brutally or delicately—of her inferiority, an experience that constantly stimulates her masculine complex" (p. 184). It was not envy of the penis that troubled women, it was envy of the freedom and power of the masculine role in society and frustration with the feminine role that denied the reality of women's experience, feelings, and abilities.

The cruel behavior of men toward women is to this day attributed to female masochism. Harold P. Blum (1982) stated: "This does not mean that an injured woman has necessarily sought her mistreatment or that she hankers for humiliation . . . . The need for punishment or masochistic gratification may be disguised, subtle, and outside awareness . . . . Masochistic women are far more likely to remain attached to abusive husbands . . . and may live out beating fantasies, which stem from childhood, in the current family situation" (p. 265). Freud's abandonment of his seduction theory was a travesty that has had lasting and detrimental effects on the "psychology" of women.

Were psychoanalysts to go back in history, however, beyond the 19th century to ancient times when the "mother right" was overthrown by the "father right," they might have a different perspective. In this context it was probably "womb-envy," the fact that women can bear children and men cannot, that was the prime factor in the development of male psychology. In this context, too, analysts today might realize that theories of penis-envy and female masochism were psychological inventions to maintain male superiority and protect father rights.

Human characteristics assigned to men and women are usually neatly packaged in terms of opposites, such as male dominance/female submissiveness or male aggression/female passivity. Interestingly enough, female masochism appears to stand alone. Psychoanalysts have not entertained the notion that male sadism is the counterpart of female masochism. However sadistic the behavior in a domestic violence scenario, the battering husband or the incestuous father, who otherwise plays the starring role in the home, has typically been depicted in the role of respondent to wife/daughter provocateurs. Theories that blame the victim tend to justify or excuse male violence against women.

When I first began my research on domestic violence in 1975, I found that the goal of most therapists was to change the wife's behavior in order to stop the beatings. It was easier to counsel the wife/victim than an uncooperative and potentially dangerous husband. Like the police, mental health professionals and religious counselors did not hold the batterer responsible for *his* behavior. Never mind the danger to the woman who, having no other resources, might become a burden to the state. More important was keeping the marriage intact and the offender free to earn the family living.

THE IMPACT ON CHILD REARING

Underlying religious, legal, and psychological emphasis on gender opposites and "appropriate" masculine/feminine roles is the presumption that such training will insure that children will become "normal" heterosexual adults. Homophobia—the fear and intolerance of homosexuality—is used to reinforce sex-role stereotyping and maintain male supremacy in personal and social relationships between the sexes.

Mothers are more apt to treat their young ones simply as children. Fathers are more likely to insist upon enforcing differential boy/girl behavior. Mothers are admonished to stop coddling their sons lest they make "sissies" or "faggots" of them. Fahters who are so obsessed with exaggerated fears their sons might not grow up to be "he-men" go to extremes in avoiding any gesture or display of affection that could in any way be perceived as "feminine." Such men recoil from father/son kissing and hugging. They hold their sons—even toddlers—at arm's length with the more male-accepted handshake.

Letty Cottin Pogrebin (1980) pointed out, "In all socioeconomic groups, boys receive more of every kind of behavior control . . . ." (p. 235). While it is true that they receive more positive reinforcement in the way of praise, encouragement, compliments, and attention than girls do, boys also receive more negative reinforcement—more frequent and severe punishment, more criticism, and more disapproval. "When a society operates according to the cult of sex differences, gender itself (especially for boys under male supremacy) becomes both a disciplinary tool and a disciplinary rationale."

Part of the disciplinary rationale is the use of homophobia as a vaccine against homosexuality. Despite the heterosexual proselytizing and conditioning that all children receive, despite social pressures against homosexuality, an estimated 10 percent of men and women identify as homosexuals. Denied physical affection from their fathers and taught that maleness is prized and femaleness to be avoided, it is no wonder that some men seek intimate relationships with men. Nor is it surprising that some women refuse to emulate the inferior and vulnerable "feminine" role model and therefore seek relationships with equals (women).

While homophobia does not prevent homosexuality, it can have negative effects upon heterosexual relationships. Homophobia can stunt a boy's emotional growth, destroy male sensitivity, and inhibit intimacy not only among men, but also with women. Compulsive masculinity—denial of tenderness and loving kindness as being womanly and the assumption of aggressiveness as the symbol of male identity—fosters contempt for all things female and makes it difficult to relate freely to the opposite sex. Boys who are taught to repress their emotions become adults who are unable to express their feelings other than anger. The women they marry often become the targets of that anger.

Ellen Morgan (1975) pointed out, too, that early differential training of the sexes "leads straight to the connection of *sex-role*—instead of actual sexuality—with eroticism . . . only those who display 'appropriate' sex-role behavior are perceived as sexy and appealing" (p. 14).

Anthony Storr (1970) stated that intense aggressiveness on the part of the male is an important element of sexuality because of the primitive necessity of male pursuit and penetration of the female. He also claimed that "fear of the more dominant male reinforces rather than inhibits erotic arousal in females" (p. 71).

P. Evans (1973) called violence sexy, "the best aphrodisiac in the world." He said that "the palm of a masculine hand on the cheek of a recalcitrant woman" established a "pleasurable" principle of man over woman. The *humiliation* in that satisfies the "sensual masochism" of the woman's makeup, which, "however slight, is undeniable" (pp. 208, 226–227).

When men equate sexuality with male conquest and violence with sexual arousal, wife battering can become an erotic pattern. It is a form of "foreplay" and may explain why a couple winds up in bed together following a violent episode. While the husband may interpret this as female sexual response, the wife may equate "making love" with the cessation of violence. Neuropsychologist James W. Prescott says that there is a reciprocal relationship between pleasure and violence, in that the presence of one inhibits the other. "When the brain's pleasure circuits are 'on,' the violence circuits are 'off,' and vice versa" (1975, p. 11).

Unfortunately, numerous images in the media and advertising that portray women as victims of sexual violence who "enjoy" their victimization have been legitimized by psychoanalytic fantasies and theories and reinforced by the criminal justice system and helping professions.

Many unwitting, well-intentioned parents give mixed messages to their children—messages that also connect violence with love and/or with sex. How a child is treated, touched, loved, disciplined, or rejected by his/her parents will determine not only one's ability to love, but also one's inclination toward the use of and response to violence.

Feedback I have received from clinicians indicates that those marriages in which both partners have a heavy investment in traditional sex roles are the most violence-prone. Lenore Walker found, however, that although battered wives "often behaved in a passive way, they did not accept their passive role. . . . Their fear of another beating often forces them into behavior in which they would not voluntarily choose otherwise" (Sonkin, Martin, & Walker, 1985, p. 154).

Instead of blindly accepting these stereotypical roles and imposing them on children, parents should be made aware of their destructive potential. In a study of more than 200 college students (Stark, 1985), Marilyn Coleman and Lawrence H. Ganong gave subjects of both sexes the Bem Sex Role Inventory to determine how masculine, feminine, and androgynous they were. Then various scales were used to measure how these groups gave and received love. The researchers found that androgynous people who have *both* masculine and feminine characteristics are more loving than those who are stereotypically masculine or feminine.

DOMESTIC VIOLENCE ON TRIAL

We cannot erase our history, but we can learn from it. The evidence on the practice of wife beating clearly supports Gil's contention (cited at the beginning of this chapter) about personal and structural violence, how one feeds into and reinforces the other. To break this cycle of violence that is passed on from one generation to the next means not only changing personal behavior and attitudes, but also social values and policies that encourage and reinforce personal and collective violence and attitudes toward women and wives.

We have seen that social attitudes and the law are inextricably bound together. Although social change is not instantaneous—old habits are hard to break—it can be accelerated by legislation. Given the force of law, behavior can be modified and attitudes subsequently changed.

Already, in the past decade (a mere moment in the annals of history), we have witnessed significant changes in attitudes toward domestic violence, its treatment, and prevention. Ten years ago there were fewer than a dozen emergency shelters nationwide that provided specialized services for battered wives and their children. Against tremendous odds—with little money and little support, if any, from the public and its institutions—a grass-roots movement of concerned and determined women began to provide refuge for victims, first in their own homes and later in rented residential facilities. These women knew that one way to break the cycle of violence was to provide sanctuary for battered wives—a safe place where they could find the space, time, support, and resources necessary for them to heal their psychological and physical wounds and consider their options. Today there are about 600 such shelters throughout the United States that are accepted and supported by the communities in which they exist.

The media were effective in increasing public awareness of the prevalance of domestic violence and the need for housing and other services for victims. Staff advocates, who were all unpaid volunteers at the start, began to unravel the bureaucratic red tape of governmental agencies (law enforcement, medical, mental health, welfare) to obtain for shelter residents necessary backup services. Researchers came forth to validate the data gathered by the shelter movement and explain the battered woman syndrome to helping agencies and professions. Workshops were sponsored by universities and other institutions for the personnel of agencies that had direct contact with families to provide information on the dynamics of domestic violence. These meetings led to the formation of community networks of a wide range of service providers, including law enforcement. Feminist shelter workers, feminist therapists, and feminist attorneys were largely involved in bringing new perceptions of domestic violence to their professions and in formulating new guidelines for responding to both victims and batterers.

As awareness and support grew, state legislators began to appropriate some supplemental funding for shelters. They examined laws that were applicable to domestic violence and passed legislation that strengthened the enforcement of civil orders of protection. Except for a few states, they fell short of reforms that would clearly estabish domestic violence as a criminal offense, entailing arrest and criminal proceedings.

Class action suits were brought against the police departments of New York City, Los Angeles, and Oakland, California, by battered wives who claimed that nonarrest policies discriminated against them as women and denied them "equal protection under the law." Resultant consent decrees led to a change in policy, which established domestic violence as a crime and changed the emphasis in police training from crisis intervention to crimes against persons. These changes of necessity required new attitudes, a whole new mind-set for police and others in law enforcement.

Of particular significance is the bill passed by the California legislature in 1984 mandating uniform statewide police training in responding to domestic violence calls. Its provisions are largely based on the 1980 general order of the San Francisco Police Department, which had been developed by top-level officials and the Coalition for Justice for Battered Women (feminist attorneys, law students, and service providers). One important provision is that an officer's course of action is *not* to be influenced by marital status, whether or not the parties live together, existence or lack of a temporary restraining order, the potential financial consequences of arrest, a history of prior complaints, verbal assurances the violence will cease, the victim's emotional state, nonvisibility of injuries, speculation that the complainant may not follow through with the criminal justice process or that arrest may not lead to a conviction—all reasons that police had used previously to avoid arrest.

With the new arrest policies came the development of diversion programs (pretrial and probation) enabling courts to mandate counseling for batterers in lieu of jail time. These programs are designed to deal specifically with the batterer's violent response patterns, not his marital relationship. The latter can only be mended, if at all, once the violence ceases. If the offender fails to attend or participate in the program or if the violence recurs, he is sent back to court and criminal proceedings resumed.

In the year following the new San Francisco police order, the Family Violence Project (which assists victims through the legal process and conducts diversion programs for batterers) found that arrests for assaults in the home increased by 60 percent. Many of the cases involved chronic patterns of abuse that may not have entered the criminal justice system had it not been for the change in police policy.

A study of Minneapolis police tactics in responding to domestic assault calls showed that the recidivism rate within a six-month period was 22 percent when offenders were ordered out of the house for eight hours, 16 percent when advice or mediation was offered, but only 10 percent when an arrest was made (Boffey, 1983). These findings suggest that arrest is the most effective approach, even more so when the criminal justice system has the backup of diversion programs for batterers.

With good police investigation and the possibility of court-mandated counseling in misdemeanor cases, district attorneys are less reluctant to prosecute. Some have also found ways to overcome the reluctance of battered wives to press charges against their husbands. These district attorneys assume responsibility for filing charges, subpoena the victim as a witness, and provide victim witness assistance. The district attorney in Santa Barbara, California, also found that when he used vertical prosecution (assigning one attorney to handle the case throughout the proceedings) victims were more apt to cooperate in the judicial process.

Some state legislatures have also been convinced of the efficacy of deleting the exemption for husbands from rape statutes. By 1984, according to Laura X, of the National Clearinghouse on Marital Rape, in Berkeley, California, 22 states had made this revision in their penal codes.

However reluctantly, even the Reagan administration has gotten into the act. Despite repeated public hearings and years of lobbying, "pro-family" members of the Senate had successfully blocked passage of federal domestic violence legislation. They were critical of advocates for battered wives as being antifamily, profeminist, and Lesbian. But when the president's conservative commission completed its national investigation of the need for domestic violence programs and made its recommendations, the impasse was broken. Legislation to appropriate federal monies to supplement state and private funding for these viable and innovative programs was quickly passed and signed into law in 1984.

Admittedly, reforms in law, its enforcement, social attitudes, and therapeutic practice have not yet been universally adopted across the country. But they show an encouraging trend toward social change, a willingness to explore new ways to deal with an age-old problem.

The following chapters provide comprehensive information on domestic violence issues and offer concrete techniques for those whose duty it is to enforce the law, for those who provide counseling for victims and batterers, and for creating an alliance between the criminal justice system and the helping professions in responding to domestic violence and preventing its recurrence.

Domestic violence is on trial. Will wife beating continue to receive social sanction, or will it be found a crime against the state? The verdict is up to you, our readers, and to the public with whom you interact and have influence.

REFERENCES

Blackstone, W. (1966). *Commentaries on the law of England*. Dobbs Ferry, NY: Oceana. (Original work published 1765)

Blum, H.P. (1982). Psychoanalytic reflections of the "beaten wife syndrome." In M. Kirkpatrick (Ed.), *Women's sexual experience: Explorations of a dark continent*. New York: Plenum.

Boffey, P.M. (1983, April 6). Arrests advised in domestic disputes. *The Oakland Tribune*.

Brownmiller, S. (1975). *Against our will: Women, men and rape*. New York: Plenum.

California Commission on Crime Control and Violence Prevention. (1982). *Ounces of prevention: Toward an understanding of the causes of violence.* Sacramento: California State Office of Criminal Justice Planning.

Calvert, R. (1975). Criminal and civil liability in husband-wife assaults. In K. Steinmetz & M. Straus (Eds.), *Violence in the family.* New York: Dodd, Mead.

Davis, E.G. (1971). *The first sex.* New York: Putnam.

DeCrow, K. (1974). *Sexist justice.* New York: Random House.

Dobash, R.E., & Dobash, R. (1979). *Violence against wives: A case against the patriarchy.* New York: Free Press.

Durbin, K. (1974, June). Wife-beating. *Ladies Home Journal.*

Engels, F. (1948). *The origin of the family, private property and the state.* Moscow: Progress. (Original work published 1884).

Evans, P. (1973, May). Do pugilists have more fun? *Cosmopolitan.*

Gil, D.G. (1978). Social violence and violence in families. In J.M. Eekelaar & S.N. Katz (Eds.), *Family violence: An international and interdisciplinary study.* Toronto: Butterworth.

Goldman, E. (1970). *Marriage and love.* New York: Times Change Press. (Essay written in 1917).

Kanowitz, L. (1969). *Women and the law: The unfinished revolution.* Albuquerque: University of New Mexico Press.

Klein, D. (1982). Violence against women: some consideration regarding causes and its elimination. In B.R. Price & N.J. Sokoloff (Eds.), *The criminal justice system and women.* New York: Clark Boardman.

Martin, D. (1981). *Battered wives.* San Francisco: Volcano Press.

Martin, D. (1982). Wife-beating: a product of sociosexual development. In M. Kirkpatrick (Ed.), *Women's sexual experience: Explorations of the dark contient.* New York: Plenum.

Masson, J.M. (1984, February). Freud and the seduction theory. *The Atlantic Monthly,* pp. 33–60.

Morgan, E. (1975). *The erotization of male dominance/female submission.* Pittsburgh: Know.

Morgan, R. (1984). *Sisterhood is global.* New York: Anchor/Doubleday.

O'Faolain, J., and Martines, L. (Eds.). (1974). *Not in god's image: Women in history.* Glasgow: Fontana/Collins.

Pogrebin, L.C. (1980). *Growing up free: Raising your child in the 80's.* New York: McGraw-Hill.

Prescott, J.W. (1975, November). Body pleasure and the origins of violence. *Bulletin the Atomic Scientists,* pp. 1–2.

Schlachet, B.C. (1978). Rapid intervention with families in crisis in a court setting. In J.M. Eekelaar & S.N. Katz (Eds.), *Family violence: An international and interdisciplinary study.* Toronto: Butterworth.

Sonkin, D., Martin, D., & Walker, L. (1985). *The male batterer: A treatment approach.* New York: Springer Publishing Co.

Stark, E. (1985, June). Androgyny makes better lovers. *Psychology Today,* p. 19.

Storr, A. (1970). *Human aggression.* New York: Bantam.

Straus, M. (1978). Wife beating: Causes, treatment and research needs. In *Battered*

Women: Issues of public policy. Washington, DC: U.S. Commission on Civil Rights.

Strouse, J. (Ed.). (1974). *Women and analysis: Dialogues on psychoanalytic views of femininity*. New York: Grossman.

Wyatt, G.E. (1982). The sexual experience of Afro-American women: A middle income sample. In M. Kirkpatrick (Ed.), *Women's sexual experience: Explorations of the dark continent*. New York: Plenum.

2

Domestic Violence Is a Crime: A Case Study—San Francisco Family Violence Project

Esta Soler

The criminal justice system is one of the primary institutions to which battered women and their families turn for help and protection. By virtue of its power to enforce existing laws, it is also the institution critical to public condemnation of violence, *wherever* it may occur. However, the criminal justice system shares the biases of society at large, biases that hold that family matters are private. Such a bias has led to selective nonenforcement of laws when violence occurs between family members. This stance of nonintervention indirectly condones violence and ignores the frequent escalation that all too often ends in homicide.

The San Francisco Family Violence Project, established in March 1980 as a federally funded demonstration project, was charged with changing the then-current criminal justice response to family violence. The Family Violence Project's working premise has always been that domestic violence is a crime—not merely a private dispute between equal partners—and so affects society at large as well as the immediate family (San Francisco Family Violence Project, 1982).

This chapter details the opposition of the project's "working premise" to the social biases that helped to create criminal justice response to family violence in San Francisco before 1980. It details the concrete strategy by which that response was changed. This chapter begins by describing what was "status quo" criminal justice response and proceeds to a discussion of how we changed the component parts of that response—i.e., the Police and Probation Departments and the District Attorney's Office. The chapter

21

concludes with a brief analysis of the critical role community groups play in this kind of systemic change.

A study showed that in San Francisco in 1981, the largest category of homicides was made up of family- and relationship-motivated murders. Forty-one percent of all assault- and weapon-related calls to the San Francisco Police Department—about 400 calls per week—were related to family violence. Despite these statistics, prior to 1980 few arrests were ever made (San Francisco Family Violence Project, 1982).

Police and sheriff's departments are generally the first line of involvement by the criminal justice system in family violence cases. The prevailing law enforcement response to most incidences of domestic violence was to attempt to arbitrate or mediate the situation. Offenders were rarely arrested and victims rarely received information on either their legal rights or social service resources available to them.

The deputy chief of the San Francisco Police Department stated: "The rule said 'Don't do anything about it; it's a civil matter . . . we weren't that much different from any other department.'" In San Francisco, policy dictated that "officers act only as referees, suggesting counseling with a minister, doctor or lawyer" (Hughes, 1985).

In any jurisdiction, the quality of police response serves as an indicator of how domestic violence cases are viewed by the entire system. Where arrest is avoided at the scene, there will be a tendency throughout the system to view domestic violence as a "family dispute" or "civil" matter: Prosecutors will dismiss cases as being "not worth" prosecuting, and the resulting unresolved violent family situations will escalate and be the material for repeated late-night calls. The irony, of course, is that such an attitude *ensures* the cyclical and escalating nature of these cases, as they become caught in the revolving door of police and prosecutorial failure to respond *effectively*.

Law enforcement plays a critical role in being the point of entry into the criminal justice system. The police are often the first—and sometimes the only—ones called for help in these situations. If a victim or her family is discouraged by the police from pressing charges, or if the police fail to respond effectively, it may be the last call made. A study of domestic violence homicide cases in Kansas City, for example, revealed that the victims had called the police at least once in 85% of the cases before the murder occurred; in 50% of the cases, they had earlier called five times or more (Stephens, 1977).

The Kansas City study dramatically underscores that the widely prevalent stances of arrest avoidance or mediation of most police departments are not only ineffective, but costly—in terms of repeat responses to a scene where no conclusive action is taken, and also in terms of human health and life. And this cost affects what is now one of the single largest categories of crime. Furthermore, arrest avoidance reinforces in the mind of the offender that these assaults are not a criminal matter (Sherman & Berk, 1983). From a psychological point of view, such a lack of sanctions ensures that the pattern will be repeated or even escalate.

The use of mediation was based on two misleading perceptions. First, domestic violence was only a family matter regardless of the seriousness of the violence. Second, this definition of domestic violence as a family matter resulted in viewing the parties as neutral and, therefore, equally responsible for the violent incident. These perceptions provided the rationale for using mediation as an intervention technique, since the parties were not seen as offender and victim but as two family members.

Further, law enforcement officers did not, for the most part, receive adequate training on domestic violence as a crime, when and how to intervene, what services and options exist for the victims, and the potential for lethality if the family violence is permitted to continue (San Francisco Family Violence Project, 1985).

The choice to prosecute a nonfederal crime was totally in the hands of the prosecuting attorney in the local district attorney's office. The district attorney also determined on what type of charge, felony or misdemeanor, a person will be tried. The charge, in turn, determines the penalties.

Nationwide, serious felony offenders were inappropriately offered pretrial diversion; misdemeanor cases were often dismissed; prosecution of a case was handled by several attorneys, thus causing confusion; and citations for release (when an offender is released on his/her own recognizance) did not take into account the potential risk to the victim.

Finally, battered women—who received virtually no support, encouragement, or protection to pursue legal redress—frequently wanted the state to drop charges out of fear of retribution from the batterer or frustration with the system. The criminal justice system used this possibility of women wanting to drop charges to justify its overwhelming reluctance to both arrest and prosecute family violence offenders.

With other crimes, it is the state, not the victim, that prosecutes criminals; and while this is also true in theory for family violence cases, it is not true in fact. The longstanding societal attitude toward the sanctity of the family makes it the individual, or victim, who must bear the onus for that prosecution.

In a recent report by the United States Commission on Civil Rights on the domestic violence problem the following seven criticisms were made about district attorney's offices. In their book *The Family Secret*, William Stacey and Anson Shupe delineate the following major reasons for prosecutorial failure in domestic violence cases (Stacey & Shupe, 1983):

1. Prosecutors enjoy wide discretion to determine which criminal cases will be prosecuted and often accord low priority to cases involving domestic violence.

2. The rate of prosecution and conviction in criminal cases drops sharply

when there is a prior or present relationship between the alleged assailant and the victim.

3. Some prosecutors hesitate to file charges against abusers, based on their belief that domestic violence is a noncriminal, personal matter or that prosecution would adversely affect the parties' marriages.

4. Prosecutors often treat victims of spouse abuse as if they, rather than the defendants, were accused of criminal conduct.

5. Prosecutors frequently attribute the low rate of prosecution in spouse abuse cases to lack of victim cooperation, which may become a self-fulfilling prophecy. Prosecutors who believe that abuse victims will not cooperate with the prosecution of their cases frequently discourage the victims from using the criminal justice system.

6. Prosecutors rarely subpoena victims to testify in abuse cases, although such action frequently could circumvent victims' noncooperation.

7. Prosecutors frequently charge spouse abusers with crimes less serious than their conduct seems to warrant.

As one lawyer put it, "the District Attorney won't typically prosecute, not until she's been put in the hospital, or is dead" (Stacey & Shupe, 1983).

This is the context in which the Family Violence Project came into being, and these are the components of the criminal justice system—the police and District Attorney's Office—on which the Family Violence Project has focused.

The Family Violence Project adopted a three-tiered approach in an attempt to renovate and strengthen the police department's approach to family violence (San Francisco Family Violence Project, 1985). The three elements included:

1. New department policies and procedures (the General Order), which reflect the serious criminal nature of the behavior; for handling domestic violence calls.
2. New training courses for dispatch officers, recruits, and advanced police personnel, and a model training curriculum.
3. Data collection systems for determining the volume of domestic violence calls and reports, and any changes over time.

The project also adopted a four-pronged approach toward changing the response of the District Attorney's Office. This included:

1. Prosecution protocols for attorney handling of felony and misdemeanor family violence cases.

2. "Vertical prosecution," so that one attorney handles a given case from beginning to end.
3. Victim advocacy units to aid battered women in their involvement with the criminal justice system.
4. Offender counseling and education programs, which constitute a comprehensive approach to changing offenders' violent behavior.

The following is a discussion of the implementation and impact of these efforts.

LAW ENFORCEMENT

In 1980, the San Francisco Police Department adopted the General Order on Domestic Violence, reversing its longstanding policy that domestic violence was a civil/family dispute (San Francisco Family Violence Project, 1982). The new policy clearly states that domestic violence should be treated as a category of crime and, as such, not appropriate for dispute mediation. "If the evidence is there, we take action like we would in any criminal assault case," states the deputy chief of the San Francisco Police Department. It took "a little pushing and shoving" to educate officers about the new order because "it was a 180 degree turnaround from what we had been saying before," the deputy chief said (Hughes, 1985).

Some highlights of the San Francisco General Order include:

1. All alleged violence should be treated as alleged *criminal* behavior. Dispute mediation *should not* be used as a substitute for appropriate criminal proceedings where violence has occurred.

2. Officers should not base their course of action on the marital status or housing situation of the parties; the existence or lack of a restraining order; the financial consequences of the arrest on either party; the complainant's history of prior complaints; or speculation about the victim's "follow through."

3. Officers responding to felonies *should* make an arrest regardless of the desires of the victim or reportee. Officers responding to a misdemeanor assault should make an arrest if they witness the crime. Otherwise, they are to inform the victims of their right to make a citizen's arrest—and they are not to discourage the complainant from doing so.

4. Officers shall write an incident report in all domestic violence incidents and give the report number to the victim.

5. Officers shall correctly enforce protective court orders.

6. Officers shall indicate that the incident involved domestic violence by

circling "yes" in the domestic violence check box on the incident report form.

To transform the General Order policies into practices, the Family Violence Project developed and implemented domestic violence training courses for San Francisco police officers. And in the first year following the adoption of the San Francisco General Order, domestic violence arrests in San Francisco increased by 60%. Between March 1980 and July 1983, reports on serious felony domestic violence assaults increased 123%. Further, there was a doubling in police report writing in domestic violence cases.

Arrests in domestic violence cases can have a deterrent effect on future violent episodes. A recent study in Minnesota has suggested, for example, that compared to traditional "cooling out," or mediating responses, arrest can have a positive effect in deterring future violence. An experiment carried out in the Minneapolis Police Department found that when nonfelony domestic violence calls were randomly responded to with arrests, as opposed to sending the suspect away for several hours to separate the parties or to giving advice or attempting mediation, those offenders were less likely to reappear in official police records of assaults in the next few months (Sherman & Berk, 1983). In San Francisco the net effect has been to disrupt chronic patterns of abuse. The police response has clarified for the parties that a criminal offense is being committed in their homes. This can lead the parties to examine their situation, it can inform victims of their options, and this can force batterers to change. The new procedures have made domestic violence more important as a police matter.

PROSECUTION

Once effective police policies and procedures are in place, the development of a domestic violence prosecution strategy is an essential next step. The Family Violence Project helped develop the following four major components of a successful prosecutorial response:

1. Prosecution protocols for misdemeanor and felony cases
2. Vertical prosecution
3. Victim advocacy units
4. Offender counseling and education programs

Successful prosecution rests on an important and incontrovertible principle: Family violence requires specialized services, services that include, at the very least, consistent and supportive victim contact and follow-up. Over the last four years, the Family Violence Project has worked intensively with more than 5,000 battered women who turned to the criminal justice system for help and protection. Working together, under the requirements of written protocols, Family Violence Project victim advocates and prosecutors have created a truly multidisciplinary professional team.

Prosecution Protocols for Misdemeanor and Felony Cases

Integral to the development of an effective prosecution response is the detailing of its principles and procedures in the form of a written protocol. The protocol, once drafted, acts as a blueprint for a systemwide standard for the prosecution of all cases. The success rate of the Family Violence Project illustrates the effectiveness of a written protocol as a central organizational force in the development of a prosecution strategy. The San Francisco District Attorney's Office implemented its felony prosecution protocol in the Family Violence Project's second year. By the project's third year:

- The conviction rate on felony cases had increased 44% from the preceeding year
- The number of cases in which charges were filed increased 136% since the project's first year
- There was a 171% increase in the positive disposition of domestic violence cases between 1981 and 1983 (a "positive disposition" is a criminal court disposition that requires continued court jurisdiction over the offender, such as probation, diversion, prison time, or parole)

The misdemeanor protocol was developed and implemented in 1983. Comparing 1982 misdemeanor convictions with those of 1983, the rate of convictions for misdemeanor cases increased by 90%.

The adoption of the felony and misdemeanor protocols represented a significant policy change for the San Francisco District Attorney's Office in handling domestic violence cases. The changes reflect the recognition that domestic violence is criminal conduct and that prosecutors have the same responsibility to respond to these cases as they do to other violent crimes.

The introduction to the protocols acknowledges that the criminal justice system is the place where victims most frequently turn for help. The system can be an effective means of stopping violence between family members. The state has a strong interest in ending this type of abuse, which tends to escalate in severity and frequency and often leads to homicide.

The successful prosecution of crimes of domestic violence, as with any crime where the victim is related to the offender, requires specialized techniques designed to overcome the victim's fear of the criminal justice system and to encourage cooperation with the prosecution effort.

The prosecution protocols identify a three-stage cycle of violence common to domestic violence cases (Walker, 1979): (1) the tension-building phase (2) the acute battering phase and (3) the contrition phase. Victims most frequently enter the criminal justice system after an acute battering episode; the contrition phase usually follows immediately. Both parties may feel horrified by what has happened. Both feel guilty about the event, and both resolve never to let it happen again. The batterer very typically will treat the victim with apparent respect, love, and affection. This is a great relief to the victim and is precisely what the victim has wanted out of their relationship all along.

The contrition phase makes criminal prosecution difficult. As long as the batterer continues to behave affectionately, the victim may become increasingly reluctant to jeopardize such good behavior by pressing charges. A prosecutor who understands the dynamics of the battering cycle can effectively intervene by reminding the victim of similar remorseful periods in the past, predicting a return to the tension-building phase, and explaining the likelihood of more frequent and severe injuries.

To introduce prosecutors to the special nature of domestic violence cases and to explain the critical need for standardized procedures in this area, each protocol contains a section outlining the psychological dynamics, the cycle of violence (Walker, 1979), and prosecution issues involved. The section also describes battered women's fears and concerns regarding the prosecution of the case, as well as alternatives available to the prosecutor and to the victim in the course of the proceedings. The following are some important elements of the protocols (San Francisco Family Violence Project, 1982):

1. *Victim Contact.* The protocol emphasizes the importance of making contact with battered women within 72 hours of rebooking or charging and of keeping them informed of the progress on their cases.

2. *Evidence Collection.* Early collection of evidence is crucial in domestic violence cases, since most involve single-witness crimes. Corroborating evidence can often be a criticial factor in successful prosecution of a case. The protocol outlines how to preserve evidence most effectively (e.g., taped as opposed to written statements).

3. *Filing Criteria.* Because of the tendency to undercharge domestic violence cases and to downplay the potential lethality of the situation, the protocol encourages district attorneys to take into account the likelihood of escalating violence, any history of prior assaults, and the tendency to minimize the extent of the battered woman's injuries, in deciding whether or not charges will be filed.

The protocol further states that it is the prosecutor's responsibility—not the victim's—to file charges against the offender. A case should be filed when a factual basis exists. The victim is to be informed by the district attorney that it is the district attorney, not the victim, who is responsible for pressing charges and prosecuting the case.

Vertical Prosecution

The use of vertical prosecution for handling serious felony domestic violence cases has proven to be the most successful method of intervention. Vertical prosecution means simply that only one district attorney is responsible for the prosecution of a domestic violence case from beginning to end.

Prior to the introduction of vertical prosecution, a battered woman had to work with three, four, or sometimes even five different district attorneys during the entire criminal proceeding. This experience was not only disruptive; it was also ineffective. The already traumatized battered woman went from district attorney to district attorney and had to repeatedly reveal the most intimate and painful details of her life. Vertical prosecution allows the battered woman to tell her story once to a specialized district attorney. With more detailed knowledge of the incident and the family situation, the district attorney becomes a better advocate for the battered woman. The woman becomes a better witness because she is more likely to cooperate fully with the prosecution effort.

Victim Advocacy Units

Family violence victim advocates are key to an effective prosecution plan. Seventy percent of the Family Violence Project cases assisted by advocates in 1981 would not have proceeded through the criminal justice system if there had not been this specialized intervention. For a variety of reasons, including fear of retailiation and lack of understanding of the criminal justice system, many victims are extremely reluctant to pursue prosecution (Martin, 1981; Fleming, 1979). The intervention of sensitive and knowledgeable advocates can reverse this phenomenon.

The role of the Family Violence Project's victim advocacy staff is to assist in locating victims and witnesses, counsel victims as to their legal rights and options, aid in case investigation and preparation, and coordinate service delivery with community and criminal justice providers. The work of the project's victim advocacy unit parallels elements in the prosecution protocols.

1. *Victim Contact and Support.* Contacting the victim is done within 48 hours after the incident, as victims are more prone to seek help immediately after the incident rather than later. Also, victims who have been hospitalized may be released soon after the incident and go into hiding.

Once the battered woman has been contacted by the victim advocacy unit of the Family Violence Project, the key factors covered in the initial counseling session include the following;

- history of violence
- current incident: facts, witnesses, evidence
- defendant's criminal or psychiatric history
- criminal, civil, and social service options (including referral to a battered women's shelter)
- what the victim would like to see happen on the case

2. *Evidence Collection.* For victims who have just recently been assaulted, the prospect of having photos of their injuries taken adds another layer of trauma to an already painful process. Being accompanied by an advocate helps lessen the victim's anxiety and fear—especially when the victim is a woman and can be accompanied by a woman staff person. Advocacy staff can also collect victim and witness statements and help determine the nature, source, and location of any weapon used.

3. *Preparation of Victim for Court.* Preparing a victim to testify in court is a long-range process, requiring a great deal of time and resources. Each contact with the battered woman—from the intake interview to a preparation session the morning of a preliminary hearing—helps her to become increasingly comfortable with the prospect of telling her story to a courtroom full of strangers. Also, recently traumatized victims need assistance in recollecting the exact details of what happened to them, since they have a tendency to minimize and deny the severity of the events. Advocacy staff review the police report with victims, and encourage them to write their own recollection of what occurred, in order to help them gain objectivity on the event. Familiarizing victims in advance with the actual courtroom and court procedures helps to bring the experience into focus and prepare the victim for testifying in court. The Family Violence Project has developed a videotape of a mock domestic violence preliminary hearing for this purpose and has begun to use it on an experimental basis in preparing witnesses for court appearances.

The victim advocate, working in tandem with the battered woman, becomes the important *human* link between the system and the victim.

Criminal justice proceedings can be dehumanizing and exceedingly painful for all victims, particularly domestic violence victims. Effective and sensitive advocates are critical to this process, not only as interpreters of the rules and procedures of the criminal justice system, but also as strong advocates for women and their desires as their case proceeds through the complicated channels of justice.

Offender Counseling and Education Programs

The offender treatment program of the San Francisco Family Violence Project involved the development and establishment of special group counseling techniques to modify violent behavior (Sonkin, Martin & Walker, 1985). The Family Violence Project also trained community agencies, and their personnel, in the use of these strategies and techniques, which are discussed elsewhere in this book. While some offenders voluntarily seek help, the majority do not. For this reason, a major focus of the Family Violence Project was the development of guidelines for the use of probation and diversion in domestic violence cases.

PROBATION/DIVERSION

The Family Violence Project supplemented the existing code on probation and diversion with written guidelines on eligibility and standards for revocation and for reinstitution of criminal proceedings so that these critical areas would not be left to the discretion of individual prosecutors or probation officers. Such uniform standards have reduced the likelihood of repeat offenses. To implement the standards, San Francisco established a special domestic violence unit in the probation department and assigned specific probation officers to domestic violence cases. This specialization afforded the Family Violence Project an opportunity to monitor and track domestic violence cases.

There is a wide range of possible sentences in domestic violence cases, depending on numerous circumstances. Successful prosecution depends partly on the prosecutor or a victim advocate explaining clearly the range of sentences to the victim. These alternatives should include probation or diversion and rule out those dispositions that may discourage the victim from cooperating. Today's ineffectively prosecuted misdemeanor often becomes tomorrow's felony or homicide.

Unlike other categories of crime, domestic violence cases require that the disposition address both the needs of the victim and the cyclical and escalating nature of such violence. A simple rule to follow here is that *any disposition that fails to meet these requirements will not force the offender to stop his violence, and may, in fact, give him implicit permission to continue his violence.* Accordingly, while incarceration may be the most appropriate and effective solution (depending on the seriousness of the injuries sustained and other factors), there are many cases where it may be inadequate. For example, many battered women seen by the Family Violence Project would be afraid or unwilling to pursue if the only disposition the prosecutor recommended was time in a county or state prison.

The inappropriate use—or even a failure to use—the probation or diversion options can actually exacerbate the domestic violence situation by failing to provide either the victim with adequate protection or the defendant with appropriate supervision. The Family Violence Project devised guidelines to ensure that probation and diversion would be recommended only where appropriate, and only when they could contribute to the cessation of violence.

Because the defendant and victim have been involved in an ongoing relationship, any disposition needs also to take into account that the defendant will continue to have access to the victim in most cases and that the violence, if unchecked, will continue, or even escalate. An inappropriate sentence can actually increase this likelihood of a reassault. For example, sometimes the imposition of jail time will so enrage the defendant that he or she will threaten to retaliate against the victim and, unfortunately, will often follow through on such threats—sometimes immediately upon release from custody. As a result, prosecutors should often consider supplementing any actual jail time with probation, so that any reassault on the victim can become a basis for revocation.

Additionally, for first-time offenders or defendants with few prior convictions, the *threat* of jail time suspended to a grant of probation can often be more effective in encouraging them to curb their violence than can actual incarceration, as many batterers fear the repercussions jail time would have on their jobs and lives. To ensure that this leverage operates fully, the defendant is closely supervised and monitored for reassaults and the victim is assured access to someone who is managing the case over time.

The sentencing must also take into account the fact that the batterer will not usually get to the root causes of his violence without professional help. Jail time may stop the violence in the short term, but it will in no way address the defendant's deep-seated rage that periodically explodes into violent episodes. Probation and diversion can be effectively used to order the defendant to seek treatment and to provide recourse for the battered woman through the courts should there be a reassault. Also, where alcoholism or drug abuse exists, substance-abuse treatment must be made a concurrent condition of the defendant's probation or diversion. If untreated, the addiction will exacerbate further violent outbreaks.

Other conditions, such as an order to stay away from the victim, may also be used to contain the batterer's impulsive behavior and to further protect the victim from future episodes. The probationary sentence or time on diversion should be long enough to allow the defendant to benefit from the treatment ordered and to give the court ample opportunity to monitor the defendant for possible reassaults.

Probation and diversion are the judicial system's mechanisms for controlling behavior. Alone, however, they do not provide individual batterers with alternatives to violence in interpersonal relationships. It is for reason that a comprehensive approach to curtailing family violence must include appropriate counseling to aid in behavioral change (Sonkin & Durphy, 1982).

BUILDING A COMMUNITY BASE FOR INSTITUTIONAL CHANGE IN THE CRIMINAL JUSTICE SYSTEM

Changes in San Francisco's criminal justice procedures could not have happened without a massive and sustained effort by a coalition of community activists, family members, feminists, and social service professionals working first to reform the institutional perception of family violence as a private matter. Years of lobbying and organizing combated the police and the courts' traditional failure to respond to domestic violence as a crime. For example, the monumental changes in the San Francisco Bay Area police and prosecution protocols described in this chapter were lobbied for by the Coalition for Justice for Battered Women (Milstein, 1985), a community coalition of attorneys and domestic violence service providers. Through their efforts and with the leadership of the Family Violence Project, both the San Francisco Police Department and the District Attorney's Office agreed to implement new procedures regarding the handling and prosecution of domestic violence cases.

As the San Francisco case study demonstrates, any criminal justice intervention strategy is dependent on a wide range of community agencies, such as battered women's shelters and mental health and social service organizations, since neither the police nor the courts alone can prevent the repeat family violence that results in homicide. A battered woman who cannot leave her home for fear of reprisal will very likely be afraid to press charges. Timely referral of the battered woman to a shelter can help to make her situation more secure and thereby allow her to consider the option of pursuing the case. Close teamwork with community agencies helps to build an effective social services referral network that then protects the victim's— and society's—interests.

As the San Francisco experience also reveals, developing an effective criminal justice response to domestic violence is a difficult challenge. For law enforcement and prosecution staff, it means reversing the historic tendency to treat domestic violence as a civil matter or "family problem." Having traditionally neglected the area of domestic violence as a crime, the criminal justice system must reestablish its credibility with domestic violence victims and the community. Victims who have previously been discouraged from pressing charges or whose cases have been repeatedly dismissed by the court must now be convinced that the criminal justice system will respond when a victim takes action to stop the violence.

Community members must also be actively involved in developing new guidelines for the criminal justice response to domestic violence, as they were in San Francisco. Through a coalition of community leaders, such as the Coalition for Justice for Battered Women in San Francisco, or the formation of a community advisory board, people gain access to the development of public policy, which then lends additional credibility to the criminal justice system's efforts. Active community leaders will also then develop a vested interest in the success of the program and become effective spokespeople for the innovations throughout the wider community. This process is particularly important in minority communities, where there has been a long history of tension between law enforcement and members of the community, and is an opportunity to acknowledge past difficulties in order to work together to improve police and prosecution response.

Finally, any criminal justice system and community-based response to domestic violence must acknowledge that family violence is a crime and is not particular to any race, class, or segment of the community. It spans all economic and cultural groups and as such demands a communitywide response. Given that public law exists to provide protection and redress for all victims of crime, the criminal justice system becomes the single most important target for institutional change and compliance. It is the criminal justice system that can intervene at the scene and provide the necessary support and protection for battered women and their children. It is the criminal justice system alone that can order counseling for the abuser, that can monitor the batterer, and that can provide the necessary motivation for change. And it is the criminal justice system that can send a message to the community at large that family violence will not be accepted.

There are committed and experienced domestic violence and social service professionals in every community who can be actively engaged as resources in the process of changing the criminal justice response to domestic violence. Working with other community activists, the Family Violence Project in San Francisco demonstrates that the criminal justice system can be changed and can *effectively* intervene in cases of domestic violence.

REFERENCES

Fleming, J.B. (1979). *Stopping wife abuse*. Garden City, NJ: Anchor/Doubleday.

Hughes, B. (1985, October 24). Hike in domestic crime reflects a new policy. San Francisco *Examiner*.

Martin, D. (1981). *Battered wives*. San Francisco: Volcano Press.

Milstein, S. (1985, June 3). Angry women who changed the landscape. San Francisco *Chronicle*.

San Francisco Family Violence Project (1982). *Domestic violence Is a crime*. San Francisco, CA: Author.

San Francisco Family Violence Project. (1985). *Family Violence Is a Crime: A revised Edition*. San Francisco, CA: Author.

Sherman, L.W., & Berk, R.A. (1983). The Minneapolis domestic violence experiment. *Police Foundation Reports*, *1*, 1–8.

Sonkin, D.J., & Durphy, M. (1982). *Learning to live without violence: A handbook for men*. San Francisco: Volcano Press.

Sonkin, D.J., Martin, D., & Walker, L.E.A. (1985). *The male batterer: A treatment approach*. New York: Springer Publishing Co.

Stacey, W., & Shupe, A. (1983). The family secret: Domestic violence in America. Boston: Beacon Press.

Stephens, D.W. (1977). Domestic assault: The police response. In M. Roy (Ed.), *Battered women: A psychosocial study of domestic violence*. New York: Van Nostrand Reinhold.

Walker, L.E.A. (1979). *The battered woman*. New York: Harper & Row.

PART II
The Battered Woman

3

The Battered Woman
Syndrome

Mary Ann Douglas

A battered woman is any woman who has been the victim of physical, sexual, and/or psychological abuse by her partner. She may be a middle-class woman whose husband holds a well-paying job, an unmarried minority woman who lives with her unemployed batterer, a single woman whose boyfriend abuses her, or the wife of a well-respected professional in the community. In the United States, an estimated 1.8 million women are physically abused by their husbands or boyfriends every year (Straus, Gelles, & Steinmetz, 1980). Physical abuse is assault that ranges from hitting or slapping at one end of the continuum to homicide at the other (Pagelow, 1981). Physical abuse may or may not be accompanied by physical injury and/or by the victims' attempts to defend themselves. Sexual abuse is "any sexual intimacy forced on one person by another" (Katz & Mazur, 1979), including but not limited to forced vaginal or anal penetration, oral sex, and sexual activity obtained by threat of force or when consent is impossible because the victim is unconscious, severely drugged, asleep, or in some other way helpless. Psychological abuse is defined using an eight-part definition borrowed from Amnesty International (Walker, 1984b). It includes (1) isolation of the victim, (2) induced debility producing exhaustion, (3) monopolization of perceptions, including obsessiveness and possessiveness, (4) threat, such as death to self, family, or friends or sham executions, (5) degradation, including humiliation, denial of victim's power, and verbal name calling, (6) drug or alcohol administration, (7) altered states of consciousness produced through an hypnotic state, and (8) occasional indulgences that keep hope alive that the abuse will cease. This chapter will discuss the battered woman syndrome (BWS), a collection of specific characteristics and effects of abuse

39

that result in a woman's decreased ability to respond effectively to the violence against her. A discussion of intervention methods with victims of battering then follows.

DEFINITION OF BATTERED WOMAN SYNDROME

The BWS is a collection of specific characteristics and effects of abuse on the battered woman. Not all women who are battered suffer from the BWS, but those who do typically are less able to respond effectively to the violence against them. Consequently, they become psychologically entrapped in a violent relationship. Indicators of the BWS can be divided into three major categories: the (1) traumatic effects of victimization by violence, (2) learned helplessness deficits resulting from the interaction between repeated victimization by violence and the battered woman's repeated victimization by violence and the battered woman's and others' reactions to it, and (3) self-destructive coping responses to the violence. The latter function paradoxically to help the battered woman minimize or endure the impact of abuse, but at great cost to her mental and physical health.

Effects of Trauma

Some traumatic effects of victimization by violence are identified using the DSM-III diagnostic criteria for the post-traumatic stress disorder (Walker, 1984a). The first criterion for diagnosis, "a recognizable stressor that would evoke significant symptoms of distress in almost anyone" (APA, 1980, p. 238), is clearly met from the occurrence of violence. Even mild forms of abuse can evoke powerful levels of distress in the victim, especially when there is knowledge and/or a history of more severe violence, since the batterer's level of control is readily apparent and the threat for future and perhaps more severe violence, however implicit, remains.

Reexperiencing the trauma, the second criterion, occurs for battered women in the form of nightmares and fear that the violence will recur. It is not uncommon for battered women to experience intrusive recollections of abusive incidents to the extent that they interfere with daily functioning. When added to the violence actually being experienced, this can create feelings of terror and desperation leading to homicide or suicide.

The third criterion, numbed responsiveness and reduced involvement with the world, occurs when the battered woman withdraws from others, including her family and friends, believing that nobody would understand her situation or that others might blame her. In some cases, the battered woman resembles a robot, with little expression of affect. She may respond automatically to anything that another, including her husband or someone in authority, may suggest to her. The affect makes it appear as if the battered woman places a protective shield around herself, often and most importantly because of her own feelings of anger, terror, and rage.

The final criterion of the post-traumtic stress disorder is a collection of symptoms, including autonomic arousal, evidenced by hyperalertness or an exaggerated startle response, sleep disturbance, and memory impairment or difficulty in concentrating. In extreme cases these indicators may mimic a manic disorder or even a psychotic reaction. Although it is possible that these disorders may precede the battered woman's exposure to violence, more often they reflect the extreme level of anxiety experienced by her as a result of the cumulative effect of the violence. These and other symptoms may intensify when she reexperiences events that symbolize or are similar to the original abusive situation. Accordingly, the battered woman may attempt to avoid certain activities associated with previous violence.

In sum, the post-traumatic stress disorder provides a standard diagnostic framework in which to understand some traumatic effects of the BWS. The diagnostic category as it is defined, however, fails to account for all of the traumatic effects often associated with woman battering.

Another major effect of the trauma of victimization by violence is the devastating impact to the battered woman's self-esteem (Hilberman & Munson, 1978). Damage to the battered woman's self-esteem parallels the effect for other victims of violence, noticeably rape. The battered woman's self-esteem may be so low as to blame herself for the occurrence of the violence, to believe that her victimization proves her to be worthless as a wife and mother, and to believe that she is worth neither the time nor attention required by others to help her create a safer environment. For one battered woman, merely noticing the words "abused wife" written on her record during a physical screening examination by her physician was sufficient to create such a state of panic that she was unable to respond successfully to simple questions like "What day is it?" When this issue was discussed in therapy, she stated that all she could think about after seeing those written words was how ugly and stupid she was and how much she hated her body.

Learned Helplessness Deficits

Walker (1981, 1984a,b) has identified the BWS in terms of the learned helplessness model of depression (Seligman, 1975). As it applies to battered women it is important to note that, whereas they may feel ultimately helpless to stop the violence against them, they are clearly not passive in their behavior (Gelles & Cornell, 1985).

For example, initially the battered woman may engage in behaviors intended to please or placate the batterer, a primary survival skill that may appear to reduce the violence temporarily. However, with time these efforts become ineffective in stopping the violence. Attempts to engage in behaviors potentially more effective in stopping the violence (e.g., calling the police, filing legal charges) are often aborted if tried at all due to several factors, including (1) the belief that they are useless anyway, (2) an increased threat of danger from the batterer when it becomes evident to the battered woman that these efforts are ineffective in stopping the violence, or (3) her fear that her efforts to stop the violence will result in loss of the relationship, an issue about which she may be highly ambivalent.

Bowker (1983) identified three groups of forces that battered women bring to bear on their husbands to end marital violence: personal strategies, informal help-sources, and formal help-sources. Personal strategies identified in his Milwaukee sample included (1) talking the batterer out of the abuse, (2) finding a way to get him to promise to end the abuse, (3) threatening him with a nonviolent act (e.g., divorce), (4) hiding from him, (5) using passive self-defense to minimize the physical damage, and (6) using aggressive defense by fighting back. Informal strategies identified in the study included telling family members, neighbors, in-laws, friends and seeking help from a shelter. As a result of the study, Bowker labeled shelter services as an informal help-source, since most women learned about it through informal friendship or acquaintance networks, not from formal efforts of seeking help. Formal strategies included use of the police, social service agencies, lawyers and district attorneys, the clergy, and women's groups.

When the battered woman employs one of these strategies, the result either strengthens her perception that she is helpless to stop the violence against her or it begins to counteract it. For example, when the battered woman is left with the batterer after the police leave her home and subsequently is beaten by her husband for calling them, she obviously learns that calling the police is ineffective in stopping the violence. Conversely, when the battered woman is told by the district attorney that battering is a crime and that her husband can be legally sanctioned for his criminal behavior, she may learn that her behavior can lead to stopping the violence. Or when she learns that she is able to say "no" to her batterer's demands on her, she has begun to counteract the BWS. Bowker's data suggest that battered women progress from personal strategies for ending the violence through informal, then formal, efforts.

The battered woman who meets with failure in her personal, then informal, and finally formal tactics to create her own safety experiences a series of lessons in the reality that neither her behavior, nor that of any other woman's, is able to stop the violence against her. It is true that the battered woman never has complete control of her own safety, regardless of her behavior, since she cannot control the actions of her partner. Learned helplessness in battered women refers to the low rate of behaviors that could potentially increase safety, based on her decreased ability or on her judgment that these behaviors are also unsafe. It is essential to remember that learned helplessness is often based on the realistic belief that it is not safe to engage in help-seeking behaviors. The implication therefore is that the presence of certain behaviors associated with learned helplessness is not necessarily irrational or unreasonable, given the violent scenario within which the battered woman lives. They may be what have kept her alive.

Self-Destructive Coping Responses to Violence

The battered woman may exhibit certain responses that enable her to cope with the violence toward her. Some of these responses, although perhaps adaptive for the purpose of minimizing the effects of the violence, occur at great cost to the battered woman. These responses are often misunderstood as indicative of the battered woman's pathology or weak character, rather than as attempts to cope with the abusive and controlling environment in which she lives.

For example, a battered woman may use alcohol or drugs as a means of numbing the effect of the violence. If her abusive partner is alcoholic, she may drink with him as a coping strategy to reduce the violence, since he may respond violently if she does not. Additionally, it is not uncommon for a battered woman to be given prescription medication by her physician for the explicit purpose of coping with anxiety resulting from abuse.

Another common reaction to coping with victimization is the minimization of the violent experience itself and of the anger felt in reaction to it (Ball & Wyman, 1978; Walker, 1981). An example illustrates this point. In being questioned about the lethal potential in her situation, a battered woman replied "no" to the inquiry about whether there were guns in the household, stating that there was only a pistol with no bullets. Her denial of the danger of the pistol and of the ready possibility of securing bullets is apparent. Another battered woman whose vagina was torn from repeated blows with her husband's fist stated in his defense that "he didn't realize what he was doing; he was pleasing himself." It is not uncommon for battered women to recall severe, long-forgotten incidents during an initial assessment interview.

OTHER CONSIDERATIONS FOR THE BATTERED WOMAN SYNDROME

In addition to the indicators of the BWS discussed above, two other areas are important to examine in identifying a battered woman who may suffer from the battered woman syndrome: (1) history of abuse and (2) susceptibility or high-risk factors.

An obvious prerequisite for the BWS is a history of physical, psychological, and/or sexual abuse. It is critical to consider not only the actual injuries or discrete episodes of violence that have occurred in assessing the abusive situation, but also the pattern of coercive control that the abusive partner exercises over the battered woman's behavior. For one woman, it required only a single incident—when her husband inserted a pistol loaded with one bullet into her vagina and pulled the trigger four times—for her to learn to respond compliantly to his slightest threat of violence. There were bruises from his punches and kicks, but no visible evidence of his near-lethal behavior. In this case, an astute observer need not require evidence of multiple episodes of physical abuse to understand the scope of his control over her and her terror associated with it.

Susceptibility factors function to influence or moderate the effects of the violence on the battered woman such that she is more vulnerable to the BWS. Bear in mind that the susceptibility factors do not refer to her increased susceptibility to being physically abused but to the BWS once the abuse has occurred. Based on the unique combination of these high-risk factors, the battered woman may be rendered even more vulnerable to the devastating effects of violence against her. These factors include both previous experiences and current attitudes.

Experiencing violence in the childhood home has been identified as one risk factor leading battered women to remain longer in the abusive relationship (Gelles & Cornell, 1985; Walker, 1984a), although Pagelow's (1981) data do not support this conclusion. Other previous victimization experiences (e.g., rape, abusive former marriages) may also contribute to the battered woman's increased susceptibility to the BWS. For one battered woman, her experience as a child who was sexually and physically abused by her father and raped by a neighbor reinforced the idea that all men are abusive and that at least her physically abusive husband was not sexually abusive.

A battered woman's attitudes and values may render her more susceptible to the BWS once the violence has occurred. Traditional values, which dictate the woman's role in marriage as one of primary responsibility to her husband, encourage her to remain in the marriage in spite of the abuse. The complex relationship between rigid sex-role socialization and the BWS has yet to be completely clarified, however (Walker, 1984a). For example, one battered woman recognized basic human rights for women, but also strongly believed in loyalty and commitment to her husband through both bad and good times. She had stayed with her husband in spite of his severe abuse toward her, with the idea that a "good enough" woman could love him out of his violent ways—a stereotypic belief that woman's role is one of nurturer and caretaker even at great cost to herself.

CRITIQUE OF THE BATTERED WOMAN SYNDROME

One major criticism of the BWS has been that it clinicalizes battered women, designating them as pathological. The BWS does not blame battered women for the occurrence of the violence, as the masochism theory does. However, some may argue that it individualizes the responsibility for stopping the violence, a responsibility that should fall on society at large. Furthermore, the BWS may pathologize women for not being successful at managing a larger social problem.

But in response to this criticism, the BWS is used to recognize and label the devastating impact on women from the battering they experience. In so doing, we can begin to examine systematically the differential effects on battered women and the factors that are associated with these differences.

In courtrooms, the BWS has been questioned on grounds of whether it is generally accepted in the psychological community (Bochnak, 1981). The American Psychological Association uses both psychological and legal literature to argue that it is (Kinports, Bersoff, & Ennis, 1983). Nevertheless, Bochnak (1981) points out that the relevant question is the adequacy and general acceptance of the methodology used by the expert in arriving at a conclusion, not the subject matter and not the specific conclusion.

INTERVENTION WITH THE BWS

Effective clinical or legal intervention with the BWS requires assessment of each of the factors identified above in the functional analysis. Intervention with the BWS can occur in three different phases, depending upon the issues that the battered woman is facing at the time. An additive model of intervention is presented; strategies of intervention are added cumulatively such that previous interventions are still appropriate and may be necessary even at later stages.

Phases of Intervention

Crisis

There are two primary objectives at the crisis phase of intervention: (1) to increase the battered woman's personal safety and that of her children and (2) to effect psychological stabilization. Following are specific behavioral goals for achieving the objective of increasing safety.

Assessing the risk of lethality is of paramount importance at this and subsequent stages of intervention. Browne (1984) identified seven factors useful for assessing the risk of lethal responses by the victims toward the batterer. These include greater frequency of violence and greater severity of injuries, the man's drug use and greater frequency of intoxication, forced or threatened sexual assault, the woman's suicide threat, and the man's threats to kill. Lethal incidents toward battered women occur at similar rates regardless of whether the batterer and victim are separated, although the risk of lethality is reduced for the batterer when the couple is separated (Bernard, Vera, Vera, & Newman, 1982).

Despite the statistics on separation, one obvious strategy for reducing the lethal potential for the battered woman is for her to leave the home and take shelter in a place unknown to the batterer, although this too may greatly increase her danger if the batterer finds out her location or if she eventually returns. Even in the light of seemingly great risk, some battered women remain in the situation. The woman's removing weapons from the home, or asking the batterer to do so, may reduce the lethal risk in some instances. However, the battered woman needs to be the one who makes this decision, since it is she who may be even more at risk then she already is if the batterer discovers her actions. Even if obvious weapons are removed from the home there are always others that can be found, including many household items like kitchen knives, hammers, and so forth. Some men may use their own body to maim and kill their partners. It remains incumbent on the battered woman to remain constantly vigilant about the level of risk in order to act defensively at the first indication of greater danger.

Assessing the pattern of violence, including cues that signal its occurrence (e.g., batterer's use of alcohol, following an argument), *and other forms of family violence* (e.g., physical or sexual assault on a child) is also extremely important. Inquiring about specific details of recent and typical incidents of abuse can facilitate identification of patterns if they exist. It is important to recognize that an obvious pattern may not exist, making it difficult for the battered woman to predict increased risk of abuse. Another caution: Even when concrete indicators have been identified for previous abusive incidents, there is no guarantee that future violence will follow a similar pattern. It is important to avoid providing the battered woman with a false sense of hope that she can control the violence if only she pays close enough attention to the pattern of its occurrence.

Again, the most certain method for increasing safety is physical removal to a secret location. However, many battered women choose not to leave the relationship, or if they do so, it is with the batterer's full knowledge of their whereabouts. Escape planning is one strategy whereby the battered woman develops a finely detailed plan of action that she is to implement at the first indication of a predetermined cue of increased danger. Some battered women resist developing such a plan, since it overtly acknowledges the possibility, and even the liklihood, that abuse will recur. The therapist may require the battered woman to develop an escape plan as a condition for continued treatment for several reasons: (1) there is no potential harm to her for doing so, (2) she must actively entertain the possibility of future violence and confront her responsibility to deal with her own and possibly her children's safety, and (3) the therapist provides a model for setting personal limits for interaction with another, much like the battered woman may need to do with the abuser.

Routinely asking the battered woman about risk to her children, either from the batterer or from her, may help identify potential instances of physical or sexual child abuse. In severe cases, a report to a social service agency is required as part of the Child Protection Act. This is a particularly sensitive issue, since reporting suspected child abuse to the authorities may increase the battered woman's risk of abuse from her partner. Also, insensitive child-protection workers may overreact and remove the child from the home, charging the battered woman with neglect and failure to protect her child. It is important to involve the battered woman as much as possible in the reporting of suspected child abuse by the man in order to devise a plan to decrease her risks.

Financial aid, social support, and emotional resources are needed to *assess the resources available for relocation* from the abusive home, whether it be to a local shelter, to the home of a family member or friend, or to an independent living situation such as a new home or apartment. Systematically evaluating the resources available and those needed is helpful in reaching a decision. Even when ample resources exist for the battered woman to relocate, the decision to do so remains her own. Otherwise, the battered woman is in a similar position with the professional as with her abusive partner: both are exercising control over her life.

Assessing the feasibility of legal action, including reports to police, obtaining restraining orders, and filing criminal charges, is important, since that may help increase the battered woman's safety. Temporary custody orders may protect children by enabling authorities to reclaim them from a batterer who may use them as yet another vehicle for control over the battered woman's life. Taking formal action of this type can be an effective strategy for enabling the battered woman to gain a sense of personal power and self-efficacy regarding her situation. However, as with other issues, it is important for the battered woman to make the final decision regarding these actions, since it is she who must live with their consequences. If a district attorney, for example, were to pursue charges without the battered woman's cooperation, it is imperative that precautions be taken, including informing her of the action, so that she may make informed choices about her safety.

The professional has an ethical responsibility to *document information about the violence* so that it will be available to assist the victim in the future. The documentation may provide the supportive evidence necessary to evict a batterer from the home or to obtain a criminal conviction for battering. The violence may be documented in the therapist's or lawyer's notes, in reports of legal action, in police or medical reports, and by photographs.

The second goal of the crisis phase, stabilizing the battered woman psychologically, can occur in two ways. First, *assessing the battered woman's mental status* can help determine the current level of psychological distress and the level of its interference with her daily functioning. Specifically, a mental-status exam should include an evaluation of the following: (1) appearance and behavior, (2) thought processes, (3) mood and affect, (4) intellectual functioning, and (5) sensorium (Nelson & Barlow, 1981). The battered woman may be able to respond effectively to the stress of the violence or it may render her unable to function independently, including providing for the care of herself or her children. Medication should rarely be considered, especially when the battered woman remains in the abusive environment, since it may only aid to numb her further to the reality of her situation. Suicide potential should be explicitly evaluated, since it is a potential risk accompanying depression and since a high suicide risk may signal an increased risk for lethal action by the batterer or by the victim toward him (Browne, 1984).

Second, *the risk of homicide* to the batterer should be evaluated by looking at the battered woman's perception of the potential for serious or life-threatening abuse toward her or her children. Examining thoughts of defending oneself using lethal means should be done explicitly. Determining the battered woman's previous pattern of anger expression can be helpful in judging risk for aggressive retaliation. Since many battered women may fantasize about the batterer's dying, it is important to examine the actual likelihood of her bringing this about. Of course, any indication of the likelihood of homicidal behavior should be taken seriously, followed by measures to reduce its likelihood of danger to the potential victims.

Decision-Making

The primary objective in this phase of intervention is for the woman to make a decision regarding continuation or separation from the relationship. In order to do this the following goals need to be addressed.

Defining the battered woman's situation as a choice point for her restructures it as one in which she has personal power. That is, rather than being controlled by the batterer, the battered woman has a choice about what to do with her life. Regardless of her decision, it is her own, one that she can maintain or alter at some future time. It is essential that the professional recognize that the decision to stay or leave the relationship is one for the battered woman to make, although not without support. The most important message to communicate to the battered woman is her right to make decisions that affect her life.

In order for the battered woman to *accept personal responsibility for her safety*, it is important to confront her with the reality that her well-being and safety are her responsibility, not one she can assume someone else will accept. In accepting this responsibility, the battered woman begins to define her situation as one over which she has control, not one in which she is controlled. Stereotypic female sex-role socialization ascribes responsibility for a woman's protection to the men in her life; thus it is often difficult for a battered woman to assume an autonomous role, even with regard to her own safety.

It is essential that the battered woman *reject personal responsibility for the violence*. To the extent that she makes internal attributions regarding the violence, she must give over that responsibility to the batterer. As long as she assumes responsibility for the violence, or even for the anger that preceded it, she may continue to look to herself for the solution to the batterer's violence. The battered woman needs to recognize that neither she, the therapist, nor her attorney can control the batterer's behavior. Only the batterer himself, or legal sanctions such as confinement in jail, can manage such a task.

A systematic and explicit *evaluation of the costs and benefits of staying in the relationship or leaving it* for the battered woman, for her children, and for her partner is a helpful strategy. An important issue to address with the battered woman is one of priorities, that is, whose costs and benefits should be considered as more weighty in her potential action. An invaluable consideration for the professional is to view the exercise as simply a process helpful in clarifying a decision for the battered woman. The weighted importance of each consideration again must be determined by the woman herself.

The battered woman needs to *evaluate her personal criteria for staying in the relationship*. A decision to stay in the relationship is often a tentative one. That is, the battered woman often decides to stay to see if temporary improvements will last or to see if the batterer carries through with the promises to change. Thus it becomes important for her to establish criteria against which she can evaluate her decision to remain in the relationship. Otherwise, it is remarkably easy for the battered woman to lose sight of her needs for change in light of the batterer's often persuasive or coercive manner. Even though a battered woman may remain even if her criteria for staying are not met, they still provide her with clear feedback regarding the status of her relationship.

Restructuring

In this final phase, the objectives for intervention are remarkably similar regardless of whether the battered woman is rebuilding her life outside of the abusive relationship or attempting to restructure her life as violence-free within the relationship. Of course, if violence recurs in the relationship, intervention necessarily needs to focus on either the crisis or decision-making phases; clearly, restructuring is not then appropriate. The objectives are (1) to reduce the traumatic effects of victimization, (2) to compensate for learned helplessness deficits, and (3) to develop more adaptive responses to stress, including violence if it recurs. Most interventions have both a behavioral and a cognitive component. All three objectives can be accomplished with the following goals.

The first goal is *increased self-efficacy and behavioral competence*. The most essential goal of intervention is to create a perception by the battered woman that she is capable of responding in ways that have a positive impact on her life, that is, that outcomes are contingent on her behavior. Since a lack of self-efficacy may have existed regardless of the level of her behavioral competence, it may or may not be necessary to develop new competencies. Instrumental skills (e.g., job and financial management skills) are necessary for greater independence in living and function to increase the woman's power over her own life, regardless of whether she remains in the previous relationship, begins a new relationship, or lives on her own.

The second goal relates to *assertiveness*. Establishing a belief in her individual rights is necessary for the woman to protect herself against the coercive control of others. An assertive behavioral repertoire enables the woman effectively to get her needs met, be they from her partner, her employer, or her social network. A women's group where role-play can be used is a particularly useful tool for increasing assertiveness.

Anger management is the third goal. Without effective intervention, the battered woman may carry around anger from the abusive relationship for a lengthy period of time. Anger may interfere with intimacy in either a new relationship or in the previously abusive one. It is important that the battered woman recognize and label her anger and effectively express it. That requires an environment where it is safe to express anger without fear of retaliation.

Relaxation training may facilitate a *reduction of anxiety symptoms* (Walker, 1984a) once the threat of violence has ceased. Of course, if violence remains, anxiety and fear are normal reactions to danger. Self-defense training (Ball & Wyman, 1978; Walker, 1984a) may also increase a woman's sense of control over her physical safety and thus reduce symptoms of fear and anxiety.

Since the battered woman has often faced extreme isolation, *increased social support* can be extremely useful in decreasing her sense of aloneness, in providing models for effective functioning, and in counteracting feelings of depression. A women's support group is helpful in that the battered woman can hear from other women about their similar experiences. Developing skills to generate additional sources of social support is ultimately necessary.

Cognitive and behavioral strategies for *decreasing the battered woman's depression* are often necessary. The use of behavioral prescriptions for activity can be extremely useful in getting the woman to experience situations that are rewarding to her. Living a life where her daily activity was often controlled and monitored has typically restricted her experience of pleasurable activity. The woman can come to learn that she can be in control of providing pleasure for herself.

Reducing alcohol/drug abuse is sometimes necessary. The use of alcohol and drugs, although initially for the purpose of numbing the effects of the abuse, may have become addicting, or at least may interfere with a productive life. Developing new coping strategies for responding to stress, including threats of violence, are necessary to replace old patterns. Referral to an alcohol or drug program may be warranted.

Economic independence is a critical issue for a battered woman. A woman cannot be free of control by another as long as she is economically dependent upon some other person. Although a woman may have the option and may choose not to become employed, it is important to explore ways in which she can gain greater control over her financial security, e.g., savings accounts and credit cards in her name.

Examining and restructuring sex-role expectations and norms concerning wife abuse are important processes in intervention with battered women. Other expectations, which bind the woman in a stereotypic role of helplessness and powerlessness and the man in a stereotypic role of all-powerful provider and protector, are important to redress in order to free both the battered woman and her partner from emotional entrapments that can ultimately lead to anger, rage, and depression (Goldberg, 1982).

CONSIDERATIONS FOR THE CLINICAL OR LEGAL PROFESSIONAL

There are a number of considerations that are equally important to the psychological and legal professional working with battered women.

First, it is important to remind oneself continually that the battered woman has a right to make decisions that affect her own life, even when they are not popular ones. The primary role of the therapist and the attorney alike is to help identify options for the battered woman and to educate her as fully as possible about the likely consequence of each. Battered women typically are faced with several major life decisions—for example, whether to leave the relationship and, if so, whether to move out or attempt to have the batterer leave; whether to pursue legal charges against her partner for his violence; and whether to trust her abusive partner with her children's safety. The latter issue may require action on the part of the psychological or legal professional if s/he determines that a child is at risk for abuse and if the battered woman is not willing or able to ensure the child's safety. As a rule, however, the battered woman's decisions do not mandate the authoritative intervention of the professional. On the contrary, the decision-making tasks she faces provide an excellent opportunity for the professional to enable her to recognize the rights to her own decisions and to provide her with the information and support to make them. All too often, both the therapist and lawyer may feel as if they have failed if the battered woman does not make the decision they believe to be in her best interest.

The relationship between the battered woman and the professional person often strikingly parallels that of the batterer and the victim. The professional, like the batterer, believes s/he knows what is best for the battered woman and attempts to control her behavior to conform to that mold in order not to feel like a failure. Like the batterer, the professional must recognize the battered woman's right to make her own decisions. The difference is that the professional has an expertise to enable the abused woman to make those decisions with the most resources possible.

A second consideration is that effective and comprehensive intervention with the battered woman involves a continual and long-term process, often punctuated by times when she is not actively engaged in change. It is necessary to identify intervention as a continual process in order not to join the battered woman in her sense of helplessness. Efforts by the victim toward removing herself from the abusive situation are frequently aborted far short of completion, much to the chagrin of her therapist or lawyer. It is at this point that all too many professionals abandon the battered woman without a continued commitment to her struggle. The challenge for the professional is to recognize the battered woman's progress toward a safer environment in however small the steps she takes.

A third consideration is that the professional may encounter situations of physical danger in working with the battered woman. It is important to take indications of danger seriously and, as much as possible, to ensure others' as well as one's own safety. It may be necessary to exercise the duty to warn when faced with a threat of potential danger from either the batterer or the victim. In his discussion of the issue, Sonkin (1986) interprets recent court rulings to indicate that clinicians must consider all threats made by patients seriously; assume that an established history of violence is sufficient evidence that future violence will probably reoccur; and use reasonable care to protect both intended and unintended victims against such danger.

The danger that the professional faces for her/himself parallels that of the battered woman; they both have equally little control over the batterer's violence. The professional has the opportunity to make use of a full range of options to maximize her/his safety, thus providing a positive model for the battered woman. As with the battered woman, however, the danger is real and is occasionally realized.

A fourth consideration is burnout, which can occur quickly. Efforts to counteract its effects include working with a team that can provide both emotional and professional support keeping a balance in one's role between over- and underresponsibility, and attending adequately to one's own mental health needs outside the professional role.

CONCLUSION

The *battered woman syndrome* is a term useful for recognizing the cumulative and devastating effects of exposure to continued and often severe physical, sexual, and/or psychological abuse. Further, identifying the BWS has enabled researchers and clinicians to begin examining the specific violence and high-risk factors that contribute to its development and maintenance. The utility of the BWS is immeasurable when it is used to educate a judge, a defense attorney, or a jury about why a battered woman does not just leave her abusive relationship if it is so bad. Finally, identifying the BWS enables clinicians to develop better, more effective methods of intervention to help the battered woman respond to the violence against her.

It is important to recognize that the BWS does not explain why violence occurs in the first place. Additionally, recognition of the BWS in no way diminishes the need to address social responses to stopping all forms of violence within the home. What are left in all cases, however, are individual women struggling with the circumstances of their own violent situations. They cannot wait for social reform; their lives are too important. Recognizing and understanding the BWS can help both the psychologist and the lawyer in working toward environments safe from violence on behalf of the individual battered woman, and thus all battered women.

REFERENCES

American Psychiatric Association. (1980). *Diagnostic and statistical manual of mental disorders* (3rd ed.). Washington, DC: Author.

Ball, P.G., & Wyman, E. (1978). Battered wives and powerlessness: What can counselors do? *Victimology, 2* (3–4), 545–552.

Bandura, A. (1977). Self-efficacy: Toward a unifying theory of behavioral change. *Psychological Review, 84*, 191–215.

Bernard, G.W., Vera, H., Vera, M., & Newman, G. (1982). Till death do us part. *Bulletin of the American Academy of Psychiatry and the Law, 10*(4).

Bochnak, E. (1981). *Women's self-defense cases: Theory and practice.* Charlottesville, VA: The Michie Company.

Bowker, L.H. (1983). Marital rape: A distinct syndrome? *Social Casework: The Journal of Contemporary Social Work, 64,* 347–352.

Browne, A. (1984, June). *When battered women kill.* Paper presented at the Second National Conference on Family Violence Research, Durham, NH.

Gelles, R.J., & Cornell, C.P. (1985). *Intimate violence in families.* Beverly Hills Sage.

Goldberg, H. (1982). The dynamics of rage between the sexes in a bonded relationship. In L.R. Barnhill (Ed.), *Clinical approaches to family violence.* Rockville, MD: Aspen System Corporation.

Hilberman, E., & Munson, K. (1978). Sixty battered women. *Victimology: An International Journal, 2* (3–4), 460–470.

Katz, S., & Mazur, M.A. (1979). *Understanding the rape victim.* New York: John Wiley.

Kinports, K., Bersoff, D., & Ennis, B. (1983). *Brief of amicus curiae, American Psychological Association.* Hawthorne vs. Florida, No. AN-635.

Nelson, R.O., & Barlow, D.H. (1981). Behavioral assessment: Basic strategies and initial procedures. In D.H. Barlow (Ed.), *Behavioral assessment of adult disorders.* New York: The Guilford Press.

Pagelow, M.D. (1981). Factors affecting women's decisions to leave violent relationships. *Journal of Family Issues, 2* (4), 391–414.

Seligman, M.E.P. (1975). *Helplessness: On depression, development and death.* San Francisco: W.H. Freeman.

Sonkin, D.J. (1986). Clairvoyance vs common sense: Therapist's duty to warn and protect. *Violence and Victims, 1,* 7–21.

Straus, M.A., Gelles, R.J., & Steinmetz, S.K. (1980). *Behind closed doors: Violence in the American family.* New York: Doubleday.

Walker, L.E. (1981). Battered women: Sex roles and clinical issues. *Professional Psychology, 12* (1), 81–89.

Walker, L.E.A. (1984a). The battered woman syndrome. New York: Springer Publishing Co.

Walker, L.E.A. (1984b). Battered women, psychology, and public policy. *American Psychologist, 39* (10), 1178–1182.

4

Battered Women in Court: Jury and Trial Consultants and Expert Witnesses

Roberta K. Thyfault
Cathy E. Bennett
Robert B. Hirschhorn

On January 29, 1985, Marian Rosen, an attorney in Houston, Texas, received a phone call informing her that one of her clients had just shot her husband. The client was Kay Sandiford. Her husband was Frank Sandiford, an internationally known heart surgeon. Kay claimed that Frank had been beating her and that she shot him as he was coming toward her with a tennis racket. The state said it was premeditated murder. If convicted, Kay faced the possibility of a life sentence.

It became Rosen's job to convince a jury that Kay had not planned her husband's death but had shot him in self-defense. To do so, Rosen had to select a jury that would listen to Kay's story as a battered woman. It was a story of violence in an expensive home in an exclusive neighborhood and during frequent trips abroad. It was also a story very different from what the public knew of Dr. and Mrs. Sandiford.

In an effort to present this story to a receptive jury, Rosen used a jury and trial consultant (Cathy Bennett) to assist her in selecting a jury and preparing trial strategy. She also presented the testimony of an expert witness (Lenore Walker), who testified about the battered women syndrome and its effect on Kay.

The jury did convict Kay of murder, but of the lesser crime of voluntary manslaughter, which carried a sentence of up to 20 years in prison. Under Texas law, the jury that renders a verdict can also determine the sentence. In this case, the jury sentenced Kay to a ten-year term of probation and a fine of $10,000. After Kay successfully completed two years of this sentence, her conviction was set aside (Sandiford & Burgess, 1984).

Kay's conviction on the lesser charge and her unprecedented sentence illustrate the impact an expert witness and a jury and trial consultant can have on a trial that involves a battered woman. The case also shows the vital roles these experts play throughout the trial, from preparation through sentencing. This chapter will explore these roles and the various ways in which these experts can assist an attorney who is representing a battered woman.

The first part of this chapter will discuss the need for expert witness testimony about battered women and how the expert can be used throughout the trial process. Some of the recent court decisions that have addressed the issue of expert witness testimony for battered women will be highlighted. The second part will address areas of special concern when selecting a jury to hear a case in which battering is a central issue, as well as special areas in which this expert can assist the lawyer during the trial. A central theme throughout this chapter is that it is only through the team effort of an attorney and experts in the area of domestic violence that our courts and public will be educated and thus responsive to the battered woman.

EXPERT TESTIMONY

Although jury and trial consultants, psychologists, and other mental health workers are often called on to be expert witnesses in the courtroom, it is only recently that they have begun to serve as witnesses for battered women. With increased attention being given to the problem of domestic violence, more and more battered women are finding themselves involved in the judicial system.

A recent Connecticut case, *Thurman* v. *City of Torrington*, 595 F. Supp. 1521 (D. Conn. 1984), is indicative of cases throughout the country that have challenged law enforcement procedures for responding to domestic violence calls. The changes that have been made in the wake of these lawsuits have placed many battered women in court as witnesses against their battering mates. Domestic violence is frequently raised as an issue in divorce and child-custody cases. Some women have also begun to bring civil suit for the batterings they received, as evidenced by a Colorado case in which a jury awarded a wife $115,000 in damages. Finally, far too often, battered women are finding themselves in court as defendants in criminal actions. These criminal charges are usually brought when a woman has wounded or killed her batterer or when she is involved in other criminal activity with her batterer. In each of these situations, the expert witness can have a critical role in the preparation and presentation of a case.

Is Expert Testimony Necessary?

Before a witness can testify as an expert in any case, it must be shown that the testimony will be of some help to the judge or jury who will be rendering the verdict. Traditionally, it was required that the testimony meet the three criteria set forth in *Dyas* v. *United States*, 376 A.2d 827 (D.C. 1977). These criteria are: (1) that the subject matter "must be so distinctively related to some science, profession, business or occupation as to be beyond the ken of the average laymen"; (2) that "the witness must have sufficient skill, knowledge or experience in that field or calling as to make it appear that his opinion or inference will probably aid the trier in his search for truth"; and (3) that "expert testimony is [admissible only] if the state of the pertinent art or scientific knowledge . . . permits a reasonable opinion to be asserted by an expert" (*Dyas*, 376 A.2d at 832). A more modern trend is to allow expert testimony so long as it will assist the trier of fact to understand the evidence in a case or to determine a fact that is at issue in the case. This is the approach followed by Federal Rule of Evidence 702 and some state courts that have adopted the Federal Rules of Evidence (Thyfault, 1984).

The first case to recognize that the subject matter of battered women was beyond the ken of the average juror was a 1977 Washington, D.C. case, *Ibn-Tamas* v. *United States*, 407 A.2d 626 (D.C. 1979). The case involved a battered woman who was on trial for the death of her husband. The trial judge would not allow an expert to testify and Ibn-Tamas was convicted of murder. On appeal, it was determined that the subject matter of battered women was proper for expert testimony because it would have "supplied an interpretation of the facts which differed from the ordinary lay perception . . . advocated by the [prosecution] . . ." that the battered woman could have gotten out of the relationship (*Ibn-Tamas*, 407 A.2d at 634–635). Although the appellate court determined that the expert testimony was beyond the ken of the jurors, it was still necessary to establish that the testimony met the other two criteria of the *Dyas* test. The trial court eventually determined that the *Dyas* test had not been met and the testimony was excluded. The case was once again appealed, however, and this time the trial court's ruling was upheld [*Ibn-Tamas* v. *United States*, 455 A.2d 893 (D.C. 1983).

Since the first *Ibn-Tamas* decision in 1979, most of the courts that have considered the issue have concluded that the subject of battered women was beyond the knowledge of most people and therefore expert testimony was proper. Only the Ohio Supreme Court, in *State* v. *Thomas*, 423 N.E.2d 137 (Ohio 1981), has held that the testimony was not necessary to help the jury.

The Ohio court concluded that a jury was well able to understand and determine if Thomas had a bona fide belief that her life was in danger when she shot her boyfriend.

One argument that has been advocated in an attempt to exclude the expert testimony goes as follows. In light of our high divorce rate, most Americans have some knowledge of, and even personal experience with, divorce and separation. Therefore, they know a great deal about the complexities of marital relationships. Furthermore, since half of the public are women, most of them would be aware of the problems that face the woman who tries to leave a relationship. Given these factors, the expert testimony will not aid the jury and thus should not be heard by jurors (Acker & Toch, 1985). This argument was apparent in the closing statement made by the prosecutor in *State* v. *Kelly*, 478 A.2d 364, 378 (N.J. 1984), when she said, "but life isn't pretty. Life is not a bowl of cherries. We each and every person who takes a breath has problems. Defense counsel says bruised and battered. Is there any one of us who hasn't been battered by life in some manner or means?" Such an argument is flawed in several respects. First, it assumes that there would be a representative number of women on a jury or that a woman judge would be trying a case. It also erroneously assumes that women jurors would be more likely to be understanding of another woman (Bochnak, 1981).

However, the most significant flaw in the argument is the assumption that the dynamics that lead to separation and divorce in a nonviolent relationship are the same as those in a violent relationship. Research has shown that there are differences between violent and nonviolent relationships (Walker, 1984; Straus, Gelles, & Steinmetz, 1980). There are also differences between violent relationships that end in homicide and those that do not result in a death (Browne, in press, 1983).

It is assumptions such as these that require expert testimony to explain how the two situations differ. Some may think they have an understanding of a violent relationship, perhaps because of personal experience. However, the testimony of an expert in this area will allow the juror to evaluate adequately the accuracy of this understanding. This is not to say that a trier of fact must accept the expert's testimony. Rather, the testimony provides additional information to be used, along with any personal knowledge or experience, to reach a verdict.

The need for expert testimony is especially critical in a homicide case where the battered woman asserts a plea of self-defense (Bochnak, 1981; Schneider & Jordan, 1981; Thyfault, 1984). The expert testimony can help the judge or jury understand why the woman believed she was in such imminent danger that she needed to use deadly force to protect herself. The testimony can also establish the reasonableness of that belief.

It is important to remember that in these situations the battered woman is not claiming, "I am battered, therefore I have a right to kill my batterer."

What she is asserting, through the expert testimony and perhaps her own testimony, is that, "Because of the history of violence in this relationship, I was sensitive to cues from the batterer that made me believe that I was in imminent danger."

The expert testimony can also help the battered woman prove that she is not mentally ill (Thyfault, 1984; Walker, 1979). In this regard, the testimony is especially important to the battered woman who is involved in a child-custody case, as well as the battered woman facing criminal charges.

It is interesting to note that expert testimony has also been used to rebut a husband's defense of insanity. In *State* v. *Baker*, 424 A.2d 171 (N.H. 1980), a husband was charged with attempted murder in the shooting of his wife. During the trial the prosecution called experts on battered women to testify that the man was a batterer and was therefore not insane when he shot his wife.

Scope of the Testimony

Unlike most witnesses, expert witnesses are usually allowed to give opinion testimony. However, the scope of their opinion will differ from court to court.

Some courts have allowed the expert to express an opinion as to the ultimate issue in a case. For example, in a case where a woman asserts a plea of self-defense, an expert may be able to express an opinion that a battered woman reasonably believed she was in imminent danger and therefore acted in self-defense. This kind of "ultimate issue" testimony was allowed in *Smith* v. *State*, 277 S.E.2d 678 (Ga. 1981).

Other courts have restricted the testimony to that of battered women in general. Still others will allow testimony about battered women in general as well as the specific battered woman who is in court. In the recent case of *State* v. *Kelly*, 478 A.2d 364 (N.J. 1984), the New Jersey Supreme Court determined that "the expert could state [the] defendant had the battered woman's syndrome, and could explain that syndrome in detail, relating its characteristics to defendant, but only to enable the jury to better determine the honesty and reasonableness of defendant's belief" her life and her daughter's life were in danger (*Kelly*, 478 A.2d at 378). The court reasoned that it was not proper for the expert to express the opinion that Kelly's belief she was in imminent danger was reasonable, because the area of the expert's knowledge only related to the reasons why she was unable to leave her husband. The court concluded that while an expert is necessary to explain the battered woman syndrome, no expert testimony is needed to tell a jury that a person who has been beaten severely and continuously might have a reasonable fear that she is in imminent danger.

Recent changes in federal law may also restrict the testimony of mental health professionals. Under this new law, Federal Rule of Evidence 704(b), an expert can no longer express an ultimate opinion about whether a person was in the mental state necessary to be convicted of a crime, i.e., whether she was insane or had the specific intent to commit the crime. However, the new rule does not preclude the expert from giving an opinion about a psychiatric diagnosis, i.e., whether she fit within a diagnosis recognized by the *Diagnostic and Statistical Manual* (DSM). Thus, it is uncertain just what effect this new rule may have on expert testimony. While few cases involving battered women appear in federal court, many states have adopted the Federal Rules of Evidence. Thus it is possible that they may also follow this new rule.

The Roles of the Expert Witness

Most of this discussion has focused on the expert who is testifying in court. However, the work of the expert witness encompasses much more than courtroom testimony.

As an expert witness, the mental health professional becomes both a teacher and a student. The expert must be willing to teach the attorney who is representing the woman about domestic violence. This will usually mean providing the attorney with reading materials in addition to being available for consultation. This role as educator is important, because there is no reason to assume that attorneys have greater knowledge than anyone else about battered women. Frequently, the expert is utilized solely as a consultant and thus never has to testify in court.

The expert must also be prepared to learn about the legal system. Each state has its own rules governing the admissibility of expert testimony. The fact that experts are allowed to testify in one court is no guarantee they will be admitted in the next case. The best example of this can be shown by two Wyoming cases. In *Buhrle* v. *State*, 627 P.2d 1374 (Wyo. 1981), the Wyoming Supreme Court ruled that the "state of the art" of the study of battered women could not support an expert opinion and thus that expert testimony would be inadmissible. However, the same psychologist who was called to testify in *Buhrle* had previously been allowed to testify in a homicide case in the same court, *State* v. *Austin*, No. 7828 (Natrona Cty, Wyo, 1979).

The expert must also be willing to learn about the attorney's theory of the case. This will usually require reading state statutes and case law. Only then will it be possible to decide if expert testimony will be helpful. The expert must also be willing to learn how to testify and how to respond to cross-examination.

The interviewing skills mental health professionals have make them especially useful to the attorney. A thorough clinical interview of the battered woman will undoubtedly provide the attorney with information he or she was unable to elicit. This interview is also helpful in preparing the woman to testify in court (Browne & Thyfault, 1981).

Finally, expert witness mental health professionals will likely find themselves in the role of crisis counselor to the woman and perhaps her family. This is especially true as the time for court appearances approaches.

JURY AND TRIAL CONSULTANT

A jury and trial consultant is a professional who assists the lawyer in trial strategy, jury selection, witness preparation, and trial observations. They give lawyers and their clients insight into the type of jury to select and the impact on jurors of women who: (1) kill in self-defense, (2) testify against their husbands, or (3) divorce and sue their husbands. A case is 85 percent over by the time the jury is selected. Therefore, extraordinary care and attention must be paid to this critical aspect of the trial.

Voir dire is a French term meaning "to speak the truth." It is the legal term for the process of interviewing jurors—the principle of encouraging people to tell the truth in the courtroom. Studies have confirmed what trial lawyers and jury consultants have consistently observed: Potential jurors are intimidated by their surroundings and fearful of being judged themselves. They have numerous biases and life experiences that must be explored in the courtroom. The peculiar problems of battered women must be handled extremely delicately so as not to discourage the openness that is necessary to uncover potential jurors' feelings regarding women on trial, domestic violence, expert witnesses, divorce and separation, racial prejudice, fear, self-defense, the use of deadly force, guns, and the battered woman syndrome.

Studies indicate that one out of three potential jurors intentionally does not tell the truth during jury selection. This phenomenon is attributable to a variety of factors: their fear of embarrassment, shyness or difficulty in speaking in groups, or their desire to be included or excluded from the jury. The fear of public speaking is overwhelming to many and needs to be handled with great sensitivity.

Potential jurors tell jury and trial consultants that they were embarrassed to talk about sensitive issues in front of the other jurors. They say that their own feelings of inadequacy, indecisiveness, fear, weakness, and failure surface during these courtroom interviews. Silence in response to these questions is often sought as an escape. Professionals who have observed a jury selection in which lawyers probed these sensitive areas have seen the pain in the potential jurors' faces and their wish to avoid answering such questions. Therefore, the lawyer should request of the court that the issues be discussed privately with each juror. If necessary, expert testimony should be presented to the judge to sensitize him or her to why potential jurors would not be as candid as they would like to be if they are interviewed in the open court.

Asking these sorts of sensitive questions requires lawyers and experts to become vulnerable themselves. This vulnerability will help the potential jurors want to hear the battered woman's side of the case.

During the jury selection process, an attorney must listen carefully, watch what the potential jurors are saying nonverbally, be congruent, and show that he or she cares about the client. It is important for attorneys to be themselves, with all of their true perception, thoughts, and feelings.

Sexual Bias

Women face sexual bias in the courtroom. The lawyer, with the help of a person experienced in dealing with this issue, needs to ask potential jurors about women's issues carefully and meticulously. They usually do not know or are unwilling to admit that they are prejudiced toward women as parties in criminal or civil proceedings involving abuse; so the lawyer must convey through good interviewing techniques a sensitivity to the problem. The following questions suggest areas of sexual bias that need to be discussed with the potential jurors:

1. What are a woman's rights in a marriage or relationship?
2. What did she do to put her on trial?
3. Are women treated more leniently than men on trial?
4. Do women overreact in many situations?
5. Are women too emotional?
6. Why did she not call the police or a family member?
7. Why did she not leave?

This discussion should not be handled by saying, "Don't you agree sexual bias exists in the courtroom?" Intimidation follows from such a question. The more delicate approach of asking potential jurors to say how they feel about each of the propositions will reap more benefits. This will lessen the threat the potential juror feels and encourage him or her to respond honestly.

Domestic Violence

Violence in our personal lives has existed for everyone in varying degrees. The magnitude of the damage and turmoil is the real crux of the problem. If individuals on the panel are afraid of their own feelings about having been battered, then perhaps they will not be open to the battered woman's feelings. Some will have battered someone themselves and will struggle to justify their own actions.

Emotional versus physical battering is a frequent conflict in potential jurors' perceptions of violence. Many feel that domestic violence only means physical episodes and that a woman loses her claim of violence if it was psychological in nature. These findings are based on numerous jury selections involving these issues and thousands of post-trial interviews of jurors. Dealing with this during *voir dire* and through the client's testimony provides the link between the potential juror's private world and the client's.

Asking persons to talk about their own experiences with domestic violence is the most difficult area in which to receive honest answers. Therefore, the questioning should be conducted in private, if possible.

Questions that need to be asked during the interview with the client and during jury selection are:

1. What does family violence mean to you?
2. What experiences in your life have affected you in a significant way?
3. Tell me about books, magazines articles, or television shows that you have read or seen regarding violence in the family.
4. In what ways do you believe that emotional violence and physical violence are alike?
5. Have you, any family member, neighbor, or co-worker ever been the victim of any crime involving violence? (Tell the juror you can approach the bench to discuss this experience.) Please tell me about the experience.
6. What organizations do you or your family belong to?
7. What is the major cause of divorce?
8. What is the main cause of domestic violence?

VIOLENCE AND RACIAL PREJUDICE

Many people believe that black, Hispanic, Asian, and Native American people are more prone to violence than are whites. They feel that members of these cultures are more apt to express feelings toward others through violent means.

Prejudice is ugly anywhere, but when it could influence the judicial process it must be thoroughly questioned. The lawyers representing a minority woman need to examine their own prejudices and work through them. Humanizing the client in one's own eyes is best done by getting to know her, by entering her world and learning that feelings of sadness, fear, and conflict cross all cultural lines. These feelings have to be communicated to the jury. The jurors must be made to see and feel how their possible racial biases prevent them from understanding the client.

Suggested questions to ask potential jurors are:

1. What does family violence mean to you?
2. Have you ever felt labeled in your life for any reason? Tell me about that.

3. What is prejudice?
4. Tell me about an incident you have seen of one person behaving in a prejudiced way toward another. How did that make you feel?
5. Some people believe that black, Hispanic, and Native American people have more violence in their cultures than do whites. Have you heard this? Tell me what you have heard.
6. Other people feel that blacks (Hispanics, Native Americans, etc.) have more violence in their families than do white people. What do you feel about that?
7. Some other people feel that violence toward a black (Hispanic, Asian, Native American, etc.) woman is more acceptable than toward a white woman. What do you feel?
8. Law enforcement officers are hesitant to go into a black (Hispanic, Asian, Native American, etc.) neighborhood to respond to a domestic violence call. What are your feelings about that behavior?

Marital Problems

Personal experiences with marital problems will affect jurors' emotions in a trial, causing them to second-guess the woman's actions. Frequently heard remarks are: "I had problems in my marriage but we worked it out; I've gotten angry with my husband but I never killed him; why didn't she leave if she was afraid; she should have gotten out, if it was that bad; why didn't she call the police, I did?" Remarks such as these evidence the barriers to empathy toward the client. With the help of an expert, a lawyer can ask questions of potential jurors that will help break down these barriers.

This is another area of questioning that should be conducted in private. No one is proud of marital problems, so this, coupled with other inhibiting factors, dictates extra effort to secure honest responses. Suggested questions are:

1. What are the causes of problems in marriages?
2. What should a woman do if she has marital difficulties?
3. What might be some reasons why a woman would not tell anyone about her marital difficulties?
4. I feel uncomfortable asking this, but I must know who has gone through the break-up of a relationship, a separation, or a divorce? (We can discuss this privately, if you desire). Tell me about this experience. What are your feelings about that? Did you hire a lawyer to help deal with this? If so, what was the result?
5. Has anyone in your family or any friend ever been through such an experience? Please tell me about what happened. Did they hire a lawyer? What was the result?

Fear

Fear is a common denominator among emotions. All other emotions are reactions in one way or another to this basic feeling. Effectively describing this to a jury brings them into the client's environment. The lawyer must ask questions about fear, experts must testify about it, and the client must learn to explain how it affected her. People constantly avoid acknowledging this emotion, though it motivates and inhibits us daily. Our limitations as human beings are brought to the surface when fear grips us. The consultant's sharing his or her own understanding of fear and its effects will help the client open up. A lawyer's sharing himself or herself with the potential jury will help them recognize how fear affects them and, thus, the client.

Questions for jury selection include:

1. How does fear affect people?
2. Tell me about an experience where you were afraid.
3. How did it affect you?
4. Tell me the difference between how you behave when you are afraid as opposed to not afraid?
5. Have you ever been in fear of your life? Tell me about that.
6. Some people feel that fear makes people do things they normally would not do. What do you think about that?

Self-Defense

Self-defense is a concept that means many things to many people. Frequently the discussion takes some moral turns. A portion of our population believes in the "turn the other cheek" stance; others feel that a person should be entitled to "stand their ground" and that using deadly force can be necessary, if dictated by fear. Because some feel that self-defense does not mean protecting one's own life or one's loved ones, this value must be explored in jury selection. Experts and lawyers find that even a battered spouse has difficulties dealing with her own self-protection instincts. Thus experts and lawyers need first to deal with the client's feelings about self-defense and then to talk with the potential jurors about the issue.

Some potential jurors say they can understand situations in which someone could shoot another in self-defense, such as an intruder into a home or a mugger on a subway (as in the *Goetz* case in New York). In the same breath, many of them deny the same right to a woman who is threatened or intimidated in her own home by her own spouse or lover. The old questions of why she did not call the police or leave if things were so bad raise their misinformed heads. Once again, the potential jurors' values must be discussed. Someone who does not feel that a woman should defend herself, use deadly force, or stand her own ground in a domestic situation should not sit on the jury.

Questions to ask potential jurors are:

1. What does self-defense mean to you?
2. Have you ever felt trapped? How did you respond? How did that make you feel?
3. Have you ever felt terrified? How did that make you feel?
4. Have you ever been in a situation where you felt you needed to defend yourself, emotionally or physically? Tell me about that.
5. Some feel that defending oneself only extends to street muggers or someone who breaks into your home. What are some other instances in which you feel you should defend yourself?
6. If someone attacked you or you feared they might, what would you do?
7. Some people feel that if their life was in danger they would not defend themselves, because it would mean hurting someone else. Who feels that way? If you do, it is o.k., many folks agree with that feeling.
8. If a woman was in fear of being hurt, should she defend herself against her husband? Why or why not?
9. If a woman fears her husband will harm her, under what circumstances would she be justified in using deadly force?
10. Who feels that being emotionally battered warrants the same self-protective measures as being physically attacked? Tell me what makes you feel that way?
11. Who feels that the emotionally or psychologically injured person should not be entitled to defend themselves? If yes, why? If no, why not?
12. Who would use deadly force if they felt endangered, emotionally or physically? Why or why not?
13. Who feels that under no circumstances would they kill another person? It is o.k. if you feel that way; please tell me about those feelings.

Guns

There are some people who would convict someone simply because a gun was used. There is a growing belief that guns should not be in the home, and there are people connected with this movement who feel a person premeditated an offense because they purchased a gun or allowed one to remain in their home. Potential jurors should be asked about their pro- or anti-gun feelings.

Suggested questions are:

1. What are your feelings about guns?
2. Do you or does any family member own a gun?
3. What purpose is served by owning a gun?
4. Have you or any family member ever owned a gun in the past?
5. Can you share with me a bad experience you or someone you know has had with a gun?
6. Have you or has anyone you know ever been the victim of a crime where a weapon was used or exhibited? How has this experience affected you?
7. Do you or does anyone you know belong to N.R.A., a gun club, or any anti-gun organization?
8. If you had but no longer have a gun, why did you get rid of the weapon?
9. Who feels that handguns should be available to the general public? Who feels they should not be available to the general public? Please explain.
10. Some people are anti-gun. Who would say they are opposed to guns in general? To handguns in particular?
11. What would you feel if a woman used a gun to protect herself from her husband (boyfriend, etc.)?
12. Have you ever shot a gun? Tell me about that.

Psychological Expert Witnesses

The John Hinkley case has drastically affected people's feelings regarding expert witnesses. Proper *voir dire* procedures must question potential jurors' feelings regarding psychology and sociology. Potential jurors' personal experiences with people in the helping professions need additional exploration. Sensitizing them to psychological issues is the lawyer's responsibility.

Questions to be asked include:

1. The fields of psychology and sociology are ones in which many of us have had an interest. Who has taken any courses in psychology or sociology? If you have, please describe.
2. Who has ever known or sought professional assistance from anyone in these or related professions? Please describe your experience with that person.
3. How helpful did you find that person to be? If not helpful, tell me about that.
4. Who has a family member or friend who has known or sought pro-

fessional assistance from anyone in these or related professions? Please describe that person's experience with the professions.

5. How did you, your friend, or family member feel about the professionals? Helpful? Not helpful? Why?

6. What are your feelings about psychologists? Psychiatrists? Social workers? Counselors?

7. If someone were to testify regarding psychological pressures on the client, how open might you be to that kind of testimony?

8. Some people are not open to such testimony. How would you feel?

9. The defendant was a battered wife. An expert on the battered woman syndrome will testify regarding this. Who feels he/she would listen openly to this expert?

10. What would make you feel open to this expert testimony?

The Battered Woman Syndrome

A battered woman knows the pressures and sense of helplessness she experiences all too well. She knows the fear of staying and the fear of what might happen if she leaves the relationship. Her life is filled with moment after moment of terror so that, no matter what she does, she cannot stop the time bomb. Physical helplessness and emotional torture are her daily treatment from a man she once loved and perhaps still does love.

There are some who think she brought this on herself and some who do not understand why she did not leave. Misunderstanding plagues this dynamic, and its mystery must be deciphered for the jury. The deciphering begins during jury selection.

Questions to be asked of potential jurors are:

1. Who has heard of the battered woman syndrome?

2. What does it mean to you?

3. Most people have read or seen a television show about the battered woman syndrome. What have you read or seen about battered wives or children?

4. Who saw the television show, *The Burning Bed*, with Farrah Fawcett? What did you feel about that show? How did you feel about how she was treated by the judicial system? How did you feel about the final result in that case?

5. Who feels that a battered wife means someone who is abused emotionally or physically or both? Tell me about that.

6. Some people feel that being emotionally battered is not as bad as being physically battered. Who feels that way? Tell me about that.

7. The defense will present a witness who will testify about the battered woman syndrome. Who would want to hear this testimony? Why?
8. Many people know someone who is battered (we can talk about this privately). Please tell me about that situation. What happened in that family? What did the battered woman do?
9. The defendant killed her husband in self-defense. She is one of the women who will be described as being a battered woman. Who feels that a battered wife could kill her husband in self-defense? For those who feel it is self-defense, tell me about that. Those who do not feel this, tell me about that.

The answers to these questions will give the lawyer and experts an insight into who will and will not listen to the defense's case. The questions also will give an attorney the opportunity to educate the jury panel on issues about which they are closed-minded or have little information. Experience tells us that the complexities of these cases are as involved as the fundamental principles in our relationships. Careful preparation and examination of potential jurors' feelings are paramount to breaking the veneer that lay people will attempt to hide behind in a courtroom.

Many citizens have been convicted or have lost lawsuits because of the questions that were *not* asked during jury selection. An effective *voir dire* of a jury panel can be accomplished if time is spent formulating and asking those sensitive questions. Equally important, an attorney must be prepared for any answer and respond accordingly. Some of the questions may be difficult to ask, and it is certain that some of the responses will not be liked. However, it is better to use that unwelcome information to exercise a preemptory challenge than to discover it during a post-verdict interview.

CONCLUSION

Mental health professionals can be used at all stages of case preparation. They can assist in the initial determination of a theory of the case. Their skills can be used to prepare a witness to testify and to select a jury as well as to provide expert testimony. Even after a trial on the merits, the expert can be called upon to assist in the determination of a sentence in a criminal case or an award of damages in a civil action.

Together, attorneys and mental health professionals can become powerful advocates for battered women. To do so, however, requires teamwork and a recognition that the skills of both professionals are needed if battered women are to be heard in, and receive justice from, a system in which they have historically been ignored.

REFERENCES

Acker, J.R., & Toch, H. (1985). Battered women, straw men, and expert testimony: A comment on *State* v. *Kelly*. *Criminal Law Bulletin*, *21* (2), 125–155. March–April, 1985.

Bochnak, E. (1981). Case preparation and development. In E. Bochnak (Ed.), *Women's self-defense cases: Theory and practice*. Charlottesville, VA: The Michie Company Law Publishers.

Browne, A. (1983). *When battered women kill*. Unpublished doctoral dissertation, University of Experimenting Colleges and Universities, Cincinnati, OH.

Browne, A. (in press). Assault and homicide at home: When battered women kill. In M.J. Sakes & L. Saxs (Eds.), *Advances in applied social psychology* (vol. 3). Hillsdale, NJ: Erlbaum.

Browne, A., & Thyfault, R. (1981, August). *When battered women kill: Psychologists as expert witnesses—interviewing techniques*. Paper presented at the meeting of the American Psychological Association, Los Angeles, CA.

Buhrle v. State, 627 P.2d 1374 (Wyo. 1981).

Dyas v. United States, 376 A.2d 827 (D.C. 1977).

Ex-wife wins $115,000.00 in beating suit. (1985, March 22). *Rocky Mountain News*, p. 7.

Ibn-Tamas v. United States, 407 A.2d 626 (D.C. 1979), *On remand*, 455 A.2d 893 (D.C. 1983).

Sandiford, K., & Burgess, A. (1984). *Shattered night*. New York: Warner Books.

Schneider, E., & Jordan, S. (1981). Representation of women who defend themselves in response to physical or sexual assault. In E. Bochnak, (Ed.), *Women's self-defense cases: Theory and practice*. Charlottesville, VA: The Michie Company Law Publishers.

Straus, M., Gelles, R., & Steinmetz, S. (1980). *Behind closed doors: Violence in the American family*. Garden City, NY: Anchor Press.

Smith v. State, 227 S.E.2d 678 (G.A. 1981).

State v. Austin, No. 7828 (Natrona Cty, WY 1979).

State v. Baker, 424 A.2d 171 (N.H. 1980).

State v. Kelly, 478 A.2d 364 (N.J. 1984).

State v. Thomas, 423 N.E.2d 137 (Ohio 1981).

Thurman v. City of Torrington, 595 F. Supp. 1521 (D. Conn. 1984).

Thyfault, R. (1984). Self-defense: Battered woman syndrome on trial. *California Western Law Review*, *20* (3), 485–510.

Walker, L.E.A. (1979). *The battered woman*. New York: Harper & Row.

Walker, L.E.A. (1984). *The battered woman syndrome*. New York: Springer Publishing Company.

5

When Battered Women Kill: Evaluation and Expert Witness Testimony Techniques

Roberta K. Thyfault
Angela Browne
Lenore E.A. Walker

Early studies of violence and victimization focused primarily on incidents occurring outside the home. Assault was believed to occur primarily on the streets of cities or in bar-room brawls; murders and rapes were committed by deranged strangers on the unsuspecting. Crimes that occurred within the family were rarely reported, and those that did become known were seen as oddities. The "average" family, it was assumed, afforded nurturance and protection to its members. Yet accumulating evidence on family violence compels us to acknowledge a hidden reservoir of victimization that has existed almost unnoticed, and in fact has been given permission to thrive, within our culture.

Although threatening or attacking another person is illegal, when it happens within the family the episodes are rarely brought to the attention of authorities. Even when such assaults are reported, they are not always accorded the serious treatment given to attacks by strangers. It is often only when someone is seriously hurt or killed that strict action is taken. Battered women reporting attacks or threats by spouses are familiar with being referred for personal mental health treatment, or asked why they don't leave home, rather than being assisted with effective and case-appropriate alternatives. A Harris poll (1979), surveying 1,793 women in Kentucky, found that 21 percent of the women reported being abused by a partner and that over two-thirds of those who had been divorced or separated during the previous year reported violence occurring in that relationship. Yet Harris found that 43 percent of women who had been abused told no one, and only 4 percent of reported assaults resulted in court action. Left without adequate recourse or intervention, some family altercations continue to escalate in severity until they result in death.

Over 17 percent of the nation's homicides occur within the family, about half of those a spouse killing a spouse (Uniform Crime Reports, 1983). Many of these lethal incidents represent the final chapter in a history of physical abuse. At home with one's intimates is not always the safest place to be. Jones, in her study of women who kill, noted: "Nine out of ten murdered women are murdered by men. Four out of five are murdered at home. Almost three out of four are murdered by husbands or lovers. Almost none are killed by strangers" (1980, pp. 320–321). Yet not all lethal incidents end with the victimized woman's death. In 1984, approximately 700 women killed men, representing about 10% of all the homicides in the United States. Many of these homicides were the result of self-defensive actions by women who found no other avenues of protection effective in stopping life-threatening attacks by their spouses on themselves or their children.

SELF-DEFENSE AND WOMEN WHO KILL PARTNERS

Women charged in the death of a mate have the least extensive criminal records of any female offenders. However, they often face harsher penalties than men who kill their partners. FBI statistics indicate that fewer men are charged with first- or second-degree murder for killing a woman they have known than are women who kill a man they have known. And women convicted of these murders are frequently sentenced to longer prison terms than are men (Schneider & Jordan, 1981). Although self-defense statutes exist in every state, until recently these were rarely applied to abused women who killed their mates. For example, a 1977 study at the Women's Correctional Center in Chicago revealed that 40 percent of the women serving time there for murder or manslaughter had killed husbands or lovers who had repeatedly beaten them (Lindsey, 1978). Many of the women now incarcerated for the death of an abusive spouse might not be considered guilty of a criminal act if they were to be tried today.

In the case of a battered woman, if a plea of self-defense is to be applied, it is necessary to document clearly that her use of deadly force resulted because she believed her life to be in imminent danger. The law requires that certain elements of an act be proven before it defines a behavior as criminal. First of all, it must be proven that the accused actually committed the behavior in question. For battered women who kill, this is rarely at issue. Most of these women call for assistance for the wounded man and readily admit that they killed or at least harmed the abuser. The second issue involves the question of individual state of mind when perpetrating the act, and it is in addressing this area—i.e., the issue of *mens rea*, or determining state of mind—that psychological evaluation and expert witness testimony can make a valuable contribution to the defense.

In the past, psychologists were typically asked to determine legal sanity; that is, did the individual have the capacity to determine right from wrong, and, in some jurisdictions, did they have the ability to conform their behavior to legal and community standards. Individuals found to have been suffering from a mental disease or defect were not held accountable for their behavior and thus could not be adjudicated guilty of a criminal act. The insanity defense, however, was only rarely used and is used even less today, because state legislatures have revised insanity laws so that they rarely apply and because this type of defense is not usually well received by jurors. In addition, as we learn more about battered women, we know that those who kill do not appear to be mentally ill, but rather seem to be reacting situationally to the level of violence perpetrated against them and attempting to protect their lives and those of their children (Walker & Browne, 1985). Thus psychologists today are asked, not to determine sanity, but to determine if the woman's perception that she was in "imminent danger of grave bodily harm or death" was reasonable at the time the lethal incident occurred. In some jurisdictions, an abused woman's "reasonable perception" must match that which any other reasonable person would presumably have had under those circumstances; in other jurisdictions, the subjective perception of the battered woman will meet the resonable person test (see Bochnak, 1981—in particular, the chapter by Schneider & Jordan—for a more complete discussion of the basis for the plea).

A number of court decisions in recent years have opened the way for psychologists to present testimony about the battered woman syndrome to judges and juries (Thyfault, 1984). This testimony has usually been used in cases of homicide or attempted murder in which an abused woman is charged with the death or serious injury of her abusive mate and claims that she acted in self-defense. However, as courts become more willing to admit testimony about the battered woman syndrome, the testimony is also being used in civil and domestic actions. In many ways, these battered woman cases have forced the courts to become more sensitive to issues that affect women in general.

For example, in *State* v. *Wanrow*, 88 Wash. 2d 881, 559 P.2d 548 (1977), the Washington Supreme Court ruled that women were entitled to a jury instruction of self-defense that took into account the effect of sexual discrimination and socialization on a woman's ability to defend herself. Traditional self-defense standards are based on altercations that occur between male antagonists, equal in strength and similar in their ability to use parts of their body as weapons. Women, of course, are usually not equal in strength to an unarmed man and are typically quite inexperienced at using their bodies in self-defense. The *Wanrow* decision recognized that, in our society, women lack the "skills necessary to effectively repel a male assailant without resorting to the use of deadly weapons." The concept of "imminent danger" as it relates to self-defense has also been changed in light of women's issues to reflect the reasonableness of a woman's belief that she is still in imminent danger some time after a violent incident (see *People* v. *Garcia*, CR. No. 4259, Sup. Ct., Monterey County Calif., 1977). This extension of time has been particularly important, as battered women become familiar with their mates' patterns of violence and sometimes kill just before the violence escalates to more dangerous proportions.

Changes that have occurred in legal processing of these cases are due, in part, to the joint efforts of attorneys and psychologists to educate the courts about women's issues and, more specifically, about abused women and family violence. Attorneys are cautioned not to use expert testimony routinely in battered woman cases (see Bochnak, 1981). However, when the testimony is appropriate, a well-informed expert witness can aid the jury and the judge in understanding the impact of the cumulative effects of repeated violent attacks and the outcomes in terms of an abused woman's thinking, feelings, and behavior.

PRETRIAL EVALUATION

A great deal of time must be spent in pretrial preparation if the testimony is to be effective and the psychologist is to be able to render an informed professional opinion. This preparation typically takes place in several stages, beginning with pretrial evaluations and continuing through the actual courtroom testimony. Even if the expert does not testify, intensive pretrial assistance can be invaluable to the attorneys as well as to the abused woman.

One of the first, and perhaps most important, steps in trial preparation is to conduct a comprehensive evaluation of the woman. The techniques used in this process are critical, in that they determine the amount and reliability of the information elicited from the woman and thus affect the preparation of the case and the expert's ability to render an informed opinion. The evaluation phase must provide sufficient data for the expert to be able to offer testimony that addresses areas critical to the woman's case. For example, a plea of self-defense would require that the expert be able to establish that the woman was within the definition of a "battered" woman; that she exhibited behavior patterns found to be typical of other abused women; and that it was reasonable, based on the battering history, for her to have been in fear of bodily harm or death when she killed her mate.

One successful method of evaluation was developed through conducting interviews with over 400 battered women who participated in a study of the battered woman syndrome funded by the National Institute of Mental Health (Walker, 1981). This evaluation involved eight or more hours of in-depth interviewing, which included the administration of a structured questionnaire, a mental-status examination, and several standardized psychological scales. The interview included a psychosocial history of the woman, beginning with her childhood; a history of the man, by the woman's self-report; a history of their relationship together; and an evaluation of the woman's current state. By using a modified version of this questionnaire for interviewing women involved in legal cases, it is possible to draw comparisons between the research sample and individual clients and to identify certain trends and commonalities in the violent relationships and women's responses to them.

In a study by one of the authors, 42 homicide cases in which a battered woman perpetrated a lethal incident against her mate were compared with 205 abusive relationships in which no lethal incident occurred. Several factors were found that distinguished the homicide from the nonhomicide group (Browne, 1983; in press). More men in the homicide group became intoxicated every day or almost every day by the end of the relationship (80 percent vs. 40 percent in the nonhomicide group), used street drugs (29 percent vs. 7.5 percent), had a history of arrest (92 percent vs. 77 percent), and had made threats to kill (83 percent vs. 59 percent). In addition, physical attacks occurred with greater frequency in the homicide group, and the women sustained more, and more severe, injuries as a result of these attacks. Over 75 percent of women in the homicide group reported that they had been raped by their mates on at least one occasion (compared to 59 percent of women in the nonhomicide group), and 62 percent (vs. 37 percent) said that their mates had forced or urged them to perform other sexual acts against their will. Both the frequency and the severity of attacks tended to increase over time. Most women in the homicide group had no history of violent, or even illegal, behavior; yet in these relationships, the women's attempts to survive with an increasingly violent and unpredictable partner eventually resulted in an act of violence on their part as well. Such a severe action by an otherwise nonviolent individual would seem inexplicable to a jury unless the pattern of prior victimization was understood.

INTERVIEWING A BATTERED WOMAN

Although battered women may not discuss their experiences with people they do not perceive as supportive, it has been consistently found that they are willing to disclose this information when questioned by skilled interviewers (e.g., Browne & Thyfault, 1981; Straus, Gelles, & Steinmetz, 1980; Washburn & Frieze, 1980). In fact, once a level of trust has been established between an interviewer and a battered woman, the woman will often want to continue talking well beyond the scheduled interview time.

Before beginning the interview, it is helpful to discuss with the woman any experience the interviewer may have had working with other battered women who have been charged with a crime or for some reason have found themselves in the criminal justice system. Just as abused women often think that their relationship was unique in that it was violent, battered women who have killed or nearly killed their abusers often feel they are the only ones involved in this kind of situation. It greatly reduces the woman's anxiety to know that the person to whom she will be revealing intimate and painful details has worked with other women in similar circumstances and has heard similar stories.

It is also important to make clear to the woman that she must be very detailed and specific about dates and events in the relationship. This is often difficult for battered women to do. Women who have been abused over a period of time tend to forget some incidents or to lump incidents together. Women who have used alcohol or drugs to cope with their fear and pain have particular difficulty in remembering specific details. The intensive, all-day approach to interviewing, in which the woman relates events in chronological order, often helps the woman retrieve much of the information she thought was forgotten. It is also an excellent way to prepare the woman to testify in court, since the process jogs her memory and she begins to recall details and to establish an order for events. It is helpful to tell the woman that she will probably continue to remember facts that might be relevant to her case as a result of this process, and to encourage her to carry a pad and pen with her in order to write these down for her attorney.

In doing such a long and sensitive interview, a balance must be maintained between gathering the information necessary for trial preparation and supporting the woman throughout the process. The interview cannot be allowed to become an unstructured therapy session, however, or adequate information will not be collected. Psychologists or others conducting this type of interview must become skilled at knowing when the woman needs support in order to continue relating painful details and yet be able to stay within the structure of the interview schedule. Although some have expressed concern that the relating of such sensitive information when the woman is already psychologically distressed and fragile might be damaging for the interviewee, experience with these cases indicates that the opportunity to tell the whole story in sequence to a nonjudgmental listener is actually therapeutic for most women.

Another concern raised about interviews with abused women relates to the reliability of the women's self-report. This is of special concern in homicide cases, when one can no longer learn the deceased's version of the story and the survivor is facing criminal charges in relation to the incident. However, it is actually easier to document abused women's stories when they are involved in a legal action, since private records become available and witnesses are called in to testify. We have noted that, when discrepancies are found between the women's accounts and information from corroborating data, it is usually in the direction of understatement in the women's accounts, both as to the severity and frequency of the violence. Battered women tend to engage in a great deal of denial and minimization in order to endure repeated assaults, and it is usually quite difficult for them to begin relating specific violent acts that occurred in a given incident. They have also learned that most people do not want to hear the details of their experiences, and thus will abbreviate their stories. However, battered women can give a detailed account of an assault if they are asked structured and specific questions.

Using the modified battered woman syndrome interview schedule, questions are asked about four different battering incidents: the first occurrence of violence in the relationship, a typical incident, the worst (or one of the worst) in the woman's opinion, and the final or lethal incident. Each of these narratives is followed immediately by matching sets of detailed questions to allow for comparison of acts, injuries, and other factors over time, before going on to the next incident. For example, in the narrative a woman may say, "He slapped me around some and then I wound up on the floor." Using neutral probers, the woman is encouraged to describe the events in more detail as she continues her narrative account and, at the completion of the narrative, is given a list of specific circumstances (e.g., time, place, duration, use of alcohol or drugs), acts of violence (slap, hit, kick, etc.), and outcomes (e.g., injuries, attempts to seek help, legal intervention) that may have occurred. Her responses to these questions help to form a more complete picture of the actual battering incident than could be drawn from the narrative alone. Obtaining consistent details on several incidents also enables the evaluator to assess the escalation in the frequency and severity of abuse and threats over time and to identify changes in behavioral patterns.

An effective technique in obtaining details that are painful for the woman to remember is to build up gradually from neutral questions to more sensitive issues in the interview format, and then close out the interview with questions about less emotional areas. A gradual buildup allows time for rapport to develop between the interviewer and the abused woman before the more intimate and sensitive topics are addressed. Thus the interview may begin with general questions about the woman's childhood, where she grew up, her family structure, and the occupations of her parents or parental figures. The battered woman syndrome (BWS) interview continues with detailed questions about any childhood physical and sexual abuse the woman may have experienced, before going on to more general questions about dating and later relationships in which she was involved.

The woman is then asked general questions about her relationship with the abuser—how they met, how long they dated, what she knows of the circumstances of his childhood (including violence in his childhood home), his education and employment history—before focusing on details of specific battering incidents themselves. After the narrative and questions on the four abusive incidents, summary questions are asked about the violent relationship pertaining to threats that the abuser may have made against her life or the lives of others, whether the children were witnesses to the violence or were abused themselves, attempts she made to leave the relationship, persons or agencies the woman contacted for help, and any other information that aids in forming an accurate and complete picture of the circumstances under which she lived. The BWS interview then concludes with questions about the woman's current state—her living and work situation, physical health, and psychological state of mind—and with the administration of several standardized psychological scales.

For especially sensitive issues, such as childhood sexual abuse or sexual assaults within the relationship, it is often helpful to ask several types of questions in order to elicit the information; some quite direct—"Did he ever force you to have sex?"—and some indirect—"Was sex ever unpleasant for you? If so, why?" In structuring indirect questions, the interviewee can be given a list of possible answers from which to choose. For example, in response to the question, "Why was sex unpleasant?", the woman might be asked to respond to the following possibilities: "He forced me to have sex when I didn't want it," "He made me do things I didn't want to do," "He compared me unfavorably with other women" (Walker, 1984a). If the interviewee indicates she was forced to do things she didn't want to do, we have found it most effective to then read from a prepared list of acts ("I'll read you a list of things he might have made you do. Please answer yes or no to each item: vaginal sex, oral sex, anal sex, insertion of objects, sex with others, sex with animals, sadomasochistic sex," etc.) so that the interviewee does not have to say those things herself. This allows the woman to answer only "yes" or "no" to questions she might be too uncomfortable to answer otherwise, while enabling the interviewer to gather important information. It has been our experience that the majority of abused women involved in homicide and attempted murder cases have been sexually assaulted by their abusers. The impact of this type of abuse on battered women cannot be overemphasized, and the possibility that a woman has experienced this type of attack should always be investigated.

Most abused women find it much easier to relate experiences of sexual assault to a female interviewer, rather than to a male. Often a male attorney or psychologist will have heard very little, if anything, about the sexual abuse. As would be expected, women are also extremely apprehensive about testifying to the sexual assaults in court and may avoid revealing them out of fear that the information will then become public knowledge. Whether this information will be used at trial should be thoroughly discussed with the woman, and whenever possible her wishes in regard to the testimony should be respected. It should also be noted that, in most states, much of the testimony about sexual assaults can be brought out by the expert witness, thus saving the woman from some of the embarrassment of talking about these details in the courtroom. In some cases, when the information is deemed critical to the woman's case, the judge may agree to hear this information in a closed session in chambers.

A battered woman who has killed her abuser may develop strong defenses to protect herself from the full impact of what has occurred. She often suffers some memory loss for a time period that may extend from the moment she picks up a weapon until she realizes that the man has been seriously hurt. Many women have no memory of firing the gun or of stabbing, nor do they generally realize how seriously the man has been wounded until sometime after the event. These memory gaps usually coincide with the time at which the fear and panic was at its highest. Such gaps often lead to inconsistencies in the women's stories when they attempt to give statements to the police shortly after the incident. They can also make it difficult to construct the defense and are frequently used by the opposing counsel at trial to call into question the truthfulness of the woman's statements. Although the use of hypnosis may be suggested to enable the woman to remember missing details, this method is fraught with legal complications and is not recommended (e.g., such testimony may not be allowed in court, because of some states' rules or evidence). In addition, it may be quite psychologically destructive for the woman to break through these defenses, even when the techniques exist to do so. Women need to remain strong enough to get through their trials, which often will not take place until several months after the evaluation is conducted. The decision to use methods to make her remember the actual facts should only be made after careful consideration by the woman, the psychologist, and the attorney.

A sequential and detailed method of interviewing is probably the most effective way to facilitate the woman's recall. When a woman begins to recount events leading up to the lethal incident, it may be necessary to move her through the account almost day-by-day, or sometimes even hour-by-hour. It is important to establish the sequence of events during the weeks immediately preceding the final incident and to try to determine why the violence escalated into a lethal event at that particular point in the relationship. The crucial questions that need to be answered for the judge and jury are: Why this time? What was different on this occasion? What changes in the pattern of abuse, or what critical events, precipitated the crisis? It is helpful to have the woman recount the fatal incident twice: once during the structured interview and again during a follow-up clinical interview, preferably with a different interviewer. This allows an evaluation of the consistency of the account, and often provides more details from which to reconstruct the sequence of events leading to the homicide. In both interviews, a description of her feelings and thoughts should always accompany her description of events.

As mentioned earlier, standardized tests should also be used as a part of the pretrial evaluation. It can be especially helpful to have women complete the Minnesota Multiphasic Personality Inventory (MMPI), as long as the results are then scored using a scale especially designed for battered women (see Rosewater, 1982). Courts are particularly receptive to the MMPI, since they are generally familiar with the test. MMPI data, along with other standardized personality tests, indicate that battered women react to their abusive environment with confusion, depression, anxiety, phobias, anger directed toward themselves, and a lack of trust. Although their test profiles may show an extremely high degree of distress, this is consistent with the crisis situation in which they find themselves. Abused women often exhibit quite unusual profiles, which would be considered indicative of pathology if the history of abuse were not known. Disturbances in interpersonal relationships and numerous psychophysiological complaints are often seen. However, it is critical to keep in mind that no specific personality pattern has been found for battered women (Walker & Browne, 1985) and that the only identifiable characteristics differentiating battered women who kill their abusers from those who do not is in their report of more extreme behaviors and more serious violence from the men (Browne, 1983; in press).

In being investigated, each homicide case must allow for the consideration of self-defense, even if at first glance the facts do not seem to support that the woman was in imminent danger. A great deal is at stake when conducting an interview for these cases. Many of the women are facing long prison sentences, even life imprisonment, if convicted. Therefore it is important to spend as much time with a woman as is needed to draw out a complete picture of the abuse and overall behavior patterns in the relationship. Information obtained from the woman can often be corroborated with police reports, hospital records, witness statements, and other materials made available to her attorney; an expert witness should always ask for and review these materials before rendering an opinion in the case.

TRIAL PREPARATION

It is customary, although not mandatory, to prepare a report once the pretrial evaluation is complete. Since the report is discoverable and thus may have to be turned over to the prosecution, care must be taken in writing the report so that it is accurate and concise. Generally, a short report of a few pages will suffice. The report should state the reason the case was referred to the expert; usually this will have been for the purpose of determining if having been battered had an impact on the woman's state of mind at the time of the homicide incident. It should also state the evaluation procedures used, dates and times of face-to-face interviews and testing, persons interviewed, and materials reviewed. Approximate time spent on the case should also be included.

Following this, a brief section on significant history is given, covering both the woman's life and the abusive relationship. Generalities should be listed here, so that the report will not become overlong. (In writing the report, the term *murder* should be avoided, since it calls for a legal conclusion and suggests that the killing was not lawful—which is exactly the issue before the court.) An account of the findings precedes the conclusion and should contain the expert's observations and a summary of current mental health status, as well as test results. Comparisons between the individual woman and findings from studies of abused women are also made here. The concluding section contains the expert's professional opinion, to a reasonable degree of psychological certainty (the legal standard). If, after examining all the information, the expert finds the woman to have been battered and to resemble what is known of other battered women, and if the expert finds that the battering so affected the woman that she was terrified that she or others would be seriously hurt or killed at the time of the lethal incident, then the professional opinion would include a statement supporting her claim of self-defense.

If the evaluation does not support a self-defense claim, however, the expert must still report these findings to the woman and her attorneys in a nonjudg-mental way. Some homicide incidents are the result of an accident, while others may be caused by a desire for revenge. What has come to be termed the "battered women's self-defense plea" may be misinterpreted by those overzealous to find a defense and to justify the actions of any woman who has been battered. In some cases, the facts may suggest a defense of diminished capacity or mitigating circumstances, which may then reduce the degree of crime with which the woman is charged. At all times, when involved with cases under litigation, the expert should keep in mind the ethics of his or her own discipline and be guided by those principles.

Decisions on whether or not to consider a negotiated plea can be especially difficult for battered women who have killed. The most common plea arrangement offered in these cases is voluntary manslaughter with no jail time and several years on probation. Most women who kill abusive mates have no prior offenses, nor do they later behave in ways that would lead to their probation being revoked. Thus a plea bargain may be a viable option. However, this requires that the woman plead guilty to a criminal offense, rather than continuing to assert her claim that the killing was justified under provisions of the law. In some states, women cannot receive any life insurance, pension, or Social Security benefits if they assume any legal guilt in their partner's death. Some battered women may be so emotionally fragile that the thought of going to trial seems overwhelming and they prefer the option of a negotiated plea, despite its drawbacks. Others need the opportunity to try for an acquittal and to break out of the pattern of giving up; taking their case to court offers a first step in standing up for themselves and their rights. These and other factors must be fully considered so that the woman is able to make an informed choice.

EXPERT WITNESS TESTIMONY

Much has already been written about techniques of effective expert testimony (Brodsky, 1977; Walker, 1984b; Weiner & Hess, in press; cf. various issues of *Law and Human Behavior*). It is most critical to be well prepared to all times while the case is pending. In a few states, prosecutors are permitted to take an expert's deposition. This is similar to cross-examination, except that no direct testimony has been given to establish limits on the range of questions. Other states permit contact to share information once the witness has been endorsed. However, care must be taken not to disclose statements the woman has made during the evaluation that might jeopardize her legal rights. Honest communication with the attorney will help guide the mental health professional. At times it is appropriate to consult with an attorney who is only concerned with *your* legal position. Statements in legal proceeding are almost always recorded in some manner and can follow an expert witness from case to case, so it is valuable to obtain as much information about the process as possible and to make your statements wisely.

It is not unusual for a psychologist's records to be subpoenaed in anticipation of testimony. It is not ethical to obey the subpoena, however, by turning over raw data (e.g., test protocols and assessment notes) to anyone not trained in their interpretation. Most psychologists' licenses are based on administrative law that incorporates the American Psychological Association's (APA) code of ethics in the state statutes. The APA ethical code and its Standards for Providers of Psychological Services clearly state that release of confidentiality necessitates the client's permission and that raw data can only be given to someone who has been appropriately trained—usually to another psychologist, if test materials are included. It is important to place any records in a sealed envelope and request a court hearing so the judge can determine whether or not to demand the records. They can then be given to the judge if so demanded, after the record is made, so that the psychologist is not held responsible for resolving the conflict between two different bodies of law, administrative and criminal.

Criminal trials usually have several different phases after the trial motions have been decided, the first phase being jury selection. Most states allow attorneys to question—or *voir dire*—possible jurors. The woman can assist her attorney by suggesting questions or by asking the attorney to have a juror excused if she senses a negative response (see Chapter 4). The next phase consists of opening arguments by each side, during which the attorneys essentially tell the jury what they intend to prove. The evidence phase follows, when facts of the case are presented through witnesses. The prosecution, which has the burden to prove the case, presents its witnesses first. After the prosecution rests, the defense presents its case. The prosecution can then reply to the defense in rebuttal, after which the defense has an opportunity to make a final reply. In the last phase, both sides give their closing arguments, summarizing the evidence they have presented and the facts they believe the evidence to have proven. Because the prosecution has the burden of proof, they are allowed to make a rebuttal argument. The judge then gives the jury formal instructions on what they are to consider, and the jury retires to deliberate. They must reach a unanimous decision, or a mistrial is declared and the process begins again at a later date.

The basic rules of testimony for expert witnesses are different from those for other witnesses. The expert's training, experience, and other qualifications are examined; if found acceptable, the witness is qualified as an expert. Being qualified as an expert allows the witness to discuss opinions as well as information that led to those opinions, including facts and hearsay that would otherwise be inadmissible. It has proven quite helpful in these cases to have the woman's way of experiencing her world communicated to the judge and jury. In some cases, the expert is the only witness who can tie everything together.

During direct examination, the expert witness is asked questions by the woman's attorney. It is essential to meet with the attorney beforehand and compose questions that will elicit appropriate information about battered women in general, including questions that will give the expert a chance to address the misconceptions and stereotypes that many individuals hold about abused women. Comparisons of the individual woman's case with data about other battered women bolsters the reliability and validity of the professional's opinion. Information should be delivered in a scholarly but easily understandable manner. If the attorney and mental health professional are well prepared in advance, all the essential information will be brought out during the direct examination.

The next phase, cross-examination, is more diffficult to prepare for in advance. The goal of the prosecutor is to lessen the expert's influence with the jury. Often the prosecutor will pick out a statement made during the direct examination and attempt to present it in a different light. Some may try to badger a witness into answering a question inaccurately, or confuse a witness bv rapid-fire questions in an accusatory tone. Staying alert, listening carefully to the questions, and responding briefly and without anger are the best techniques for handling this type of cross-examination. An expert witness should always feel free for clarification when that is needed. This is also an effective technique for interrupting an onslaught of questions.

TESTIMONY AT SENTENCING HEARINGS

If a plea bargain is made, or if a battered woman is found guilty, expert witness testimony can also be offered at the sentencing hearing. This testimony is generally the same as would be offered at trial, unless the judge has already heard it. The goal at sentencing is to educate the judge about mitigating circumstances that had bearing on the act. The data available from battered women who have killed their abusers also indicate that such women are extremely low risks for repeating violent behavior and thus present no risk to the community if they are not incarcerated. Many of these women are raising children who would have to be housed by relatives or would be at the mercy and expense of the state were their mother sent to prison. Again, the expert should be well informed and should present the facts about the individual battered woman in the context of what is known about abused women in general.

CONCLUSIONS

In conclusion, expert testimony from a psychologist or other mental health service provider is often necessary to educate a judge and jury about the dynamics of a violent relationship and the effects that repeated assaults and threats can have on an abused woman. Through the use of an intensive interview and evaluation, data can be gathered that will help in the preparation of the woman's case. Throughout the process, adherence to psychological principles, including a primary concern for the psychological well-being of the woman, is important. When attorneys and psychologists are willing to work together, they can have a powerful and positive effect on the manner in which battered women are dealt with in our criminal justice system.

REFERENCES

Bochnak, E. (Ed.). (1981). *Women's self-defense cases: Theory and practice.* Charlottesville, VA: The Michie Company Law Publishers.

Brodsky, S.L. (1977). The mental health professional in the witness stand: A survival guide. In B.D. Sales (Ed.), *Psychology in the Legal Process*. New York: Spectrum.

Browne, A. (1983). *When battered women kill*. Unpublished doctoral dissertation, University of Experimenting Colleges and Universities, Cincinnati, OH.

Browne, A. (in press). *Assault and homicide at home: When battered women kill*. In M.J. Sakes & L. Saxe (Eds.), *Advances in Applied Social Psychology: Vol. 3*. Hillsdale, NJ: Erlbaum.

Browne, A., & Thyfault, R. (1981, August). *When battered women kill: Psychologists as expert witnesses*. Paper presented at the meeting of the American Psychological Association, Los Angeles, CA.

Harris & Associates. (1979). *Survey of spousal violence against women in Kentucky* (Rep. No. 792701) New York: Louis Harris & Assoc., Inc.

Jones, A. (1980). *Women who kill*. New York: Fawcett Columbine Books.

Lindsey, K. (1978, September). When battered women strike back: Murder or self-defense. *Viva*, pp. 58–59, 66–74.

People v. Garcia, CR. No. 4259 (Sup. Ct., Monterey County, Calif., 1977).

Rosewater, L. (1982). *An MMPI profile for battered women*. Unpublished doctoral dissertation, University of Experimenting Colleges and Universities, Cincinnati, OH.

Schneider, E.M., & Jordan, S.B. (1981). Representation of women who defend themselves in response to physical or sexual assault. In E. Bochnak (Ed.), *Women's self-defense cases: Theory and practice*. Charlottesville, VA: The Michie Company Law Publishers.

State v. Wanrow, 88 Wash. 2d 881, 559 P.2d 548 (1977).

Straus, M., Gelles, R., & Steinmetz, S. (1980). *Behind closed doors: Violence in the American family*. Garden City, NY: Anchor Press.

Thyfault, R. (1984). Self defense: Battered woman syndrome on trial. *California Western Law Review, 20*, 485–510.

Uniform Crime Reports. (1983, September). *Crime in the United States*. Federal Bureau of Investigation. U.S. Department of Justice, Washington, DC.

Walker, L.E.A. (1981). *The battered woman syndrome: Final report* (Grant #RO130147). Rockville, MD: National Institute of Mental Health.

Walker, L.E.A. (1984a). *The battered woman syndrome*. New York: Springer Publishing Co.

Walker, L.E.A. (1984b). Battered women, psychology, and public policy. *American Psychologist, 39*, 1178–1182.

Walker, L.E.A., & Browne, A. (1985). Gender and victimization by intimates. *Journal of Personality, 53* (2), 179–195.

Washburn, C., & Frieze, I.H. (1980, March). *Methodological issues in studying battered women*. Paper presented at the meeting of the Association for Women in Psychology, Santa Moncia, CA.

Weiner, I.B., & Hess, A. (Eds.) (in press). *Handbook of Forensic Psychology*. New York: John Wiley & Sons.

6

The Clinical and Courtroom Application of Battered Women's Personality Assessments

Lynne Bravo Rosewater

For years we as a society have asked why so many women "allow" themselves to be beaten, instead of asking why there are so many violent men. In an environment that tends to victimize the victim (Ryan, 1976), battered women are often blamed for the violence in their lives and condemned for their alleged stupidity or passivity in remaining in an abusive situation. This skewed perception of the dynamics of battered women extends to the mental health and legal professions.

Bias against the battered woman persists in the courtroom. In civil cases involving custody issues, battered women are often viewed as "unfit mothers" because of their "crazy" behavior, while their abusive husbands are seen as "healthy" and "normal." In criminal cases, including murder trials, battered women commonly are seen as "vindictive." These prejudicial views highlight the necessity for expert testimony on the battered woman's syndrome (Thyfault, 1984; Walker, 1984; on the battered woman's syndrome, see Douglas, Chapter 3 of this volume).

Misconceptions about battered women pervade in the clincal arena as well. Battered women have been viewed as masochistic, provocative, and passive/aggressive. Because many mental health professionals do not understand why a battered woman stays in an abusive situation, they assume that battered women either like the violence or are "crazy." These practitioners often confuse the *symptoms* of mental illness and the *effects* of battering, frequently leading to misdiagnosis of battered women as suffering from schizophrenic disorders or borderline personality disorders (Rosewater, 1985b).

Battered women, whether in court or in therapy, are often re-victimized. It is my hope that this chapter will lead to a better understanding of the dynamics of battered women and the usefulness of testing for both mental health and legal professionals so that the quality of intervention with these women can be improved.

TESTS: CAN YOU TRUST THEM?

The personality assessment I use in the courtroom is the Minnesota Multiphasic Personality Inventory (MMPI). I will use the MMPI as a prototype in order to discuss the ramifications of personality tests.

The MMPI is a personality inventory consisting of 566* self-reference true/false questions. Hathaway and McKinley state, "subjects sixteen years of age or older with at least six years of successful schooling can be expected to complete the MMPI without difficulty" (1967, p. 9). The test, based on a sixth-grade reading level (Hanes, 1953), usually takes an hour to an hour and a half to complete. Constructed by Hathaway and McKinley and first published in 1943, the MMPI was originally developed to be an objective aid in determining diagnostic assessment and severity of psychological symptoms. As used today, the MMPI is described by Hathaway and McKiney as "designed to provide an objective assessment of some of the major personality characteristics that affect personal and social adjustment" (1967, p. 7).

Personality assessments have been criticized as being racist (Erdberg, 1970) and sexist (Rawlings & Carter, 1977). Because the control group, the "Minnesota normals" used for the MMPI, contained no blacks, the norms developed were clearly white norms. Several researchers have found that blacks score higher on certain clinical scales (4, 6, 8, and 9), as well as validity scales (? and F) (Baughman & Dahlstrom, 1972, Harrison & Klass, 1968). While some argued that special norms for clinical scales for blacks were not necessary (Gynther, Lachar, & Dahlstrom, 1978), most experts on the MMPI agreed that accurate interpretation for the MMPI had to take into account the race of the individual test-taker. Much less has been written about the sexist bias of the MMPI. I have argued that while the MMPI *is* sexist, the method of interpreting the test is more important than the nature of each individual question (Rosewater, 1985a).

Tests cannot be interpreted in isolation; the social-psychological context

---

* The MMPI actually consists of 550 items, 16 of which are repeated. The repetition of the 16 items was to insure the accuracy of computer scoring, when such scoring was first introduced.

must always be considered. For instance, how does one accurately define paranoia? Fearfulness is considered excessive if there is no reality basis for such apprehension. Battered women are an excellent example of misinterpretation based on inadequate consideration of the social-psychological context. Because battered women are ashamed, they often keep silent about the physical violence in their lives (Walker, 1979). Misunderstanding the real basis for their fear, mental health professionals often see such women as paranoid. In my own research with currently battered women (n = 106), I found that the severity of beatings is directly correlated to elevation on scale 6 of the MMPI, which measures paranoia or extreme fearfulness (Rosewater, 1982).

I have previously argued that interpreting personality tests is similar to the Supreme Court's interpreting the Constitution: Like the justices we must use a basis of standardization; but, again like them, we also use our own judgment and discrimination, which are influenced by existing cultural values (Rosewater, 1985a).

WHY USE TESTS?

If properly interpreted, psychological testing can be an asset in the courtroom. Individuals tend to trust quantifiable data; the same test scored by anyone will have the identical numerical results. Hence the term *objective* connotes a sense of fairness and accuracy. An established test instrument like the MMPI, in use for over forty years, has already been proven reliable and valid, giving it an aura of respectability.

An objective test instrument can lend credibility to a defendant's tale. Prosecutors are quick to argue to the jury that the defendant has not told the truth, either to the expert witness or to them. The MMPI offers several ways to confirm a defendant's credibility. The validity scales of the MMPI indicate the candor of the test-taker. Using a special formula (the F-K ratio), it is possible to determine if a test has been exaggerated in a negative or positive direction (Graham, 1977). A valid test-taking effort reinforces the notion of the honesty of the test-taker. Additionally, the MMPI clinical scales and subscales give an accurate description of personality functioning. Dynamics that match the behavior the defendant describes reinforce the credibility of the defendant. The personality test results then can be used as collaboration for the defendant's story.

Another advantage of a personality test like the MMPI is that the results can be graphically displayed to the jury. Such visual test results make explanations easier.

All of the reasons that personality tests are helpful in a public arena like the courtroom apply equally in a private arena such as the therapist's office.

CURRENT RESEARCH ON BATTERED WOMEN USING THE MMPI

My research (Rosewater, 1982) was with 118 battered women, all but 12 in currently abusive situations. These women, 58 of them white, 54 black, and 4 Hispanic, ranged in age from 17 to 53. The major focus of the discussion of these test results will be the 106 currently battered women in the research population.

A three-point code type of 486 (468) emerged for currently battered women. The highest scale elevation was for the scale measuring anger (scale 4). The subscales show that battered women direct their anger inward rather than outward. Their highest scores were on the subscales that measure alienation, a sense of feeling personally responsible for the bad things that happen in their lives. This sense of alienation is culturally cultivated by the expectation that it is a woman's responsibility to "take care of her man." Women who experience violence from their men feel that somehow they have failed. Batterers heighten this sense of failure by blaming the women for the violence ("I wouldn't have hit you if . . .").

The currently battered women also had significant elevation on the scale that measures confusion (scale 8). The subscale elevation indicates that the violence in their lives affects their ability to think clearly and drains their energy. These data seem to suggest that the battered women in this research sample feel out of control of their lives.

In addition to elevation on anger and confusion, the currently battered women in the research population had significant elevation on the scale that measures paranoia/fearfulness. The subscale elevation indicates, not surprisingly, that battered women are fearful of others. The Frequency of Battering and the Violent Hurt (at the .01 level) and the Violent Action (at the .05 level) are significantly correlated with elevation on the scales that measure fearfulness, suggesting that the frequency of battering, the amount of violence used, and the damage done are the key variables related to this fear.

Scales on the MMPI can be significantly low as well as significantly high. Two scales were exceptionally low for the currently battered women tested: those that measure intactness (K) and ego strength (ES), indicating that currently battered women do not feel they possess inner strength and are exceptionally pessimistic about their ability to cope.

Formerly battered women had a three-point MMPI mean profile of 849. Formerly battered women tended to have similar configurations (especially on the subscales) but lower elevations than the currently battered women. The greatest difference between the two groups seems to be that the formerly battered women suffer less from alienation, fearfulness, and feelings of inferiority than currently battered women.

Race proved to be a relatively unimportant variable in terms of defining differences, leading to the conclusion that the commonality of being battered is a stronger variable than race. The expected racial differences (Erdberg, 1970) were not found. The only significant differences found were cultural. Black women in the sample were tougher, less passive, less willing to be passive, and more abusive with alcohol and/or drugs, all externalizing behaviors; white women in the sample were more self-critical, more introverted, more passive, and more willing to be passive, all internalizing behaviors. In a society that is both racist and sexist, black women are understandably tougher—but still vulnerable to sexual stereotypes and the resulting victimization.

The 468 profile as a general type has been described by Lachar as one that "suggests a chronic emotional disturbance, must likely a character disorder or paranoid type of schizophrenia" (1973, p. 82). I compared a composite mean profile of the women in the battered women study ($n = 118$) with a "cookbook" chronic (female) schizophrenic profile ($n = 133$) from Lanyon (1968). Since only the clinical and validity scales are used in Lanyon's book, it was not possible to compare differences in research scales or any of the subscales. Because of the similarities between these two profiles it is essential that the clinician keep in mind that *these two profiles may be indistinguishable*; thus the clinician must determine if what appears to be a schizophrenic women is not, in fact, a battered woman. It is also possible that a woman may be schizophronic *and* battered. Given clinicians' general lack of awareness about battered women, it is possible that some women previously diagnosed as schizophrenic may have been better diagnosed as suffering from post-traumatic stress disorder (i.e., suffering from the effects of being battered).

LINKAGE

Walker (1979) has adapted Seligman's (1975) construct of learned helplessness. She found that battered women learn that beatings occur randomly regardless of their behavior and that their attempts to avoid beatings are ineffective. My research supports Walker's findings. The low mean scores on K and ES indicate that currently battered women perceive themselves as lacking internal strength and are exceptionally pessimistic about their ability to cope. These personality dynamics are similar to those behavior descriptors that comprise learned helplessness.

Further, Walker's research initially found (1979) and later confirmed (1984) that a battered woman syndrome exists. This syndrome consists of a repetitive cycle of abuse that starts with a tension-building stage, moves into overt violence, and ends with a stage of loving contrition. What keeps battered women in the relationship (along with a lack of options or support to leave) is this last stage of remorse, apologies, and promises to change—not the acts of violence. Believing that the batterer will indeed change his behavior and stop the abuse, the woman remains.

Battered women stay because they are afraid (Davidson, 1978; Martin, 1976). My research confirms this fearfulness. The fact that the severity and frequency of the violence were significantly correlated with the level of elevation of the scale measuring fearfulness indicates that the more violent the batterer, the more fearful the victim.

Browne's research (1983) found seven variables that predicted when a battered woman was likely to kill. All but one of these were based on the batterer's behavior. When the battered women Browne studied finally perceived that the violence was not going to stop but would only escalate until someone died, they killed to defend their own lives.

Women, via their social and cultural conditioning, are taught that their expected role is to be wife and mother and that keeping the family together is their responsibility and obligation (Davidson, 1978; Martin, 1976; Walker, 1979). A battered woman is caught in a Catch-22: If she does not take care of her family, she is labeled a failure; if she does not take care of herself, she is labeled a masochist. The dynamics of this double-bind are evident in my research. While the battered woman is angry about what is going on in her life, she tends to turn that anger inward toward herself. Believing the abuse is *her* failure, the battered woman feels guilty, responsible for the violence in her life.

The feelings of guilt are heightened by the batterer's tendency to blame the woman for his violence (Walker, 1979). Further, his denial of her perceptions leads her to feel crazy. The currently battered women in my research sample felt overwhelmed and confused, dynamics associated with a sense of feeling "crazy."

USING TESTS TO EDUCATE JURIES, CLINICIANS, AND CLIENTS

"Why didn't she just leave him if he was so violent?" is one of the most commonly asked questions about battered women, especially those who kill. Such a question reflects the asker's ignorance about the dynamics of victims of domestic violence.

The results of a personality assessment like the MMPI can provide a unique tool in educating others about these dynamics. Its format of graphed results produces a useful visual aid, which can help make concrete the abstract concept of victimization. Although the following discussion will focus on informing juries, that process is similar for informing others, including mental health professionals and the victims/survivors themselves.

Why a battered woman did not leave her abuser is the most difficult issue for jurors to understand. The majority of murder trials for battered women are based on a plea of self-defense (see Chapter 5 of this text). Why should she have stayed and then been forced to defend herself, asks the juror, when she could have simply left?

Understanding the battered woman's syndrome (see Chapter 3 of this text) and the construct of learned helplessness (Walker, 1979) is necessary to help answer the question of why the battered woman didn't leave. Trapped in the cycle of violence, seduced by the hope of change, and feeling personally responsible for the batterer's violence—all are reasons why battered women stay. The woman who winds up in the courtroom tends to be someone who lacks access to outside resources that can change these perceptions. In the courtroom I show the significant elevation of the scale that measures anger. Then I show the subscale configuration, which shows that the anger is directed inward rather than outward. I can explain what this alienation represents: blaming oneself rather than blaming the batterer. It is this level of insecurity that keeps women believing and hoping that things will change.

Add to this alienation/insecurity the construct of learned helplessness, the battered woman's belief that it doesn't matter what she does. The low scores on K (which measures intactness) and on ES (ego strength) validate the woman's sense of lacking strength and her feelings of extreme pessimism about her own ability to cope. Her sense of confusion add to this paralysis.

In addition, fear keeps her rooted where she is. Batterers make threats— and often carry them out. One battered woman in my research sample did leave her husband. He had threatened to burn her mother's house down if she did; the day after she left, her mother's house burned to the ground. "I went back," this woman stated, "because I just couldn't expose my relatives to that kind of danger. Besides," she added, "sometimes I feel safer when I live with him, because then I know where he is. Otherwise I'm always afraid he'll show up when I'm not expecting him."

Violence needs to be assessed not only by the amount of overt physical damage (violent hurt), but by the severity of the *threat* to cause damage (violent action) (Frieze et al., 1980). Pointing a loaded gun at a woman's head for hours at a time and threatening to shoot is an example of such a violent action, which may cause no measurable physical damage but may result in considerable psychological trauma. The fear generated by such violent action may be as considerable as that created by violent hurt. In a court of law, physical injuries may be given much more serious consideration than psychological ones. Yet the fear of imminent bodily harm may well be heightened by repeated episodes of threats to kill. Ironically, for purposes of pleading self-defense the most credible battered woman is a dead one. Thus the argument that the batterer had never yet killed her is one favored by prosecutors.

Inside or outside the courtroom, the very real danger these battered women face needs to be kept in the foreground. Like Walker (1985), I develop an escape plan with each battered woman with whom I work in a clinical setting. Keeping a spare set of car keys hidden and readily accessible, having some emergency money, making provisions for children (if applicable), and knowing when and where to go are all facets of this escape plan.

CONCLUSIONS

Victims of domestic violence frequently are re-victimized by both the mental health and legal professions. Lack of credibility has been a major obstacle, because victims are often silent, out of fear and guilt, about the abuse they have borne. One way of enhancing credibility, in the courtroom as well as the clinic, is through understanding the dynamics presented by victims of violence on standardized personality assessments such as the MMPI. Such tests can bolster credibility and help others—juries, judges, lawyers, therapists, and the victims themselves—be more aware of the observable patterns of behavior presented by victims of domestic violence.

To be victimized is a tragic occurrence. To have this victimization repeated in the guise of legal or mental health intervention is unconscionable.

REFERENCES

Baughman, E.E., & Dahlstrom, W.G. (1972). Racial differences on the MMPI. In S.S. Guterman (Ed.), *Black psychotherapy model: Personality patterns of black Americans*. Berkeley, CA: Glendessary.

Browne, A. (1983). *When battered women kill*. Unpublished doctoral dissertation, Union Graduate School, Cincinnati, Ohio.

Davidson, T. (1978). *Conjugal crime: Understanding and changing the wifebeating pattern*. New York: Ballentine Books.

Erdberg, S.P. (1970). MMPI differences associated with sex, race, and residence in a southern sample. *Dissertation Abstracts International* (University Microfilms No. 340 5236B).

Frieze, I.H., Knoble, J., Zomir, G., & Washburn, C. (1980, March). *Types of battered women*. Paper presented at the Annual Research Conference of the Association of Women in Psychology, Santa Monica, CA.

Graham, J.R. (1977). *The MMPI: A practical guide*. New York: Oxford University Press.

Gynther, M.D., Lachar, D., & Dahlstrom, W.G. (1978). Are special norms for minorities needed? Development of an MMPI F scale for Blacks. *Journal of*

Consulting and Clinical Psychology, 46 (6), 1403–1408.

Hanes, B. (1953). Reading ease and MMPI results. *Journal of Clinical Psychology*, 15, 350–353.

Harrison, R.J., & Kass, E.H. (1968). Differences between Negro and White pregnant women on the MMPI. *Journal of Consulting Psychology*, 10, 262–270.

Hathaway, S.R., & McKinley J.C. (1967). *Minnesota Multiphasic Personality Inventory manual*. New York: The Psychological Corporation.

Lachar, D. (1973). *The MMPI clinical assessment: Automated interpretation*. Los Angeles: Western Psychological Services.

Lanyon, R.I. (1968). *A handbook of MMPI group profiles*. Minneapolis: University of Minnesota Press.

Martin, D. (1976). *Battered wives*. New York: Pocket Books.

Rawlings, E.I. & Carter, D.K. (Eds.). (1977). *Psychotherapy for women*. Springfield, IL: Charles C. Thomas.

Rosewater, L.B. (1982). The development of an MMPI profile for battered women. Unpublished doctoral dissertation, Union Graduate School, Cincinnati, Ohio.

Rosewater. L.B. (1985a). Feminist interpretations of traditional testing. In L.B. Rosewater & L.E. Walker (Eds.), *Handbook of feminist therapy: Women's issues in psychotherapy*. New York: Springer Publishing Co.

Rosewater, L.B. (1985b). Schizophrenic, borderline or battered? In L.B. Rosewater & L.E. Walker (Eds.), *Handbook of feminist therapy: Women's issues in psychotherapy*. New York: Springer Publishing Co.

Ryan, W. (1976). *Blaming the victim*. New York: Vintage Books.

Seligman, H.E.P. (1975). *Helplessness: On depression, development and death*. San Francisco: W.H. Freeman.

Thyfault, R.K. (1984). Self-defense: Battered woman syndrome on trial. *California Western Law Review*, 20 (32), 485–510.

Walker, L.E. (1979). *The battered woman*. New York: Harper & Row.

Walker, L.E. (1984). *The battered woman's syndrome*. New York: Springer Publishing Co.

Walker, L.E. (1985). Feminist therapy with victims/survivors of interpersonal violence. In L.B. Rosewater & L.E. Walker (Eds.), *Handbook of feminist therapy: Women's issues in psychotherapy*. New York: Springer Publishing Co.

PART III
The Children

7

The Child Witness to Family Violence: Clinical and Legal Considerations

Gail S. Goodman
Mindy S. Rosenberg

> Anyone who has listened to Mahler's music will
> know how frequently the expression of tragic feeling
> is interrupted by frivolous turns or simple melodic
> themes that appear banal. Mahler offered Freud a
> psychological explanation for this. He spoke of his
> father's callous attitude to his mother and of the ugly
> scenes he had witnessed. During one of their painful
> quarrels he had rushed out of the house. And outside
> he ran into an organ-grinder churning out the trivial
> tune *O du lieber Augustin alles ist hin* . . . . The brutal
> dissonance of tragic events with the frivolous and
> commonplace haunted him all his life, dominating
> him even at moments of maximum inspiration.
> Because of this he felt that he would never achieve
> his ideal, never compose music of the highest order.
> —KURT BLAUKOPF, *Mahler*

Children are often the unintended victims of family violence. Child witnesses to interparental conflict—even if not directly assaulted themselves—have an increased risk of developing behavioral and emotional problems. Empathically, children suffer from the blows inflicted by loved ones on loved ones. As with the composer Gustav Mahler, memory for violent events witnessed in childhood may last a lifetime and shape the person's very core.

97

In this chapter we discuss two issues related to child witnesses to family violence. The first concerns the effects of witnessing violent events on children's emotional well-being. The second concerns children's memory of the violent incidents. These two issues are intimately interrelated: Memory is affected by one's emotions, and emotions are affected by one's memory. Understanding the interplay of these two factors is of substantial importance for mental health and legal professionals who work with and evaluate child witnesses. We argue in this chapter that, while children may be emotionally damaged by the violent incidents they have witnessed, they can nevertheless accurately recount much about what they have observed.

DYNAMICS OF FAMILY VIOLENCE

Statistics on intrafamily violence in the United States indicate that there is greater risk of injury in intimate relationships than there is on the city streets. National estimates of marital violence (including such acts as hitting, beating, and threatening with or use of guns or knives) suggest that approximately 1.8 million wives are physically abused each year by their husbands (Straus, Gelles, & Steinmetz, 1980). When less stringent definitions of violence are employed (such as pushing, slapping, grabbing, or throwing an object), the estimates increase to approximately 6 million women victimized annually by their spouses. According to FBI statistics (U.S. Department of Justice, 1984), nearly 20 percent of all homicides involve family relations and almost one-third of female homicide victims are murdered by their boyfriends or husbands.

These estimates of violence between partners assume even greater significance when one considers the number of children who are likely to witness such violence. While precise statistics are unavailable, Carlson (1984) extrapolated from national survey data to project that 3.3 million children, at the minimum, annually witness spousal abuse.

Rosenberg (1984) recently interviewed battered women and their children about the types and frequency of verbal and physical spousal abuse witnessed by the children. Nearly all such incidents were witnessed by the offspring. This finding confirms previous clinical and police descriptions (e.g., Bard, 1971). In Rosenberg's sample, children observed verbal threats of injury; verbal assaults on their mother's character; objects or boiling water being hurled across a room; beatings; threats with and actual use of a gun or knife; suicide attempts; sexual torture; and, in all too many instances, homicide. Although one or both parents may want to shield the children from the violence, their good intentions appear to be rarely accomplished.

In addition to witnessing spousal abuse, children may themselves become victims of the assaults, either indirectly or directly. They may, for example, become targets of either parent's displaced anger, frustration, and helplessness. One pattern of couple violence that increases children's vulnerability to physical abuse is a mutually combative pattern where escalation of violence between parents has a high probability of spilling over to the children (Barnett, Pittman, Ragan, & Salus, 1980). Even in the absence of a mutually combative pattern, children often try to protect the victimized parent. When they do, their risk of physical injury substantially increases (Barnett et al., 1980). One of the most frequent reasons given by women for leaving a battering partner is that he threatened to abuse the children or had already injured them physically (Giles-Sims, 1983).

Violence and discord within the family, in general, have a negative effect on children. Substantial evidence documents the relationship between marital discord and children's behavior problems (e.g., see Emery, 1982). Research on intrafamilial violence reveals striking correlations between spousal abuse and various forms of violence involving children, including child abuse (e.g., Finkelhor, Gelles, Hotaling, & Straus, 1983; Reid, Taplin, & Lorber, 1981), sibling abuse (Steinmetz, 1977), and violent offenses committed by juvenile delinquents (Lewis, Shanok, Pincus, & Glaser, 1979). Only recently, however, have clinicians and researchers turned their attention to understanding the effects on children's development of *witnessing* recurrent battering.

EFFECTS OF WITNESSING INTERPARENTAL VIOLENCE

Given the relatively high frequency of couple violence and the strong likelihood that offspring will witness it, what are the resulting emotional effects on children? Research that addresses this question, while still relatively sparse, is growing. In discussing the budding literature, we focus on studies relating to children's behavior, emotional distress, cognitive abilities, and coping strategies.

Behavioral Problems and Emotional Distress

Early clinical studies of child witnesses to interparental violence were anecdotal in nature. These studies catalogued serious behavioral and emotional consequences of living in a violent home. For example, Gayford (1975) and others (Hilberman & Munson, 1977–78; Levine, 1975) described a range of children's reactions that included enuresis, stealing, temper tantrums, truancy, violence toward others, insomnia, anxiety, tics, and the presence of fears and phobias. In general, the early clinical work strongly suggested that child witnesses to interparental abuse suffer from exposure to the violence.

Hilberman and Munson (1977–78) were the first to describe a developmental pattern for child witnesses. Characteristic problems of pre- and elementary-school children included psychosomatic complaints, school phobias, enuresis, and insomnia. Older children showed sex-specific reactions. Boys typically engaged in aggressive, disruptive behavior, while girls were reported to have difficulty concentrating on schoolwork. In other studies, adolescents, particularly females, were noted to suffer from feelings of worthlessness, depression, negative attitudes toward marriage, and distrust of intimate relationships. Male adolescents were reported to view the use of force as a legitimate means of solving interpersonal conflict. They were also found to be vulnerable to behaving violently toward their girlfriends and, at times, toward their mothers (Roy, 1977). Thus, these clinical impressions reinforce other findings that a connection exists between family discord and behavioral problems in children.

While the findings seemed intuitively and theoretically reasonable, many methodological problems plagued these early reports: specifically, the lack of standardized methods, the absence of appropriate comparison groups, and the confounding of victimization with witnessing. These problems limited the inferences that could be made from these studies.

Improvements in methodology are apparent in much of the recent research on child witnesses. Studies are starting to include comparison groups, standardized measures (typically, Achenbach's child behavioral checklist), and documentation of the amount and type of violence witnessed and directly experienced. The findings from the more methodologically sound studies generally support the notion that witnessing interparental violence adversely affects children's emotional adjustment, although the findings are, as yet, less than conclusive.

For example, Porter and O'Leary (1980) correlated measures of overt marital hostility with children's behavioral problems in a sample of clinic-referred boys and girls, ranging in age from 5 to 16 years. Significant correlations between overt marital hostility and a variety of behavioral problems emerged for the boys but not for the girls. For the boys between 5 and 10 years of age, marital hostility significantly correlated with conduct disorders and total pathology scores; for boys between 11 and 16 years of age, marital hostility significantly correlated with socialized delinquency, personality disorder, inadequacy-immaturity, and total pathology. In a later study of 10-year-old boys, Rosenbaum and O'Leary (1981) report that boys from violent families exhibited more behavioral problems than did boys from either discordant but nonviolent families or satisfactory marital relationships. The mean differences between these groups failed to reach statistical significance, however. Emery, Kraft, Joyce, and Shaw (1984) report that the severity of child witnesses' internalizing problems correlates with parents' use of high degrees of verbal aggression and limited use of reasoning.

In general, most of the controlled studies to date report either small differences between child witnesses and comparison-group children (e.g., Rosenbaum & O'Leary, 1981) or significant differences for only a particular age group or sex (Brown, Pelcovitz, & Kaplan, 1983; Cohn, Christopoulos, Kraft, & Emery, 1984; Hughes & Barad, 1983; Porter & O'Leary, 1980; Rosenberg, 1984; Wolfe, Zak, Wilson, & Jaffe, in press). When behavioral problems do appear, they can take an internalizing form, such as depression (e.g., Cohn et al., 1984), an externalizing form, such as delinquency and aggression (e.g., Porter & O'Leary, 1980; Rosenberg, 1984), or both internalizing and externalizing forms (e.g., Brown et al., 1983).

While these recent studies are methodologically advanced compared to the early clinical reports, they suffer from their own share of flaws, which may explain the inconclusiveness of their findings. One limitation concerns the conditions under which the children are assessed. Typically, researchers assess the children in shelter settings within three to five days after admission. Research has not separated the effects of witnessing interparental violence per se from the effects of leaving home, entering and living in an unfamiliar environment, and being separated from one's father.

A second methodological issue concerns the almost complete lack of longitudinal research on child witnesses. We know of only one longitudinal study (Emery et al., 1984). In this study, child witnesses and their mothers are being followed from shelter admission to a year after shelter residence. Data from a 4-month post-shelter intake assessment (the only data available to the authors at present) indicate that the children had significantly more internalizing problems at shelter admission than they did four months later. This finding raises the possibility that assessments made shortly after the move to a shelter may not reflect later adjustment. More longitudinal research is needed to determine the course of behavioral and emotional problems evidenced by child witnesses.

A third methodological problem, alluded to earlier, is the frequent lack of distinction between children who are bystander witnesses to interparental violence and children who have themselves been victims of abuse. This confusion, evident in the early clinical studies, is still present in some recent research, but not all. At least two studies have directly compared child witnesses and child victims of abuse and found more severe behavioral symptomatology in abused children (Hughes & Hampton, 1984; Jaffe, Wolfe, Wilson, & Sluscarzck, 1985). In a third study, comparisons were made between child witnesses to interparental violence and child witnesses to their siblings' abuse (Pfouts, Schopler, & Henley, 1982). Children who had witnessed marital violence suffered the most emotional turmoil and evidenced greater tendencies to model their parents' behavior. Findings such as these lend support to the importance of identifying and distinguishing between violence witnessed and violence experienced.

A fourth and final methodological point relates to the advisability of using parents' responses to child behavioral checklists as the primary means of assessing children's adjustment. These measures rely on parents' perceptions of their children's behavior. In the future, it will be important to gather corroborating evidence of children's behavior from observations across different settings and across a variety of reporting sources, such as day-care personnel and teachers.

Cognitive and Social-Problem-Solving Skills

In addition to behavioral problems, a few studies have investigated the effects of witnessing spousal abuse on cognitive and social-problem-solving skills. In a study of 2-½- to 8-year-old child witnesses, Westra and Martin (1981), found preliminary evidence of decreased cognitive abilities and poor school performance relative to the children's age norms. Documentation that child abuse victims suffer delayed cognitive abilities is already available (e.g., Hoffman-Plontkin & Twentyman, 1984). If Westra and Martin's results can be replicated in future studies, it may be found that family violence in general correlates with cognitive delays.

Related to cognitive abilities are social-problem-solving abilities. Even if future research reveals that child witnesses do not have general cognitive deficits, these children may have specific difficulties. A prime candidate for specific deficits would be the realm of social-problem solving, since this is an area in which their parents seem to have difficulty. Rosenberg (1984) studied the social-problem-solving abilities of a group of children, ranging in age from five to eight years, who had witnessed parental violence but had not themselves been victims of violent attacks. The social-problem-solving measure tapped a range of social-cognitive skills and problem-resolution strategies in several problem situations (e.g., a child being blamed unjustly for starting a fight; a child witnessing a parental argument). Compared to the children who had observed relatively low levels of spousal abuse, children who had observed high levels (i.e., many types and a high frequency of violent behavior) performed poorly on a submeasure of interpersonal sensitivity. This measure concerns the ability to understand social situations, including the thoughts and feelings of people involved in those situations. Thus child witnesses to spousal abuse may have difficulty seeing the other person's perspective in conflict-laden situations. Perhaps these situations have aroused so much anxiety in the past that the children have not been able to build the skills necessary for a normal level of development in this domain. Or the anxiety aroused when confronted with hostile situations may interfere with the child's ability to use the necessary skills that he or she possess (Fischer & Pipp, 1984). Alternatively, the children may have learned from their parents that the other person's point of view is, in a sense, of little relevance.

Coping Strategies

The coping strategies used by child witnesses to deal with recurrent violence is a topic worthy of research, yet not a single published study has directly examined this issue. Recent reports suggest that severely abused children may employ defenses of denial and fantasy to such an extent that multiple personalities or psychosis results (Fagan & McMahon, 1984). We do not know, however, whether children who witness spousal abuse are likely to resort to these same defenses. If a continuum of violence could be established, perhaps the severely abused children would be at the far end of the scale, with child witnesses at not such an extreme. If the use of denial and fantasy were to correlate with severity of abuse, perhaps child witnesses would use these defenses to a lesser extent than the child victims but more so than "normal" children. Because of the lack of research, we must remain tentative in our discussion of coping strategies. It is interesting, however, to consider several case studies indicating that at least some children who witness parental violence do indeed employ defenses of fantasy and denial.

The first case involves a divorced woman who was brutally battered over a period of 10 years. Her 9-year-old daughter was also severely abused by the father. An 8-year-old son escaped direct abuse. The most striking finding of a clinical assessment of the family was the boy's complete denial of violence or discord in the home, despite the fact that both his mother and sister were repeatedly abused in front of him (as reported in separate interviews with the mother and daughter) and showed obvious bruises and black eyes at the time of the interview. In addition, the family was residing in a shelter for victims of domestic violence. Nevertheless, the boy did not waiver in his presentation of a happy family without any problems. Denial seemed to be the dominant defense this boy used, at least during the interview, in talking about his family.

A second case involves a 4-½-year-old boy who had witnessed his mother's frequent battering and psychological abuse. Many times the boy and his sisters were awakened from a deep sleep in the middle of the night as the mother tried to escape from a life-threatening situation. Intimidation with weapons was commonplace, as were the batterer's threats of suicide and homicide. The boy was evaluated in a local shelter after the mother decided to terminate the marital relationship. During the administration of an IQ test, the boy at first answered questions appropriately but then spoiled his answers with words and phrases from cartoons, movies, or creatures of his own imagination. This boy's fantasies seemed to intrude uncontrollably into his thoughts.

Finally, another example of the use of fantasy to cope with extreme inter-parental violence concerns a 6-year-old girl. After years of battering and psychological abuse, the mother of this child left her husband. Shortly there-after, the husband committed suicide. An evaluation of the child indicated that she was depressed, plagued with social problems at school, and with-drawn into a fantasy life lived in a fantasy land. In this make-believe world, her thoughts focused on death and destruction. While this child suffered the effects of multiple traumas—parental suicide and witnessing spousal abuse—the violent home environment undoubtedly contributed to her emotional difficulties.

These examples are meant to highlight the possibility that children who witness extensive family violence may use coping strategies that perhaps are adaptive initially, but that interfere with general psychological adjustment. Futhermore, as we discuss later in the chapter, these particular strategies may be problematic for professionals who wish to conduct forensic interviews of children about their parents' violence. Interestingly, however, the chil-dren's coping styles seem to minimize rather than exaggerate the extent of violence.

In summary, the research reviewed here tentatively suggests that children who witness spousal abuse are at risk for a number of psychological distur-bances. Depending upon age, sex, and the extent of violence observed, these children tend to feel worthless, to mistrust intimate relationships, to be aggressive, to have trouble seeing the perspective of others in tense social situations, and possibly to be somewhat delayed intellectually. Nevertheless, as we discuss in the next section, these children may remember much about the violent episodes they have all too often witnessed.

CHILDREN'S MEMORY

Children who witness family violence will be exposed to repeated, personally significant events that involve familiar people in familiar settings. The assaultive events may last minutes, hours, or even days, and go on for years. The dynamics of family violence play an important role in determining how well children will remember what happened.

Unfortunately, scientific studies of children's memory for violent parental interactions do not exist, but there is good reason for their absence. In order to evaluate a person's memory, an objective record of the witnessed event must be available. The objective record permits one to know exactly what happened. Without an objective record, one easily falls into the following dilemma: If two people witness an event and their accounts differ, whom are we to believe? One person may be correct and the other incorrect, but it is impossible to know which is which. It is also possible for both people to be correct about much of what happened, but for each of them to have had slightly different perspectives and to have interpreted the acts differently. It can also occur that both are wrong, perhaps because both are lying or because their memories distort the event in the same way. For real-life, family inter-actions—particularly those that are violent—objective records (such as videotaped recordings) are generally unavailable. Thus, scientifically sound research on children's memory for interparental violence has been impossible to conduct.

Instead, one must turn to laboratory studies. To the extent that such research provides a general understanding of memory and its development, it can be used to predict children's memory for violent family incidents. Furthermore, to the extent that laboratory research simulates important characteristics of abusive incidents, one can generalize from research to real-life problems.

Does a general understanding of children's memory exist? The answer to this question is "yes." There have been literally hundreds, if not thousands, of studies conducted on children's memory, enough that certain highly repli-cable findings have emerged. Does some of this research simulate the im-portant aspects of violent family interactions? The answer to the second question is also "yes," although this affirmation must be qualified. While some relevant research does exist, variables that might be expected to affect a child's memory for repeated interparental violence have been studied separ-ately rather than in unison. That is, some studies have examined memory for stressful events, but not for repeated ones. Other studies have examined memory for repeated events, but not stressful ones. To the extent that these variables interact (i.e., affect one another), there is the danger that the litera-ture may not generalize to actual incidents of interparental violence. More-over, some variables that may exert an important influence on children's memory, such as the stressfulness of the event, are only beginning to be addressed by researchers.

With these caveats in mind, we will consider what is known about various factors that are likely to affect children's memory for acts of spousal abuse. Since spousal abuse typically involves incidents of repeated violence, one factor concerns the repetition of the event. Children's memory for repeated, real-life events is currently a topic of much interest (for reviews, see Mandler, 1984; Nelson, 1983; Perlmutter, 1980). A second factor concerns whether the child is actively involved in the incident or helplessly observes it. For most acts of spousal violence, the child is likely to be a bystander witness. Studies of child bystander witnesses do indeed exist. Third, child witnesses are likely to observe stressful events that have personal significance to them. Fortunately, studies are currently being conducted on children's memory for stressful, personally significant events. In sum, laboratory research is available upon which to draw insights into children's ability to remember repeated incidents of family violence.

General Principles of Children's Memory for Witnessed Events

When a child or an adult witnesses an event, his or her memory of it will not be perfect. For example, certain details of the incident will become lost over time. Parts of the event may be "reconstructed" to conform to the witness's expectations or needs (Loftus, 1979). Nevertheless, much about the traumatic incident can be retained accurately.

Studies of eyewitness testimony indicate that the most accurate reports are obtained from witnesses shortly after the event (at least for more or less neutral events) and when free reports are obtained (Dent & Stephenson, 1979; Loftus, 1979). Free reports (also called "free recall") refer to answers to open-ended questions, such as "What happened?" Unfortunately, these reports are the most incomplete. Especially with children, free reports typically elicit little information.

When comparing the free reports of children and adults, it is consistently found that children recall less than adults do, and the younger the child is, the less he or she will recall (for reviews, see Flavell, 1985; Kail, 1984). We have seen young children (e.g., 3-year-olds) who will say that "daddy hurt mommy," but when asked what else happened will say "nothing." The limited, verbal responses of these children is not necessarily due to repression or denial, since similar findings often emerge even if children are asked about neutral events (Fivush, Hudson, & Nelson, 1984). In the typical eyewitness testimony study (which involves a one-time event), a 3-year-old child might recall only one or two items of information and a 6-year-old child only three or five items, whereas an adult will recall much more (Goodman & Reed, in press; Goodman, Reed, & Hepps, 1985; King, 1984; Marin, Holmes, Guth, & Kovac, 1979). There are wide individual differences, however. Even though, on average, children tend to recall less than adults do, what they do recall is usually quite accurate. Children's errors tend to be those of omission rather than commission (Johnson & Foley, 1984).

There appear to be only a few exceptions to the general rule of less detailed recall by children than adults. One is that, when children are more familiar than adults with the information to be recalled, children's memory can exceed adults' (Chi, 1978; Lindberg, 1980). Also, children at times notice events that adults miss, making children's memory better than adults' for those particular pieces of information (Neisser, 1979).

Retrieval demands are high in free recall, and we know that children often have more difficulty than adults retrieving information from memory when cues are not available to support retrieval (Ackerman, 1985). Asking children objective (i.e., nonleading) questions is likely to lead to more complete reports and is generally considered the method of choice after free recall has been attempted (Goodman & Helgeson, in press; Loftus, 1979). It does, however, lead to a slight increase in inaccuracies (Lipton, 1977; Marquis, Marshall, & Oskamp, 1972). The inaccuracies are mainly about peripheral details or physical descriptions, however, so that responses to objective questions about central actions remain highly accurate (Dent, 1982; Goodman, Reed, & Hepps, 1985; Pear & Wyatt, 1914). Props also aid children in retrieving information from memory (Price & Goodman, 1985).

The most inaccurate testimony is obtained through the use of leading or suggestive questions (Dent, 1982; Loftus, 1979; Marquis et al., 1972). Legally, leading questions are defined as questions that suggest an answer to the witness. A question such as "There were three chairs in the room, weren't there?" would be highly leading. The question "Were there three chairs in the room?" would be less leading but still somewhat so, since it suggests that there might have been chairs in the room. The question "Was anything in the room, and if so can you describe what was there?" would be considered nonleading since it does not suggest that anything was in the room. Unfortunately, psychologists have not always conformed to the legal definition of a suggestive question, so that what psychologists call objective questions would often be called mildly suggestive by attorneys.

In any case, several factors are known to affect suggestibility. First, people are more likely to be suggestible when their memory for the original event is weak (Loftus, 1979). Second, children and adults tend to be more suggestible when they are interviewed by someone of relatively high status compared to themselves (Ceci, Ross, & Toglia, 1985; Loftus, 1979).

There is currently great debate about the extent of children's suggestibility. Unfortunately, the modern research literature is inconclusive. Some studies find children to be more suggestible than adults (Ceci et al., 1985; Cohen & Harnick, 1980; Goodman & Reed, in press); other studies find children to be no more suggestible (Marin et al., 1979); still other studies find that, at times, children may be even less suggestible than adults (Duncan, Whitney, & Kunen, 1982; see Loftus & Davies, 1984, for a review). Even when children are more suggestible than adults, the suggested information is not likely to appear in either's later reports (Goodman & Reed, in press). Only three studies that we know of have included children as young as 3 years of age (Ceci et al., 1985; Goodman, Reed, & Hepps, 1985; Goodman & Reed, in press), with all of them finding 3-year-olds to be quite suggestible, at least about peripheral information (e.g., the color of a person's hat). It is possible that 3-year-olds are generally more suggestible than older children or adults. Their low status—socially and intellectually—may make them especially susceptible to suggestion.

With the exception of the research on 3-year-olds, most of the modern studies indicating children are more suggestible than adults have examined memory for stories (e.g., Ceci et al., 1985) or films (Cohen & Harnick, 1980; Dent & Stephenson, 1979; Duncan et al., 1982), materials that raise serious questions about the "ecological validity" (i.e., generalizability) of this research. We do not know, for example, whether studies such as these will predict a child's degree of suggestibility about personally significant real-life events, such as whether or not the mother's live-in boyfriend beat up the child's mother. Events of personal significance seem to be retained with unusual strength by adults (Brown & Kulik, 1977; Keenan & Baillet, 1977), and it is probably fair to assume that this finding will also hold for children. In one study of personally significant events, age and suggestibility were highly correlated only when 3-year-olds were included (Goodman, Reed, & Hepps, 1985).

Another criticism of the current suggestibility research is that these studies almost invariably examine age differences in suggestibility for fairly peripheral information or fail to differentiate between central and peripheral information. It seems unlikely that a child's account of peripheral detail would often be of crucial importance to legal authorities or clinicians who are trying to determine the extent and type of family violence the child had witnessed. Goodman and Reed (in press) found that adults, 6-year-olds, and 3-year-olds did not significantly differ in their suggestibility about a central action that occurred in a real-life event.

No modern study has attempted to create an entire fantasy event through the use of suggestion, even though children's reports are often attacked on the basis that an adult led the child into claiming an entire event occurred when it did not. For example, it might be claimed that the child did not see her father and mother have a fight but rather that the mother, an interviewer, or a police officer suggested such information to the child, and the child could not distinguish the truth from the suggestion. Only one study that we know of attempted to suggest an entire, false event to children, and this study was conducted at the turn of the century (Varendonck, 1911). It indicated that children as old as 11 or 12 years could be easily led to fabricate an entire event, but the researcher was so biased that one must question the results. Moreover, the event suggested—that a man came up and talked to the teacher—was of little concern or consequence to the children involved.

There is much more for future research to uncover about children's suggestibility. For example, we do not know if suggestibility is increased if the subject believes he or she will receive positive attention or approval for a conforming response. We do not know the effect parental pressure and questioning has on children's suggestibility. Even if children are highly suggestible, we do not know if interviewers can recognize questionable responses to suggestive questions and discount them in forming their opinions. Many of these issues may arise when a child is interviewed about spousal abuse.

Memory for Repeated Events

Battered women report that the frequency of their partner's attacks escalates over time (Walker, 1979). Given that children are likely to witness much of the violence, they will be exposed to a repeated event. When a child or an adult experiences a repeated, real-life event, generalized "event representations" (also called "scripts") develop. These mental structures consist of organized knowledge about the event, such as what actions typically occur, how the event typically unfolds, and what people are typically involved. When asked about what happens, children can, with high accuracy, tell an adult interviewer about the actions that generally occur and the sequence of events. Interestingly, one omission in their statements tends to concern physical descriptions, which are not frequently mentioned (Fivush, 1984; Hudson & Nelson, 1985; Nelson & Gruendel, 1981), although the inclusion of them increases with age (Hudson & Nelson, 1985).

Nelson and her colleagues (e.g., Nelson, 1978; Nelson, Fivush, Hudson, & Lucariello, 1983) have interviewed children about what happens during such repeated events as going to McDonalds, going to preschool, or going to a birthday party. She finds that even quite young children—3-year-olds, for example—accurately report the core actions. For example, a young child asked about what happens when one goes grocery shopping might say "You buy things and then you go home." The description is quite skeletal, but what is said is accurate. With age, children are able to describe much more about what happens. Their descriptions become more detailed and they are able to articulate more complex relations. For example, 5- to 8-year-old children articulate "if-then" relations. If asked to tell about going to restaurants, they might say, "If we go to McDonalds, we get hamburgers, but if we go to Pizza Hut we get spaghetti." Thus child witnesses of elementary-school age, might be able to articulate that "If daddy is drunk, he hits mommy, but he doesn't otherwise."

In contrast to children's ability to recount what *generally* occurs, when asked to describe a *specific episode* of a repeated event (such as the second incident when the father hit the mother), certain predictable errors often result. Children sometimes confuse similar episodes in their recall. Hudson and Nelson (1985) provide the following example of a 5-year-old child who was asked to remember what happened one time when he went to the zoo: "I remember only a time that I went to the Israel one. There was a wolf there, I think . . . . No, that was another zoo. There was no wolf . . . . There was a duck. There wasn't no zebras . . . . I think there was zebras, but I'm not sure." What appears to be happening here is that the child is confusing different trips to various zoos. Thus, even though the child might be highly accurate if asked what happens when one goes to the zoo (the general question), the child might show some confusion when asked about a specific incident of a repeated event. The confusion would result from the fact that the various episodes become combined in memory. The same types of confusions appear in adults' reports of repeated events as well. For adults, and probably for children, too, the first incidence of a repeated event is retained more clearly than subsequent incidents (Linton, 1982).

When children are asked about a specific, one-time (novel) experience, they show less of this confusion than when asked about a specific incident of a repeated event (Fivush, 1984; Hudson, 1983). Fivush (1984), for example, took kindergarten children to a special archeology museum and then interviewed them either immediately afterwards, six weeks later, or one year later. The children were highly accurate in their reports of the experience, and their memories remained strong at the six-week test. After a year, they could recall less about what happened but, again, what they recalled was accurate. In other studies, children have been found to provide more detailed reports about novel than about familiar events (Hudson, 1983).

Based on these studies, one would predict that the memory that a repeated event occurred (e.g., that the father hit the mother on multiple occasions) should be strong but that the exact details of each incident may become confused as the number of incidents increases (Fivush, 1984; Hudson & Nelson, 1985; Linton, 1982; Neisser, 1981). That is, the child may not be able to remember which time the father hit the mother in the face and which time in the stomach, or which time the father was drunk and which time sober, but still be quite accurate that the mother had been repeatedly assaulted by the father. If the incident is novel, however, the child's memory may remain accurate and strong over a long period of time. Thus, the one time the father brandished a knife might be retained quite well. These findings are not, by the way, peculiar to children: The same memory phenomena have been reported in adults (e.g., Linton, 1982).

Repeated events will typically involve highly familiar people in highly familiar surroundings. The child's memory for the people involved should be quite accurate: It is known that adults' memory for familiar people can be strong over spans of 35 years (Bahrick, Bahrick, & Wittlinger, 1975) and that children can also remember familiar faces well (Diamond & Carey, 1977; Levy-Schoen, 1964).

Bystander Witnesses to Neutral and Personally Significant Events

When interparental violence occurs, children are likely to be bystander witnesses, that is, they observe the events but are not victims themselves. Most of the research on children's testimony has concerned bystander witnesses, albeit to fairly neutral events. Marin and colleagues (1979), for example, exposed children and adults to a 15-second argument between a researcher and a stranger. The subjects' memories were tested after a short delay.

Despite the large age range examined (5 years to adulthood), developmental differences in memory occurred for free recall only, and not in the ability to answer objective or suggestive questions or in the ability to recognize the culprit in a photo line-up.

Active participation in an event versus merely observing it may lead to even better memory, although the studies that directly test this notion have concerned adults' memory for neutral events rather than children's memory for personally significant events. MacWhinney, Keenan, and Reinke (1982) found that subjects who were actively involved in a conversation had better memory for it than did bystanders (see also Hammersley & Read, 1985).

When the witnessed event is personally significant, however, memory may endure regardless of whether the person is actively involved or a bystander. Keenan, MacWhinney, and Mayhew (1977) found that bystander's memory for the exact wording of sentences heard as a part of a lecture was excellent if the sentence had "interactional content," a form of personal significance for the listener.

Violence and Stress

Children who witness family violence are not only likely to be bystander witnesses to repeated events but also to events that are highly emotional and stressful. Linton (1982), in a long-term study of her own memory, found that events that are strongly emotional at the time they occurred tended to endure in memory. This principle probably holds true for children as well.

But there may be some aspects of stressful events that are retained well and other aspects that are retained poorly. The exact relation between stress and memory for real-life incidents appears to be a complex one that has received insufficient study in adults (Deffenbacher, 1983), not to mention children. Several notions have been advanced, however. One, captured by the Yerkes-Dodson law, is that performance on a task—including memory tasks—increases with moderate levels of arousal but then decreases as arousal becomes intense. The exact function that describes this law varies depending upon the complexity of the task. If the task is relatively easy, higher levels of arousal are needed before a decrement in performance occurs. Unfortunately, it is not possible to predict the exact level of arousal that will lead to optimal performance versus decrements in memory for witnessed acts. Nevertheless, it is probably reasonable to expect that experiencing life-threatening events or witnessing highly traumatic acts (e.g., the murder of one's parent) would elicit levels of arousal that might interfere with the completeness of a child's memory.

Even if memory is reduced overall for traumatic events, parts of the event might be retained with clarity. Easterbrook (1959) proposed that the Yerkes-Dodson law results from a narrowing of attention as arousal increases. As arousal reaches moderate levels, attention becomes narrowed onto salient items; irrelevant, more peripheral information is less likely to be attended. As arousal increases, attention becomes more and more restricted. But whatever the person is attending to during stressful moments might then be retained particularly well, since a great deal of the person's attentional resources will be brought to bear on that information.

Preliminary data suggest that this may well be the case (Goodman, Reed, & Hepps, 1985). Children ranging in age from 3 to 7 years were videotaped while having their blood drawn at a hospital's walk-in clinic (the experimental group). The children were scheduled for venipuncture (blood testing) for medical purposes, although none of the children were sick. Venipuncture is a stressful procedure for many children—almost all of the children in the experimental group of our study cried, for instance. A comparison group of children, matched to the experimental group in terms of age and sex, came to the clinic but did not have their blood drawn. These children experienced a similar sequence of events with the laboratory technician, but instead of having their blood drawn, they merely had a design rubbed onto their arm. Three or four days later, the children's memory was tested.

When asked objective questions about the event, the two groups were equivalent in their overall accuracy scores, and both groups remembered central information (e.g., information about the actions that took place) better than peripheral information (e.g., information about the room). But the children who had their blood taken were more accurate than the comparison group in answering questions about central information. In contrast, the comparison group was more accurate than the experimental group in answering questions about peripheral detail. It appears from these results that the more stressed (experimental) group's attention was narrowly focused on the main event, whereas the less stressed (comparison) group's attention was less constrained, freeing these children's attention to process peripheral information. On the other memory measures employed in the study (e.g., photo identification, free recall, suggestive questions), the two groups showed no statistically reliable differences. The results are consistent with the notion that high arousal causes attention to narrow but does not necessarily lead to an overall decrement in memory.

The idea of "flashbulb memories" suggests that memory will be strong for certain aspects of a traumatic event (Brown & Kulik, 1977; Winograd & Killinger, 1983). Brown and Kulik (1977) proposed that memories for personally significant events can be quite vivid and strong and remain so for many years. The prototypical example concerns memory for events surrounding the assassination of John F. Kennedy. Adults who were in late childhood or early adolescence in 1963 seem to be able to recall unusually well what they were doing and where they were at the time they heard the news of the president's death. In order for a vivid memory to be formed, the significance of the event appears to be more important than its recency, since subjects are more likely to report flashbulb memories for the killing of John than Robert Kennedy, the latter event having occurred in 1968 (Winograd & Killinger, 1983). Unfortunately, in these studies, objective records of the subjects' actual whereabouts and behavior are not available to substantiate their reports, so it is still unclear whether the memories are as vivid and real as implied by the metaphor to a photograph (Neisser, 1982).

While memory for salient actions of a stressful event can be strong, if the event becomes too stressful to endure, some children might flee, close their eyes, or cry—activities that would interfere with a vivid recollection of what happened. The child might still be able to report accurately that a violent incident took place, who was involved, and the general outline of the event, but might not have complete memory for all of the details. Other children, however, may be glued to the events or try to protect their parent (Pynoos & Eth, 1984). In this case, their memory for much of the incident is likely to remain vivid for some time.

In summary, child witnesses are likely to evidence predictable accuracies and inaccuracies in their reports. The gist of children's statements is likely to be correct, although they may be confused about specific details. As noted above, the maladaptive strategies seem to minimize the violence witnessed rather than exaggerate it. This principle is consistent with the general finding that children's errors are mainly those of omission rather than commission. Inaccuracies result in large part from inappropriate interviewing.

THE THERAPIST AS FORENSIC INTERVIEWER

Because of the increased possibility of emotional problems and because of the dynamics of human memory, interviewing child witnesses to interparental violence is no easy task. Nevertheless, it may become necessary to interview children about the violence they have observed. If criminal charges are being considered or a social service investigation is underway, a clinician might be asked to attempt a forensic interview of the child; that is, to obtain information from the child that could be used in an investigation or in a court of law.

Clinicians are often hesitant to assume the role of forensic interviewer. They see their role as one of helping children recover from traumatic events and become healthy, well-adjusted individuals, not as obtaining evidence from a child. We argue below, however, that mental health workers need to be informed about forensic issues and how their therapeutic work might affect a child's credibility if the case does go to trial. Even if the clinician does not expect or want to become involved in the investigation, she or he can be subpoenaed to appear in civil or criminal court. The clinician's interviewing techniques may then come under examination. If, for example, the clinician's interview can be attacked as being overly suggestive, the credibility of the child's and the clinician's testimony may be severely damaged. Below, we provide several guidelines for conducting a forensic interview of a child.

In working with child witnesses, the first thing a clinician will want to do is develop a relationship with the child. A supportive relationship will help the child feel comfortable enough to express what happened. The clinician will also need to inform the child that what is said may have to be communicated to authorities. The clinician must decide whether to include a battery of standardized tests in addition to conducting verbal and play interviews. Information obtained from standardized tests, such as intelligence tests, projective instruments, and behavioral self-reports, can provide valuable background information about a child's overall psychological functioning and coping abilities. The more information the clinician has about the child, the better prepared the clinician will be in court should questions arise about the child's overall development. It should be kept in mind, however, that there is no evidence that these tests predict the accuracy of a child's report.

It may take multiple sessions before the clinician wants to broach the topic of the abusive incidents. When the time comes, the clinician should begin by asking open-ended questions that could not be construed as leading. The question, "What happened on the night your mother was killed?", would be nonleading (assuming it is known the mother was killed at night). Or a clinician could ask, "Do your parents ever fight?" If the child responds affirmatively, the interviewer could say, "Tell me what happens when they have an argument." These questions are open-ended and do not suggest a specific answer to the child. Pynoos and Eth (1984), who see child witnesses shortly after they have witnessed the homicide of a family member, ask the children to draw a picture. These clinicians report that the traumatic incident often comes out in the child's drawing, opening the way for discussion.

If the child is not able to provide a detailed verbal response, props can be very useful in aiding the child recount events. A study by Price and Goodman (1985) found that children who had repeatedly experienced an event increased their ability to recount what happened by many fold when given realistic toy props. Interestingly, the props did not elicit fantasy responses or incorrect recall. Most child clinicians have toys in their offices, which could be used by the child to recount what happened (e.g., a doll house). It is sometimes possible to have police or district attorneys' offices construct very realistic models of the child's home so that the props will maximally remind the child of the actual incident. To the extent that children engage in post-traumatic play, clinicians may be in a position to obtain the child's report regardless of attempts specifically to elicit such information from the child. In most cases, however, it will be necessary to ask the child to show what happened. The clinician must let the child take the active role and not manipulate the toys for the child. Otherwise, the interview is open to attack as leading.

Objective questions, such as "Did he hit your mom?," can generally be employed without later legal problems, but clinicans need to be careful not to suggest information to the child. Questions such as, "Didn't he hit your mom?" or "It was your mother who shot your dad, wasn't it?," must be avoided. Not only might such questioning distort the child's report, but it is also likely to be used later to discredit the child in court. It is often difficult for interviewers to restrain themselves from asking leading questions because children can be so difficult to interview. But given the common belief that children can be led to make false accusations through improper interviewing, it is essential to be as nonleading as possible when interviewing a potential witness. Sometimes the interviewer may feel that he or she already has a good idea of what must have happened, making it even more tempting to try to confirm the idea through leading questions. Dent (1982) reports that interviewers who have preconceived notions about what happened are most likely to lead a child into false statements, so clinicians, like others, need to examine their own biases and not let preconceived notions intrude into their interactions with the child.

In general, the interviewer will want to obtain information about who the abuser was, how the event of interest unfolded, and when the event occurred. Consulting with legal professionals before talking to the child is important in order to learn exactly what information is needed and how best to proceed.

Child witnesses who exhibit emotional problems or maladaptive coping mechanisms may pose special problems to the forensic interviewer. It is even more tempting to ask a child leading questions if, for example, the child is denying that his or her parents ever fought when, in fact, a long string of domestic violence complaints exists. A similar problem is often faced when interviewing a child whose life has been threatened if he or she tells and who is thus denying the violence out of fear. In attempting to overcome the child's resistance, clinicians should consider several issues. First, it is of utmost importance that the clinician can assure the child that he or she will be physically safe after the information is told. If necessary, the clinician may need to help make arrangements to ensure the child's safety. Second, the child may need to know that someone in the immediate or extended family supports the clinician's efforts to obtain information about the spousal violence. The clinician should be aware of the potential for family members to help assure the child that "it is OK" to tell "what happened." Likewise, the clinician should also be aware of family members' efforts to obstruct the child from providing information and the reasons for their interference (e.g., loyalty to one of the parents; misinformation about the court process; or attempts to remain uninvolved by withholding information). Here, the clinician will need to decide how to approach the individual(s) to discuss the situation and work toward a family atmosphere that supports the child's efforts to provide testimony. Finally, the clinician needs to validate the child's feelings (e.g., feelings of fear, loyalty to a parent, vulnerability, or distrust of the therapist) and recognize that the child may need time to gain the courage to tell about the violent events.

When the child is ready to describe the events, what might appear to be hedging, recanting, or denial may really be the result of poor communication between interviewer and child. For example, if the child is young, the interviewer needs to be careful in using indefinite terms such as *it* or *that*. If the interviewer asked the child about the abuse and then refers to it as "that" (e.g., "Didn't you say that happened?"), the child may not be sure what "that" refers to and so may say "no." Children can be very literal in their interpretation of language and easily confused, making communication difficult. Re-asking the question in a slightly different way can help ferret out possible miscommunications.

In closing the interview, it is important that the clinician communicate support and validation to the child for telling a very emotionally difficult story. It is also necessary for the clinician to be well informed about the series of events that will happen next and to help the child understand what to expect. How this information is transmitted will, of course, vary according to the child's age and cognitive abilities. Consideration should be given to the possibility of conducting a follow-up session with the child and family members to process the aftermath of the court appearance if the child testifies.

There is currently some debate over whether clinicians should videotape their therapy sessions with children who are potential courtroom witnesses, whether or not a forensic interview is attempted. The advantages of video-taping are numerous. If the sessions are videotaped, an objective record will exist of the interview and of the types of questions employed. The fact that a complete record will exist places pressure on interviewers to conduct a "proper" interview and thus helps guard against the use of leading questioning. Furthermore, a spontaneous report by the child that is captured on video tape may be particularly convincing to a jury. The child's nonverbal responses, such as depictions of an event with toys, may also be preserved and possibly shown in court.

Disadvantages of videotaping must also be considered, however. It is possible that the therapist's discussion with the child will be attacked if it involves suggestion. Also, a child may at times give contradictory statements, and these contradictions may be used to discredit the child in court. Children who at first deny that the abuse took place but then later feel comfortable enough to talk about it will have their credibility severely tainted if their contradictory statements are preserved on video tape. (See MacFarlane,

1985, for a more thorough discussion of these issues.) If child witnesses to family violence are likely to feel particularly conflicted, to deny what occurred, or to recant, then these issues become especially problematic. Nevertheless, we feel it is best to have an objective record of the child's responses and of the interviewing practices used, since this record contains the truth of what actually happened in interviewing the child.

CRIMINAL COURT INVOLVEMENT

Most children who witness spousal abuse will probably not have to testify in criminal court. But some children will. This is particularly likely when criminal charges are brought against the alleged offender and the child is the only or the key witness. We know of a number of homicide cases in which children have been star witnesses against one of their parents or a parent's lover (e.g., see Pynoos & Eth, 1984).

If a child does become involved in a criminal investigation and prosecution, a fairly standard sequence of events is likely to unfold (Soderman & O'Connell, 1962; Swanson, Chamelin & Territo, 1977). The child will first be interviewed by a police officer. This interview will take place as soon as possible after the crime is reported. The police officer will attempt to establish the sequence of events, the actors involved, and the actors' motivations. The interview may take place in the child's home, at a shelter, in a hospital (if the child has been injured), or at the police station. Recounting the events may force the child to, in a sense, relive what happened and may be cathartic or not, depending in part on the interviewer's and the family's reactions and the child's ability to deal with the event.

Pynoos and Eth (1984) report that the police often separate the child from other family members so that the witnesses do not influence each other, despite the extra stress this may cause the child. The child is likely to have other emotional concerns as well, for example, fears about where he or she will spend the night, that he or she is being accused of the crime, that he or she will have to implicate a loved one in the crime, that the culprit will seek revenge if the child tells what happened—all of which may interfere with the child's ability or willingness to recount the events. In some cases, children may be pressured to lie about what happened to cover up the assailant's guilt (Pynoos & Eth, 1984).

Child witnesses are often questioned repeatedly by authorities. They typically have to tell their stories many times to police officers, detectives, protective service workers, attorneys, judges, and juries (Whitcomb, Shapiro, & Stellwager, 1985). Anecdotal evidence indicates that children often resent the necessity of telling the story over and over again. Some children, perhaps understandably, become resistant to the repeated interviews and begin to refuse to talk to authorities. If a clinician attempts a forensic interview, he or she must realize that it may be the umpteenth time the child has been asked about the violent events. Efforts are being made in some jurisdictions to limit the number of interviews a child witness must endure. In such cases, a clinician may be asked to conduct the interview, with attorneys, police, social service workers, and judges all submitting questions to be asked by the clinician.

If the case goes to trial, the chances that the child will become revictimized by the legal system may be particularly high for the child witness to parental violence. These children are likely to suffer from a disorganized, disruptive family environment and to have suffered emotional effects from years of witnessing brutality. To then immerse the child in an adversary process developed for adults in which the child may have to testify against his or her own parent would seem to hold the seeds of revictimization unless it is handled with care. Unfortunately, our criminal court system is not noted for the care with which child witnesses are treated.

For example, it is common for trials to involve many continuances. The child may not have slept well the night before because of having gathered all of his or her courage to appear in court. The child comes to the courthouse ready to testify but is told that a continuance has occurred and that he or she will have to come back another time. Such delays can occur over and over again. By the time of the actual court appearance, the child may be traumatized by this process (in addition to having been traumatized of the event), and the child's testimony and believability may suffer.

Depending on the jurisdiction and the specific case, the child may testify to a grand jury, in preliminary hearings, and at the actual trial. At a preliminary hearing, children under the age of 10, 12, or 14 years (depending on the state) will typically have to undergo a competency examination (Whitcomb et al., 1985). The goal of the examination is to determine if the child: (1) knows the difference between the truth and a lie, and understands the obligation to speak the truth; (2) had the mental capacity to register the event at the time it happened; (3) possesses an uncoached memory of the event; and (4) can communicate his or her memory in court (*American Jurisprudence*, 1960). The examination consists of direct examination and cross-examination by the attorneys, although in some cases the judge may decide to do the questioning. The determination of the child's competence is entirely in the hands of the judge. If the judge decides the child is a competent witness, the child will be permitted to testify before the "factfinder" (jury or judge). If not, the prosecution may lose its key witness and may not be able to pursue the case.

In a competence examination, there is no set type or style of questioning, but it is clear that inappropriate questions are sometimes asked of children. For example, in one case we know of, a judge asked a 5-year-old child who had flown back to Denver for a preliminary hearing if she knew how many seats were on the plane that brought her to Colorado. The girl began to cry, and the judge found her incompetent to testify.

In many jurisdictions across the country, the requirement of a competence examination is being dropped for children. In some jurisdictions, however, the requirement is being eliminated for child victims of sexual abuse only. The rationale for dropping the requirement only for a subset of children is not clear. In any case, even when the requirement for a competence examination is dropped, an attorney can—and generally will—challenge a child's competence. When this occurs, a competence examination may be ordered regardless of the new laws.

At the time of the competence examination, it may be necessary for the child's clinician to appear in court as an expert witness. The clinician may be asked to discuss the child's credibility and thus to advise the court about the child's competence to testify. It is also possible for the clinician to be asked to testify in the actual trial and to recount what the child said. It is here that the clinician's techniques are most likely to be attacked under cross-examination.

If the child is permitted to testify, the child will testify much like any other witness. For example, the child will be required to submit to direct and cross examination. The Sixth Amendment of the Constitution guarantees the accused the right to confront all witnesses, and this guarantee has so far been interpreted as applying to children as well as adults (Bulkley, 1985). Some states are now permitting children to testify via closed-circuit TV, however, in the hope that distancing the child from the defendant will reduce the trauma of testifying.

During cross-examination, children, like rape victims, are especially likely to have their credibility attacked. This attack may not be as overt as that levied on an adult but may still do damage to the child's credibility and sense of self-esteem. Attorneys' tactics to discredit children vary, but a few common ones can be described. If the child is young, attorneys often try to confuse the child by using inappropriate language in relation to the child's age. The attorney may also use leading questions to confuse the child and to demonstrate to the jury that the child is suggestible. Children may be asked mainly about irrelevant details, such as what they ate for breakfast the morning of the assault, in the hope of undermining their confidence and credibility. If the child is older, attorneys may, in addition, be overtly hostile (Goldstein, 1959; Goodman, Golding, & Haith, 1984; Thomas, 1956). However, open hostility may offend the jury. Instead of using this tactic, an attorney may start a fierce argument with the opposing attorney immediately before questioning the child in order to intimidate the young witness. One wonders if cross-examination that employs such techniques is the best way to obtain the truth from a child.

Children's credibility is often viewed by adults as being relatively low (Goodman, Golding, & Haith, 1984; Yarmey & Jones, 1983). But, as discussed above, children who have witnessed parental violence may have developed a variety of coping strategies that damage their credibility even further. To the extent that these children are more likely than many other children to "act out," become delinquent, do poorly in school, or develop emotional disturbances, these problems may be brought out in court in an attempt to discredit the child's testimony.

One type of coping—the use of fantasy—may be particularly damaging to children's credibility. For example, an accurate statement that the father shot the mother might be followed by a fantasy statement such as "and then he sewed her up in a horse." To the extent that such fantasy responses occur, they are probably more likely to be evidenced by younger rather than by older children, but such responses may raise serious questions in jurors' minds about the validity of the child's other statements.

If the child's coping response is denial of the violence, the child may be unwilling to talk about the event or may deny that it ever occurred. Especially when denial takes the form of recanting, the child's credibility is likely to suffer enormously. If the child refuses to talk about the event and the child is the key witness, the case may have to be dropped or a plea bargain arranged. Finally, if the child's coping style is to withdraw emotionally from the event, he or she may appear uninvolved or numb at the trial. In this case, the child may be able to repeat the story without showing the emotional reactions that a jury might expect, leading to questions about the child's credibility. We believe, however, that most children will be able to testify about what happened without these problems severely interfering with the accuracy of their reports.

Both the judge and the attorney who call the child witness can play important roles in protecting the child from revictimization and hence in avoiding the degree of stress that leads to the intrusion of maladaptive coping responses. The judge, for example, can limit the number of continuances of the trial, refuse to permit harassing questioning, allow a supportive other to sit with the child, call needed recesses, and try to make the situation as unintimidating as possible. The attorney who calls the child can object to hostile and repetitive questioning, clarify ambiguous statements made by the child, and request special procedures to be used (e.g., videotaped testimony). Especially if both sides and the judge agree, many accommodations can be made to protect the child from trauma and to elicit the most accurate testimony from the young witness. If the child is emotionally supported, the experience of testifying may actually be cathartic. In fact, Pynoos and Eth (1984) report that children's overriding concern is often to report what occurred as a means of coming to the defense of the injured parent.

In many states, laws have been passed or are under consideration to limit the presumed stress experienced by child witnesses in courts of law (Bulkley,

1985; Whitcomb et al., 1985). Unfortunately, these laws typically apply only to child victims of sexual assault. There is no reason to assume that a child who has witnessed the murder or assault of his or her parent will be less traumatized by a court appearance than a child victim of sexual assault. In many cases, one can easily imagine that a child witness to parental violence will be even more traumatized than the child who has been sexually assaulted, especially if the sexual abuse involves fondling by a stranger but the parental violence involves murder of and by a loved one. Children who testify in spousal abuse or intrafamily homicide trials are likely to have to testify against a parent, and conflicts of loyalty can be expected to be as great if not greater than they are in incest cases. The chances of revictimization by a court appearance apply to children who witness family violence as well as to children who experience sexual assault.

One trauma that might result for a child after a court appearance concerns the verdict. In parental homicide cases, if the child is the main witness but the verdict is "not guilty," the child may be returned to the custody of the abusive parent. We can speculate that the child may fear retaliation or a similar fate. Fears of retaliation may also occur in cases of spousal abuse that do not involve murder. In any case, the child will have to live with the fact that he or she was not believed and with a sense that justice is not always served. After the trial, as well as before, the child may need a good deal of emotional support and therapeutic intervention.

CONCLUSION

In this chapter, we have reviewed much of the literature relating to child witnesses to parental violence. We have examined the evidence indicating that these children are at greater risk than the average child of developing behavioral and emotional disturbances. We have also examined research relevant to the question of children's memory for real-life events. While we have been able to suggest that child witnesses' emotional reactions do not necessarily preclude accurate testimony, it will be necessary to conduct much more research before we can know with certainty how child witnesses' emotions affect their memory. In the end, some child witnesses, like the composer Gustav Mahler, may find that many of their memories of interparental violence—the parts of family life they would like to put behind them—are not only accessible but impossible to forget.

REFERENCES

Ackerman, B.P. (1985). Children's retrieval deficit. In C.J. Brainerd & M. Pressley (Eds.), *Basic memory processes in memory development* (pp. 1–46). New York: Springer-Verlag.

American Jurisprudence Proof of Facts, 6 (1960). San Francisco: Bancroft-Whitney Co.

Bahrick, H.P., Bahrick, P.O., & Wittlinger, R.P. (1975). Fifty years of memory for names and faces: A cross-sectional approach. *Journal of Experimental Psychology: General, 104,* 54–75.

Bard, M. (1971). The study and modification of intra-familial violence. In J. Singer (Ed.), *The control of aggression.* New York: Academic Press.

Barnett, E.R., Pittman, C.B., Ragan, C.K., & Salus, M.K. (1980). *Family violence: Intervention strategies* Publication No. (OHDS) 80-30258. Washington, DC: U.S. Department of Health and Human Services.

Brown, A.J., Pelcovitz, D., & Kaplan, S. (1983, August). *Child witnesses of family violence: A study of psychological correlates.* Paper presented at the annual meeting of the American Psychological Association, Anaheim, CA.

Brown, R., & Kulik, J. (1977). Flashbulb memories. *Cognition, 5,* 73–99.

Bulkley, J. (1985). Evidentiary and procedural trends in state legislation and other emerging legal issues in child sexual abuse cases. In J. Bulkley (Ed.), *Papers from a national policy conference on legal reforms in child sexual abuse cases.* Washington, D.C.: American Bar Association.

Carlson, B.E. (1984). Children's observations of interparental violence. In A.R. Roberts (Ed.), *Battered women and their families: Intervention strategies and treatment programs* (pp. 147–167). N.Y.: Springer.

Ceci, S.J., Ross, D.F., & Toglia, M.P. (1985). *Suggestibility of children's memory: Psycho-legal implications.* Unpublished abstract. Cornell University, Ithaca, NY.

Chi, M.T.H. (1978). Knowledge structures and memory development. In R. Siegler (Ed.), *Children's thinking: What develops?* (pp. 73–96). Hillsdale, NJ: Erlbaum.

Cohen, E.L., & Harnick, M.A. (1980). The susceptibility of child witnesses to suggestion. *Law and Human Behavior, 4* (3), 201–210.

Cohn, D.A. Christopoulos, C., Kraft, S., & Emery, R.E. (1984, June). *The psychological adjustment of school-aged children of battered women: A preliminary look.* Paper presented at the 92nd Annual Conference for Family Violence Research, Durham, N.H.

Deffenbacher, K.H. (1983). The influence of arousal on the reliability of testimony. In S.M.A. Lloyd-Bostock & B.R. Clifford (Eds.), *Evaluating witness evidence* (pp. 235–254). New York: Wiley.

Dent, H.R. (1982). The effects of interviewing strategies on the results of interviews with child witnesses. In A. Trankell (Ed.), *Reconstructing the past* (pp. 279–298). Deventer, The Netherlands: Kluwer.

Dent, H.R., & Stephenson, G.M. (1979). Identification evidence: Experimental investigations of factors affecting the reliability of juvenile and adult witnesses. In D.P. Farrington, K. Hawkins, & S.M. Lloyd-Bostock (Eds.), *Psychology, law and legal processes* (pp. 195–206). Atlantic Highlands, NJ: Humanities Press.

Diamond, R., & Carey, S. (1977). Developmental changes in the representation of faces. *Journal of Experimental Child Psychology, 23,* 1–22.

Duncan, E.M., Whitney, P., & Kunen, S. (1982). Integration of visual and verbal information in children's memories. *Child Development, 53,* 1215–1223.

Easterbrook, J.A. (1959). The effect of emotion on the utilization and organization of behavior. *Psychological Review, 66,* 183–201

Emery, R. (1982). Interparental conflict and the children of discord and divorce. *Psychological Bulletin, 92,* 310–330.

Emery, R.E., Kraft, S.P., Joyce, S., & Shaw, D. (1984, August). *Children of abused women: Adjustment at four months following shelter residence.* Paper presented at the 92nd Annual convention of the American Psychological Association, Toronto, Canada.

Fagan, J., & McMahon, P.P. (1984). Insipient multiple personality in children: Four cases. *Journal of Nervous and Mental Disease, 172* (1), 26–36.

Finkelhor, D., Gelles, R.J., Hotaling, G.T., & Straus, M.A. (Eds.). (1983). *The dark side of families: Current family violence research.* Beverly Hills, CA: Sage Publications.

Fischer, K.W., & Pipp, S.C. (1984). Development of the structures of unconscious thought. In K.S. Bowers & D. Meichenbaum (Eds.), *The unconscious reconsidered* (pp. 88–148). New York: Wiley.

Fivush, R. (1984). Learning about school: The development of kindergartners' school scripts. *Child Development, 55,* 1697–1709.

Fivush, R., Hudson, J., & Nelson, K. (1984). Children's long-term memory for a novel event: An exploratory study. *The Merrill-Palmer Quarterly, 30,* 303–316.

Flavell, J. (1985). *Cognitive development.* New York: Prentice Hall.

Gayford, J.J. (1975). Wife battering: A preliminary survey of 100 cases. *British Medical Journal, 1,* 194–197.

Giles-Sims, J. (1983). *Wife battering: A systems theory approach.* New York: Guilford Press.

Goldstein, I. (1959). Child eyewitnesses. *Trial Lawyers Guide. 3,* 45–51.

Goodman, G.S., Golding, J.M., & Haith, M.M. (1984). Jurors' reactions to child witnesses. *Journal of Social Issues, 40*(2), 139–156.

Goodman, G.S., & Helgeson, V.C. (in press). Children as witnesses: What do they remember? In L. Walker (Ed.), *Handbook of child sexual assault.* New York: Springer.

Goodman, G.S., & Reed, R.S. (in press). *Age differences in eyewitness testimony.* Manuscript submitted for publication.

Goodman, G.S., Reed, R.S., & Hepps, D. (1985, August). The child victim's testimony. In R. Toglia (Chair), *Current trends in children's eyewitness testimony research.* Symposium presented at the American Psychological Association Convention, Los Angeles, CA.

Hammersley, R., & Read, S.D. (1985). The effect of participation in a conversation on recognition and identification of the speaker's voice. *Law and Human Behavior, 9,* 71–82.

Hilberman, E., & Munson, K. (1977–1978). Sixty battered women. *Victimology: An International Journal, 2,* 460–470.

Hoffman-Plotkin, D., & Twentyman, C.T. (1984). A multimodal assessment of behavioral and cognitive deficits in abused and neglected-children. *Child Development, 55,* 794–802.

Hudson, J. (1983, April). Scripts, episodes, and autobiographical memories. In K. Nelson (Chair), *Memory in the real world.* Symposium held at the Society for Research in Child Development meetings, Detroit, MI.

Hudson, J., & Nelson, K. (1985). *Repeated encounters of a similar kind: Effects of familiarity on children's autobiographic memory.* Unpublished manuscript.

Hughes, H.J., & Hampton, K.L. (1984, August). *Relationships between the affective functioning of physically abused and nonabused children and their mothers in shelters for battered women.* Paper presented at the 92nd Annual Convention of the American Psychological Association, Toronto, Canada.

Hughes, H.M. & Barad, S.J. (1983). Psychological functioning of children in a battered women's shelter: A preliminary investigation. *American Journal of Orthopsychiatry, 53,* 525–531.

Jaffe, P., Wolfe, D.A., Wilson, S.K., & Sluscarzck, M. (1985). *Similarities in behavioral and social maladjustment among child victims and witnesses to family violence.* Manuscript submitted for publication.

Johnson, M., & Foley, M.A. (1984). Differentiating fact from fantasy: The reliability of children's memory. *Journal of Social Issues, 40,* 33–50.

Kail, R. (1984). *The development of memory in children.* New York: W.H. Freeman.

Keenan, J., MacWhinney, B., & Mayhew, D. (1977). Pragmatics in memory: A study in natural conversation. *Journal of Verbal Learning and Verbal Behavior, 16,* 549–560.

Keenan, J.M., & Baillet, S.D. (1977). Memory for personally and socially significant events. In R.S. Nickerson (Ed.), *Attention and Performance, VIII* (pp. 651–669). Hillsdale, NJ: Erlbaum.

King, M.A. (1984). *An investigation of the eyewitness abilities of children.* Unpublished doctoral dissertation, University of British Columbia, Canada.

Levine, M. (1975). Interparental violence and its effects on the children: A study of 50 families in general practice. *Medical Science Law, 15,* 172–176.

Levy-Schoen, A. (1964). L'image d'antrui chez l'enfant. Publications de la faculte' des lettres et sciences humaines de Paris. Serie, Recherches, tome XXIII. Paris: Presses Universitaires de France.

Lewis, D.O., Shanok, S.S., Pincus, J.H., & Glaser, G.H. (1979). Violent juvenile delinquents: Psychiatric, neurological, psychological and abuse factors. *Journal of the American Academy of Child Psychiatry, 18,* 307–319.

Lindberg, M. (1980). Is knowledge base development a necessary and sufficient condition for memory development? *Journal of Experimental Child Psychology, 30,* 401–410.

Linton, M. (1982). Transformations of memory in everyday life. In U. Neisser (Ed.), *Memory observed* (pp. 77–91). San Francisco: Freeman.

Lipton, J. (1977). On the psychology of eyewitness testimony. *Journal of Applied Psychology, 62,* 90–93.

Loftus, E.F. (1979). *Eyewitness testimony.* Cambridge, MA: Harvard University Press.

Loftus, E.F., & Davies, G.M. (1984). Distortions in the memories of children. *Journal of Social Issues, 40(2),* 51–68.

MacFarlane, K. (1985). Diagnostic evaluations: Interview techniques and the uses of videotape. In J. Bulkley (Ed.), *Papers from a national policy conference on legal reforms in child sexual abuse cases.* Washington, DC: American Bar Association.

MacWhinney, B., Keenan, J.M., & Reinke, P. (1982). The role of arousal in memory for conversation. *Memory & Cognition, 10,* 308–317.

Mandler, J. (1984). *Stories, scripts and schemes.* Hillsdale, NJ: Erlbaum.

Marin, B.V., Holmes, D.L., Guth, M., & Kovac, P. (1979). The potential of children as eyewitnesses. *Law and Human Behavior, 3*(4), 295–306.

Marquis, K.H., Marshall, J., & Oskamp, S. (1971). Testimony validity as a function of question form, atmosphere, and item difficulty. *Journal of Applied Social Psychology, 2,* 167–186.

Neisser, U. (1979). The control of information pickup in selective looking. In A.D. Pick (Ed.), *Perception and its development: A tribute to Eleanor Gibson* (pp. 201–219) Hillsdale, NJ: Erlbaum.

Neisser, U. (1981). John Dean's memory: A case study. *Cognition, 9,* 1–22.

Neisser, U. (Ed.) (1982). *Memory observed.* San Francisco: Freeman.

Nelson, K. (1978). How children represent their world in and out of language. In R. Siegler (Ed.), *Children's thinking: What develops?* Hillsdale, NJ: Erlbaum.

Nelson, K. (1983). The derivation of concepts and categories from event representations. In E.K. Scholnick (Ed.), *New trends in conceptual representation: Challenge to Piaget's theory* (pp. 131–150). Hillsdale, NJ: Erlbaum.

Nelson, K., Fivush, R., Hudson, J., & Lucariello, J. (1983). Scripts and the development of memory. In M. Chi (Ed.), *Trends in memory development research* (pp. 52–70). Basel, Switzerland: Karger.

Nelson, K., & Gruendel, J. (1981). Generalized event representations: Basic building blocks of cognitive development. In A. Brown & M. Lamb (Eds.), *Advances in developmental psychology* (Vol. 2). Hillsidale, NJ: Erlbaum.

Pear, T.H., & Wyatt, S. (1914). The testimony of normal and mentally defective children. *British Journal of Psychology, 3,* 388–419.

Perlmutter, M. (Ed.). (1980). *Children's memory: New directions in child development* (No. 10). San Francisco, CA: Jossey-Bass.

Pfouts, J.H., Schopler, J.H., & Henley, H.C. (1982). Forgotten victims of family violence. *Social Work, 27,* 367–368.

Porter,, B., & O'Leary, D.D. (1980). Marital discord and childhood behavior problems. *Journal of Abnormal Child Psychology, 8,* 287–295.

Price, D.W.W., & Goodman, G.S. (1985). *The development of children's comprehension of recurring episodes.* Paper presented at the Society for Research in Child Development Meetings, Toronto, Canada.

Pynoos, R.S., & Eth, S. (1984). The child as witness to homicide. *Journal of Social Issues, 40*(2), 87–108.

Reid, JB., Taplin, P.S., & Lorber, R. (1981). A social interactional approach to the treatment of abusive families. In R.B. Stuart (Ed.), *Violent behavior: Social learning approaches to prediction, management and treatment.* New York: Brunner/Mazel.

Rosenbaum, A., & O'Leary, D.K. (1981). Children: The unintended victims of marital violence. *American Journal of Orthopsychiatry, 51,* 692–699.

Rosenberg, M.S. (1984). *The impact of witnessing interparental violence on children's behavior, perceived competence, and social problem solving abilities.* Unpublished doctoral dissertation, University of Virginia, Charlottesville, VA.

Roy, M. (Ed.) (1977). *The abusive partner: An analysis of domestic violence.* New York: Van Nostrand Reinhold.

Soderman, H., & O'Connell, J.J. (1962). *Modern criminal investigation.* New York: Funk & Wagnalls Company.

Steinmetz, S.K. (1977). *The cycle of violence: Assertive, aggressive and abusive family interaction.* New York: Praeger.

Straus, M.A., Gelles, R.J., & Steinmetz, S.K. (1980). *Behind closed doors: Violence in the American family.* Garden City, NY: Doubleday.

Swanson, C.R., Chamelin, N.C., & Territo, L. (1977). *Criminal investigation.* Santa Monica, CA: Goodyear Publishing Company, Inc.

Thomas, R.V. (1956). The problem of the child witness. *Wyoming Law Review, 10,* 214–222.

U.S. Department of Justice, Federal Bureau of Investigation (1984). *Uniform Crime Reports for 1983.* Washington, DC: U.S. Government Printing Office.

Varendonck, J. (1911). Les temoignages d'enfants dans un proces retentissant. *Archives de Psychologie, 11,* 129–171.

Walker, L.E. (1979). *The battered woman.* New York: Harper & Row.

Westra, B., & Martin, H.P. (1981). Children of battered women. *Maternal Child Nursing Journal, 10,* 41–54.

Whitcomb, D., Shapiro, E.P., & Stellwager, C.D. (1985). *When the victim is a child: Issues for judges and prosecutors.* Washington, DC: National Institute of Justice.

Winograd, E., & Killinger, W.A.(1983). Relating age at encoding in early childhood to adult recall: Development of flashbulb memories. *Journal of Experimental Psychology: General, 112,* 413–422.

Wolfe, D.A., Zak. L, Wilson, S., & Jaffe, P. (in press). Child witnesses to violence between parents: Critical issues in behavioral and social adjustment. *Journal of Abnormal Child Psychology.*

Yarmey, A.D., & Jones, H.P.T. (1983). Is the psychology of eyewitness identification a matter of common sense? In S.M. Lloyd & B.R. Clifford (Eds.), *Evaluating witness evidence* (pp. 13–40). New York: Wiley.

8

Domestic Violence and Determination of Visitation and Custody in Divorce

Lenore E.A. Walker
Glenace E. Edwall

A decade of experience within the battered women's movement has helped us learn that dissolution of battering relationships does not always end the violence. One of the most common areas in which batterers continue their harassment and other abuse involves determination of custody and visitation of the children. It is not unusual for battered women to lose custody of their children, be forced to co-parent them with their abuser in some kind of formal joint custody agreement, or continue to be violated around the time of visitation. For a variety of reasons, to be discussed in this chapter, the courts have not recognized the high risk of further abuse to battered women or their children. Often mental health professionals, child-custody evaluators, and guardians *ad litem* have encouraged the courts to respond in a punitive or nonsupportive manner. The lack of professional and judicial knowledge of the negative effects of witnessing the violence fathers commit against mothers needs to be reversed if we are to realize our goal of battering-free relationships in the next generation.

DEFINITIONS

The definition of what constitutes harm to children has not been consistent, given the amount of discretion judges have in American law. Most look to the definitions of physical and sexual abuse set forth in the state's criminal law and the children's codes and operationalized by child protective services. If the abuse is overt and results in obvious serious injuries, it is readily defined as harmful and its negative impact can be ascertained. But in the majority of cases, the abuse is less obvious and injuries may not be visible. This is especially true for psychological harm that prevents normal development in children. Few child protective service workers have the authority or ability to investigate allegations of abuse that occur during a child-custody dispute, thus turning these cases back to the divorce courts, which generally rely on appointed children's attorneys (guardians *ad litem*) and mental health professionals for guidance. Unfortunately, few of these professionals have any knowledge or understanding of the dynamics or impact of domestic violence.

In this chapter we define *physical abuse* as an act or behavior that is intended to or actually inflicts bodily harm on a child. This includes, but is not limited to, shaking, hitting, shoving, punching, kicking, choking, throwing objects, and using weapons. Naturally, the impact of some acts will differ with the age of the child. *Child sexual abuse,* usually called *incest* in families, is defined as any kind of exploitive sexual contact or attempted sexual contact, including but not limited to the genital areas of the body.

In defining *psychological abuse* of the child, it is much more difficult to define specific acts or behaviors, although inattention to the child's needs or exposure of the child to situations that disrupt his or her normal development must be considered. There are two major ways to abuse a child psychologically: intentionally, through specific acts, and unintentionally, through exposure to violence. Vulnerabilities and strengths of individual children will result in different impacts from similar acts. Nonetheless, certain situations can be expected to produce a traumatic effect. One such unintentionally abusive situation is witnessing degrading acts towards others, especially the name-calling and verbal humiliation that usually accompanies the father's physical abuse of the mother. Another is exposure to the batterer's poor social skills and inability to control anger in a variety of situations. Children who are subjected to witnessing their father's temper tantrums are psychologically injured by them (see Chapter 7 of this text). Experiencing threats of or witnessing family abuse creates a high probability of psychological harm that compromises a child's present and future development. The psychological evidence is presented below.

PSYCHOLOGICAL DYNAMICS

Theoretical and Empirical Findings about Aggression

Social learning theory postulates that behavior is learned by both direct and indirect experiences. Bandura (1977) discusses the importance of modeling on repetitive behaviors, especially after witnessing influential persons exhibit the same acts. Children, then, would be expected to model violent behavior they have witnessed as well as experienced. The theory suggests that witnessing parental conflict can directly cause a child to use aggressive or violent behavior, whether or not the child has actually been physically abused. This theoretical principle, widely accepted by psychologists, is rarely applied to child-custody evaluations. Yet learning theory can predict the future expression of aggression.

Empirical studies have helped clarify how learning actually occurs in children who have been exposed to family violence. Burgess (1984), like most other researchers in the field, has found that abused children are likely to repeat the abusive and aggressive behavior they have experienced unless mediating factors occur. His study suggests that competence in social relationships with peers can mitigate some of the transmittal of aggression. Kalmuss, in comparing the use of violence by those children who directly experienced and those who only witnessed it in their families, found that "the results indicate that observing hitting between one's parents is more strongly related to involvement in severe marital aggression than is being hit as a teenager by one's parents" (1984, p.15). Her data also show that there is a dramatic increase in the likelihood of marital violence if an individual was both abused and witnessed abuse as a child.

Gender differences in the transmittal of aggression and violence have also been empirically studied by Patterson (1982) and his colleagues (Reid, Taplan, & Lorber, 1981). Their research pioneered the use of behavioral observations at home to study family interactions in aggressive boys. They found that there was greater cross-gender aggression observed in abusive than in nonabusive homes with both aggressive and nonaggressive boys. Thus, aggressive acts at home may be more likely to become abusive when males and females fight. Their work begins to shed light on how males learn to be more abusive while females learn to be more receptive to male aggression. Children learn more than aggressive acts in these families; they also learn the roles and attitudes that cause spouse abuse. They learn that love and violence can co-exist in a family.

Straus, Gelles, and Steinmetz (1980) analyzed data from 2,000 randomly selected families and found that men who had witnessed their parents hit each other were three times as likely to abuse their own wives. They also compared rates in nonviolent and violent childhood homes and found that, "sons of the most violent parents have a rate of wife-beating that was one thousand percent greater than that of the sons of non-violent parents" (p. 175). Walker's study (1984) found similar data given by battered women about the childhood homes of their violent and nonviolent partners. It seems clear that both the theoretical expectations and the actual empirical data are consistent. Witnessing and experiencing family violence places children at higher risk to grow up and repeat the abusive behavior patterns of their own homes.

Divorce in Battering Relationships

There has been much discussion among those treating battered women about whether the best way to stop the violence is to terminate the relationship (see, for example, Walker, 1979, 1984; Martin, 1976; Sonkin, Martin & Walker, 1985; Douglas, in press; Rosewater, in press). In fact, one of the most frequently asked questions is why the woman doesn't just leave the relationship. Some have labeled her masochistic, while others claim she is to blame for her own victimization because she stays. Although it has been said that there is a symbiotic relationship between men who batter and the women with whom they live (Walker, 1979), our empirical data suggest that battering relationships do not last any longer than other marriages (Walker, 1984). We found that the average battering relationship lasts the same six years that the U.S. census data found all marriages to last on average.

It is difficult to estimate the number of divorces in which violence has played a part, since no-fault divorce laws rarely permit disclosure of such facts. Prior to the widespread adoption of the uniform dissolution act by many states, the available data suggested that almost one-third of the divorce actions filed were for grounds of mental and physical cruelty. This statistic compares well to the data of Straus and colleagues (1980), who found that almost one-third of those interviewed admitted to at least one physically abusive incident during the year inquired about. Thus, one way to estimate incidence is to use these figures and approximate that in one out of three dissolving marriages there has been domestic violence. However, this may be a low estimate, given some of the properties known about men who batter women.

Sonkin and colleagues (1985) found that batterers pursue their wives relentlessly. Their research is consistent with other studies, which find that it is the men who commonly will not let the women leave. One way to continue the relationship, for those men who cannot disconnect from the women they abuse, is to use the legal system as a new arena of combat. Thus there may well be a high percentage of contested divorces where there has been abuse. I estimate that at least one-half of all contested child-custody cases involve families with a history of some form of family violence. Recent communication with Colorado district court judges suggests that in approximately 40 percent of those contested cases, fathers are being awarded sole custody of the children irrespective of their history of violence.

Many states have moved to a presumption of joint custody as a way of preventing a bitter court battle. Although risk of harm to the child is a justified reason for awarding one parent sole custody, the burden of proof in such cases would fall to the battered woman to demonstrate the potential harm from joint custody. Because many battered women are too worn down emotionally or are too frightened of losing contact with their children, they give in rather than fight the batterers' demands for control. It is not known how many joint custody arrangements are made without knowledge of the potential for direct or indirect abuse to the children involved. But it is reasonable to estimate a large number of children are damaged by this arrangement.

Battered Women's Anecdotal Reactions

Battered women interviewed at our offices tell of the difficulties they have with the courts once they decide to go forward with terminating their relationships. It is not unusual for battered women to have to leave home without their children in order to assure everyone's immediate safety. Gloria is an example:

> Gloria ran away from home unexpectedly one afternoon when her drunken husband began beating her. She managed to get outside the house and hide in the surrounding woods. Soon she heard him coming after her, shooting his 357 Magnum while shouting obscenities and demands for her to return. Her three young children were inside the house. Since he had never physically harmed them before, Gloria chose to leave them and flee to safety, fearing for her own life. The judge later gave custody to her batterer, angry that she had not rescued the children, too.

Some battered women flee from their homes, without court permission, because they are afraid to tell the court where they are going.

> Lois ran away with her 2-year-old son and hid in a battered women's shelter in another state. Although she wrote the judge a letter explaining her continued fear for her own and her child's safety, he became irate at her willful disrespect of his previously issued visitation order and immediately transferred custody to her former husband. This enabled the child's father to contact the local missing children's agency, with the new judicial orders in hand, and they broadcast the child's picture on television and/or posters nationwide. No one at the agency ever reviewed the divorce file, which is a public record and would have given the details of the violent acts committed by the father. Nor was the risk of danger to the child important to the judge, who was exercising his power to punish Lois for not trusting the court to act in the best interests of her child.

Many battered women lose custody to child protective services who believe they are acting in the best interests of the child:

> Diana's violent husband called our office the day she left home, leaving behind our telephone number on a scrap of paper. He sounded quite paranoid on the telephone, insisting he would never recognize what any judge or psy-

chologist says since in God's eye there is no such thing as divorce. "She ran away and left her two baby boys," he told me, "because she is crazy. Why one time she even burned the house down. Can't she make up her mind," he continued. "This must be the fifteenth time she's gone." Responding to gentle questioning, he revealed that he had hit her the night before but insisted it was only after she hit him. "I mean what's a guy to do when you women want to have liberation. If you want independence, then you have to learn to be treated like a man. Ain't no man I know who wouldn't have hit her head against the wall after she slapped him." Because he was obviously a high risk for abusing his children, protective services took custody of them. However, Diana, safe in another state, cannot get them to release the children to her care. She is seen as unable to protect them.

Some battered women need time to get their own lives straightened out before they can continue to meet their children's needs. But when they do, they may find that others did not see the arrangement as temporary.

Pamela didn't really want to let her father and stepmother raise 9-month-old Scottie, but she was young and tired from all the abuse. The judge gave her parents custody, with the unwritten provision that it was just for a year or two. Pam planned to live with them, so it seemed like a reasonable judicial decision. Pam couldn't follow her parent's rules, and after much conflict, she moved to another state. Her parents soon followed, as did her former husband. Pam got a job and remarried within the next two years. But her parents wouldn't let Scottie live with her and restricted her visitation with Scottie to the same number of hours they let him see his dad. Eventually, Scottie's dad went to court for custody. Strategically, Pam's lawyer advised her not to file for custody, too. Her parents got to keep Scottie, and in this state another custody change cannot be proposed for two more years.

Or there may be retaliation for the battered woman's pursuing legal action against her husband.

Jeanie wanted to give her child up for adoption because of her partner's violence. She was persuaded by her batterer's parents to let them have custody of her newborn daughter. She continued to visit her baby sporadically while she was living with the child's father. She feared he'd abuse their daughter, like he did her older child from a previous marriage, and so limited their time with the baby. Now Jeanie no longer lives with the batterer. He was successfully prosecuted for assault and battery, and she won a civil suit against him for damages he caused her during a beating. When his mother couldn't persuade Jeanie to drop the lawsuits, she began denying her the right to visit the baby. Jeanie's only recourse is costly litigation. She has filed contempt charges and requested a change of custody to her, but while it slowly winds through the court process, she is not able to see her daughter.

By the time some battered women terminate the relationship, they no longer can persuade their children to go with them. These are often teenage children who have learned that their aggressive father has the power and, often, the money.

> Sally was one such case. She left home following a bad beating in the middle of the night and drove for 24 hours to her parents' home in another state. They told her to go home. When she got back, she found her husband had gone to court in an *exparte* hearing and won a temporary order locking her out of their home and giving him custody of their 14-year-old son. At the hearing several days later, her son testified that he wanted to live with his dad. The judge granted his request. Sally found herself feeling rejected and betrayed by her husband, her son, and her parents.

> Sandy's case was somewhat different. Her 13-year-old daughter wanted to stay with whoever offered her the most freedom, love, and money. Having learned to manipulate as a coping style in her abusive home, the daughter set up a contest between parents and would go back and forth between each of them as her mood and the ante got higher. Sandy suspected sexual abuse or at least emotional incest but was unable to prove it, since her daughter denied that anything inappropriate was going on. After two years, Sandy finally was awarded custody of the daughter. But the length of time it took to get resolution contributed to the daughter's out-of-control behavior, and Sandy was unable to parent this child effectively by the time the court made this ruling.

Many children refuse to take a side in their parents' dispute, accurately perceiving that in violent families, to chose one parent is effectively seen as a rejection of the other. In those cases, someone has to help make the decision. Often mental health professionals are asked to do an evaluation of both parent's "fitness," although the Center for Women and Family Law in New York indicates there is case law in some states that are automatically deciding in favor of the mother as custodian in battering cases. The Montana Supreme Court recently issued an opinion in *In re: Custody of Tiffany Cherewick* that a man known to have beaten a woman could not be expected to have the personality characteristics to parent his 3-year-old daughter adequately and upheld a state court's award of custody to the mother—despite the recommendation of a psychologist who said the father should have custody and discounted the impact of the violence on the child. It is possible that the courts will return to an absolute standard, such as that no custody be awarded to men who batter women or children, if mental health professionals do not take the impact of witnessed or experienced violence on children more seriously.

Impact on Children's Development: Clinical Findings

Children's reactions to divorce, as compared to other issues, have been little reported in the empirical or clinical literature, although anecdotal evidence abounds.

The available studies show that when there is parental cooperation during and after the divorce, the children continue to develop normally (cf. Wallerstein and Kelly, 1980). This finding, of course, has guided the attempts to legislate and force parents into cooperation *in the best interests of the child,* the current legal standard. Unfortunately, there are no studies specifically measuring the impact on the child when the forced cooperation does not work. Clinical impressions suggest that one healthy, strong parent may be more beneficial to the child than two parents with different values who continue the battering relationship during visitation and when litigating custody issues.

The available empirical data on the impact of physical, sexual, and psychological violence on children's development is consistent with clinical findings. Goodman and Rosenberg review these findings in detail in Chapter 7 of this book. In general, being exposed to abuse can produce aggressive acting-out behaviors, conduct disorders, anxiety disorders, panic attacks and other phobias, affective disturbances, learning disabilities, and gross developmental delays. Speech problems, enuresis, ecopresis, poor motor control, eating and sleep disorders have been observed. Disturbance in interpersonal relationships may come as a result of the abusive situation which then prevents the development of good peer relationships that the Burgess (1984) study suggests may mediate against intergenerational transmission of violence. Cognitive disturbances including thought disorders, confusion, lack of concentration, memory deficits, and confused belief systems are also seen. Rumination about previous violence and a hypervigilance to cues of future violence occurs.

Many of the psychological symptoms are consistent with the posttraumatic stress disorder classification in the American Psychiatric Association's (1981) *Diagnostic and Statistical Manual of Mental Disorders, Third Edition* (DSM-III). They can be distinguished from other childhood disorders by the pattern in which they are seen, which is similar to those of other abuse syndromes, and by a careful history. Comparisons of symptoms with historical data, expected reactions to trauma, behavioral principles, and social learning theory can provide the necessary clarification. For example, it is probable that a child fears the father she has seen beating her mother because of the exposure to abuse. We have, however, seen custody reports that blame the mother for instilling such a fear in her daughter because of her own fears and anger toward the child's father. Yet given the information we have about batterers, it is not parsimonious to interpret the battered women's anger alone as sufficient cause to turn a child against her father. Even well-known clinicians can make such errors in interpretation, sometimes as a result of trying to fit their own theory to the domestic violence issue (cf. Minuchin, 1984), when they do not take into account the direct impact on the child of witnessing the father's abusive behavior.

Physical Abuse

The impact of physical abuse on children has been widely reported elsewhere and will not be detailed in this chapter (cf. Burgess, 1984; Patterson, 1982; Reid et al., 1981; Straus et al., 1980). It is not unusual for men who batter women to hit, shove, push, kick, punch, throw, shake, and otherwise beat their children. Their uncontrolled expression of anger may take different forms with children of different ages. Their difficulties with boundary issues extends to the various members in the family. It is as though each person is thought of as an extension of the man's own sense of self. Thus, he reasons, he has the duty and the right to discipline and manage each family member by methods of control he chooses. This rationalization, unfortunately, is supported by the sanctity with which the privacy of the family is endowed by American culture.

Much has been written about the frequency with which women also physically abuse their children. In our research sample, the battered women interviewed were eight times more likely to abuse their children when living with a batterer. We found, however, that only 0.5% of those women interviewed had physically battered the children, whereas they reported 55% of the batterers had done so (Walker, 1984). However, the women admitted disciplining the children to control their behavior so that their abusive mate would not get upset and possibly hurt the children or the women themselves. Many went to great lengths to protect their children, only to find that the children then resented their being the disciplinarian. Although the women often knew how they would prefer to parent their children, they said they felt restrained by the ever present threat of more violence. The no-hitting rules so popular in most battered women's shelters offer them an opportunity to try out nonphysical means of discipline, such as time-out techniques and positive reinforcement for appropriate behavior.

Sexual Abuse

Sexual abuse of children has become more commonly known than ever before (Russell, 1983). Some men who batter women also sexually abuse their children. In fact, the profile of the batterer found by Sonkin and colleagues (1985) is remarkably similar to the data obtained on sex offenders by Wolf, Conte, and Engle-Menig (in press) and Peters and McGovern (in press). It is not uncommon for mothers to notice sexually inappropriate behavior between the batterer and his children. Sometimes it is the impetus for terminating the relationship. However, unless there is overt sexual abuse that is witnessed by others or supported by other evidence, neither the mother nor the child is likely to be taken seriously during a divorce and custody determination. Some child protective service departments are so inundated with cases that they refuse to investigate reports if a divorce is pending. Once again, the angry woman is expected to seek revenge against the man by making these false accusations. It is our experience, however, that in most of these cases it is quite likely that presexual conditioning has taken place even if actual sexual abuse has not yet occurred. A thorough investigation is critical to the safety of the child.

Rosalie's situation illustrates this point:

Rosalie is a 7-year-old girl whose parents were in the process of divorcing when she was referred to our offices for therapy. Although her mother had temporary custody, Rosalie's time was pretty equally spent between her mom and dad's homes. She began reporting that she watched movies with her dad that had explicit sexual and violent content. Then her mom noticed her dad making sexual comments to Rosalie like, "You've got a great ass in those tight jeans." He was keeping Rosalie on his lap for too long a time, nibbling her ear and kissing her neck. He told Rosalie that it was important for daughters and dads to have secrets with each other and she'd get special favors if she kept the secret. When Rosalie spontaneously told her mom that she thought her dad was touching her "weird" with little further explanation, her mom reported possible sexual abuse to child protective services. She knew her husband had been sexually abused as a child and had been violent toward her. The caseworker interviewed the child, who told her very little, and the mom. Perhaps Rosalie was being conditioned for sexual abuse to begin within the next year, the investigation determined; but there is nothing they can do at this time.

This information was used at the custody hearing, with one evaluator stating that the mother was overreacting and not allowing the father-child relationship to develop fully and another evaluator testifying that Rosalie was at high risk for sexual abuse and in need of greater protection. The judge awarded custody to the mother and continued the liberal visitation arrangement, but ordered the father into therapy for his violent behavior.

In another case, the outcome was not as good for the children.

Julie and Carol were sisters; Julie was 13 and Carol was 7 when their parents got divorced. During the year and a half between the separation and pending divorce action, the children were ordered to live with their mother and visit their father frequently. Julie ran away from her mom's house to live with her father shortly after the temporary orders. Although the judge ordered her back to her mom's, neither the father nor the judge enforced the order. Julie was seen accompanying her dad to dinners and parties, much like her mother did prior to the separation. Her make-up and style of dress were more appropriate to an older teenager. But she felt special. She told her mother she thought she had an eating disorder, since she was binging and vomiting in the pattern of bulimia. She vehemently denied any sexual misconduct with her dad or anyone else and resented her mother's raising the question. When her father beat her and threw out of the house a 13-year-old boy who was her friend, Julie voluntarily returned to live with her mother. No one but her mother was paying any attention to the possibility that Julie was sexually abused by her dad, nor was Carol's safety ascertained.

The judge in this case listened to the testimony of the mother's therapist, who said that sexual abuse had not been ruled out and that Carol, the 7-year-old, might also be in jeopardy. The court-appointed evaluator said it was not enough of an issue to warrant an investigation or even to ask social services to get involved. The judge became angry with the therapist for not reporting the suspected abuse to child protective services and threatened her license for willful nonreport of a child abuse case. Yet the report made to the children's lawyer and the court-appointed evaluator did not result in any support for the mother's suspicions. The judge did award custody of Julie to the mother but gave custody of Carol to her father, unmindful of his potential to sexually abuse her also.

Psychological Abuse

Often children's self-esteem is threatened by the father's cruel and abusive verbalizations. Nasty and degrading comments, cursing, and threats of harm frequently are reported by children. Fear of being cut off from the love they need may cause some children to accept what they get. Others become oppositional and use acting-out behavior to protect themselves from some of the psychological abuse. Forcing children to watch their mother get hurt, spanking one child for the misdeeds of another, severe punishment which does not fit the misbehavior, and humiliation as a form of discipline can all be used as psychologically abusive techniques. We apply the Amnesty International definition of psychological torture in evaluating these cases.

In addition to direct negative outcomes, exposure to violence may prevent the development of desirable characteristics in children. Cummings, Iannoth, and Zahn-Wexler (1985) report evidence that children observed in battered women's shelters do not develop *empathy*, or the ability to put oneself in another's shoes and feel for them, at the age-appropriate time, which is between 4 and 7 years old. Preschool children, particularly boys, have been observed to have a greater identification with abusive father's than with nonviolent fathers. Adolescents, struggling with abandonment issues, may also take on a greater identification with and defense of the abusive father, perhaps knowing they will lose him otherwise. Sexually abused girls have been found to be unable to create intimate bonds with their adolescent girlfriends, causing difficulties in distinguishing between emotional and sexual intimacy. The children all learn to be good at manipulation, often fearing they will not get their needs met otherwise. Sometimes the manipulation takes the form of coercive behavior; at other times, compliant and pleasing acts. Rarely do they learn to trust.

There is also reason for concern about children's cognitive and emotional development when parented by a batterer who has a paranoid-like pattern of projecting his fears of his own inadequacy and lack of impulse control onto others. Such a man perceives threat in the actions of others regardless of their intent; he may respond with angry, impulsive attacks, a "first strike" sort of defensiveness. In addition to posing an obvious physical danger to the child, such a father cannot provide a stable cognitive-perceptual world for the child. Since there are no contingencies between the child's actions (let alone intents) and the father's reactions, there is fertile ground for learned helplessness to develop (Seligman, 1975; Walker, 1979, 1984). Cognitive-perceptual consistency is necessary for the child to develop his or her own cognitive structures as well as to learn impulse control. Emotional and behavioral problems can also develop in such an environment.

Children's Reactions to Divorce in the Battering Family

The reactions of children in abusive families to divorce have not been empirically studied. The few systematic research studies available count on cooperation between divorcing parents in order to study the family. Experience has shown that it is unusual for abusive men to be cooperative in a divorce; it is known to be the most stressful and, thus, most dangerous point in the relationship. In fact, sometimes the abuse that previously had been kept a carefully guarded secret becomes known because of the vehement fights around the division of property and children.

The anecdotal data suggest that children have mixed reactions to their parents' separation. Some have already strongly identified with one parent, while others want to maintain a relationship with both. The dynamics of the abusive family often create different alliances, which may not permit the child to perceive equal access to both parents. Sometimes different children align with each parent, also reflecting the unhealthy alliances created in the violent home. Older children frequently express relief that the fighting may stop. In too many cases, however, the abuse continues by using the children. Low self-esteem has been observed as a frequent outcome of such battles.

John was 4 when his parents began their divorce action after many years of sexual, physical, and psychological abuse. He would become tense and irritable whenever he made the twice weekly shift from mom's to dad's house. Mom was somewhat unstructured and preferred John to be creative and develop an independent character. Dad, on the other hand, was quite rigid and compulsive, demanding a military-like obedience to his rules. John was scared of his father but couldn't let him see it or he feared he'd lose all contact with him. The temporary orders mandated a joint custody arrangement, with the child going back and forth 50% of the time each week.

John developed stomach aches, crying spells, and a depressed affect. His relationships at school deteriorated, he became more aggressive with his mother, and he became more dependent on whichever parent he was living with. He couldn't shift focus from the extreme structure at his dad's house to the more liberal, find-it-yourself attitude at his mom's. A videotape evaluation of the two extreme parenting styles was shown to the court, and the judge eventually gave sole custody to the mother. Again, liberal visitation was awarded to the father, with no demands that he learn more flexible parenting skills.

In some cases, children are aware of their mother's fragile mental health and choose to live with their father, confident they can control his violence even if their mother could not do so. Others deny or minimize the father's abuse toward the mother or even identify with the aggressive father, justifying why mom deserved to be hit. Many of these mothers cannot adequately parent their children while trying to protect themselves and their family from further harm. They may be abusing alcohol or drugs, or be otherwise emotionally unavailable. Some become so depressed or angry when the relationship is over that they neglect the children's emotional needs for a time. It can be difficult to ascertain whether this emotional instability is temporary or part of a characterological disorder. Injuries sustained during beatings, such as epilepsy, may also interfere with parenting.

Juliette was 14 when her mother and father separated. One of the precipitating factors was her mother's suspicions and later accusations that her father was behaving in a sexually inappropriate way toward Juliette. Juliette acknowledged an incident where there was some "horseplay" but adamantly denied anything else. Her father got a job in another state, while Juliette stayed in the family home with her mother. She accused her mother of being paranoid and hysterical, minimized her father's earlier violence, and became verbally abusive of her mother.

As her mother heard her using language similar to her father's, she became more suspicious and less trusting of her daughter. Juliette became more manipulative, often calling her guardian *ad litem* for support against her mother; the attorney readily supplied such support, including reinforcing Juliette's belief that the mother was "crazy." Their relationship deteriorated, both mother and daughter becoming aggressive and making unsuccessful suicide gestures. Juliette ran away to her father. The mother became frightened for her daughter's safety but also decompensated emotionally, becoming unable to parent her daughter effectively. By the time of the final custody determination, Juliette perceived her abusive father as a better choice than her significantly emotionally disturbed mother. The mother's condition worsened as her daughter separated from her. There were no options in the best interests of Juliette by the time the court intervened.

CUSTODY EVALUATIONS

The typical posture for courts to take where custody is disputed is to order a custody evaluation. In some jurisdications, mediation or reconciliation hearings are mandatory. Others utilize the state department of social services to conduct evaluations, especially when the family does not have much money. It is most common to have an evaluation performed by one or more mental health professionals known to the court. Given the time and costs involved, most divorcing couples would prefer not to have the court resolve a custody dispute. In battering relationships, however, the men rarely compromise, often hiring known father's rights attorneys and using the children to further hurt their spouses or to try to protect themselves from their fear of abandonment. Women are frightened to leave their children with a man they know can be as violent as he can be loving. Joint custody, the attractive compromise being used as a presumption in many states, is impossible for most relationships where there has been spouse or child abuse because mutual decision making cannot occur.

Custody evaluations are usually biased against battered women for a variety of reasons. Few evaluators have any substantial training in understanding the psychological impact of battering on the women, men, or children. Many believe that if there is no overt physical abuse to the child, it does not matter what the man does to the woman. Sexist views of mothering and fathering abound in custody evaluators' values and fill the pages of their reports. If a woman demonstrates any nontraditional behavior, her ability to mother her children is suspect. In one case, a child protective services caseworker recommended removing a formerly battered woman's children when she made an unannounced visit and found them eating McDonald's hamburgers for dinner. In another case, the custody team recommended custody to the abusive father because the mother was not "making men central in her life" and the child might not learn to live in a family! Juggling a job, a home, a social life, and parenting is seen as appropriately creating great stress for married mothers and single fathers. But single mothers are more likely to be penalized for reacting poorly to the stress; if they do not manage perfectly, they are viewed as less capable than single men or couples.

When a woman who has been abused is in the process of terminating the relationship, all of her suppressed, repressed, and denied feelings come to the surface. There may simultaneously co-exist anger, fear, and the need to be fair to this man they once loved and still fear. Low ego strength, confusion, flooding of emotions, lack of trust, fear of betrayal, little ability to distinguish how much to tell, lack of long-term plans, and poor performance on standardized tests (see Rosewater, 1986) will further handicap battered women's performance during the custody evaluation. Since many custody evaluators have had little or no training in understanding the impact of abuse on any member of a family where there is a battered woman, there is great likelihood that her poor performance will be misinterpreted as a pathological disorder that will interfere with her ability to parent her children. In Chapter 3 of this text, as well as in other writing on the subject, Mary Ann Douglas provides important knowledge to further mental health professionals' understanding of the situational responses of battered women.

On the other hand, the batterer's ability to charm and con selected important people for short-term interactions stands him in good stead in the custody evaluation. Many of these men genuinely want to be nice and consequently only show their good sides, successfully hiding the violent sides of their personalities. The batterer may be viewed as genuine and sincere; the part of his personality that evidences his difficulty with others who have some power over him remains hidden. His fear of losing his family is seen by untrained custody evaluators as a genuine reason to give him as much contact as possible with his children. If he is young, his ability to nurture his children is seen as a benefit for them. What is not recognized is that the batterer's nurturing behavior is contingent on the children's not requiring their own independence.

Many children can give up their individuality for the security of peace when living within such narrow limits. However, they lose their creativity, spontaneity, and ability to think for themselves, qualities often seen as desirable by women. Thus the two different value systems can and often do cause anxiety disorders and depression in the children. Some begin to act out their anger when they reach adolescence. Others demonstrate a pseudomaturity that can threaten their development, even though they appear more sensible than the adults in their lives. Sonkin and colleagues (1985) found that 68% of the children had seen their fathers' violent behavior. Also, 93% of the batterers admitted to having had a previous partner whom they also had battered. It can be expected that, without treatment, these men will continue their violent behavior. It is important to weigh risk factors that might interrupt a child's development. Few evaluators have the skills to do such an analysis.

Also of concern is the custody evaluators' inability to conduct an appropriate assessment of parents' long-term ability to raise children. Lengthy childhood and social histories with analytical guesswork in interpreting their significance are often used as substitutes for accurate measurement of the mothers' and fathers' skills, abilities, and values in parenting their children. Currently, there are no professional standards to guide evaluators as to what constitutes an appropriate custody evaluation, although several American Psychological Association divisions are discussing guidelines. Interestingly, experts in family violence have not been a significant part of such discussions. Psychometric testing is often used routinely rather than selectively to answer specific questions. Computerized scoring and interpretations are often filled with sex-role bias against women. Violent, aggressive, and impulsive tendencies seen on men's psychometric test results may never be related to their risk for abusing children. Individual factors for each parent, e.g., narcissism and impulse control, may be less important than how they interact with one another. Basic child-raising values may never be evaluated by those who have not kept up with the literature.

Court Attitudes

The attitude of the courts toward child-custody cases sometimes borders on the shameful. Parents may be treated with disdain for troubling an overburdened court with their inability to decide together what is best for their child. Issues of violence are typically seen as irrelevant to the proceedings about children. A parent's motivation for making an allegation is given more significance than it deserves; the children should be carefully examined for the impact of abuse without confusing the evaluation process with speculation about why the battered woman is accusing the batterer. There is a presumption that children are entitled to be raised by both parents, even if the father has serious mental health problems or trouble keeping his temper under control. The recent *Fedders* case in Washington, D.C., is a good example of such judicial bias. Although Mr. Fedders was fired by President Reagan from his position as head of the Securities and Exchange Commission when the details became public of his battering of his wife "only eight times in the past eighteen years," the judge refused to grant the divorce for 90 days. "The children need an intact family," the judge was quoted as saying, "so I'm giving you time to think about reconciliation!" (*Washington Post*, February 24, 1985).

Courts liberally assign such cases to professionals, supposedly to gain their help in making determinations. There are no generally agreed-upon guidelines or standards to determine the adequacy of the evaluations; the courts usually either accept the professionals' recommendations uncritically or ignore them. Rarely is sufficient time allowed for a second opinion, and noncourt-appointed evaluators are often treated with little respect if they should testify. The testimony of shelter workers or battered women's therapists, which could enlighten the court about what the experience has been like for the woman and how it impacts on her ability to parent, is often discounted as biased. The message is clear: The courts think mental health professionals cannot tell the truth if it contains negative statements about their clients. Feminist advocacy is defined as legal advocacy rather than in the supportive manner in which it is used by mental health professionals. Women are quickly labeled as *"man-hating"* when they demonstrate anger at one man for his abusive behavior. And child advocacy is discounted by the many ways the legal profession and courts use to move on to what they define as more important matters. Jody is an interesting case in point.

Jody was 7 years old when her adoptive parents decided to dissolve their marriage. She had always been closer to her mother than her father and was developing well in all areas, including academic excellence at a school where her mother's family were administrators. There had been much psychological abuse during her parent's marriage, as well as several physically abusive incidents that frightened Jody and her mother. Her father's behavior caused Jody to fear him, and she would refuse to go on visits by getting stomach aches and other somatic complaints. During a custody evaluation, Jody's mother discussed some physical problems she had had corrected by surgery prior to her marriage. The custody evaluators attributed her anger at her husband to being caused by a lack of resolution of these earlier problems and totally discounted the role of the husband's angry, impulsive, frighteningly unpredicatable abusive behavior. They labeled the mother as seriously disturbed with no objective evidence to support that diagnostic impression, claimed her anger at her husband would destroy the child's relationship with her father, and recommended custody to the father with limited visitation with the mother.

Jody was crushed by the decision, which was upheld by the judge. She had been confident she'd get to live with her mother and had told everyone who asked her, including the custody evaluation team and her therapist, that that was what she wanted. She wrote an angry letter to the judge, chiding him for asking children what they want and then not listening to them. Her father took her out of her school and switched her therapy to a male therapist of his choosing. Jody's grades began to fall; she also developed oppositional, acting-out behaviors, refused to talk with her new therapist, and went in and out of major depressive episodes. Two years later, she had developed resentment and hatred for her father and spoke about him in an angry, contemptuous manner. She described his temper tantrums as though they were continuous behavior and would often run away to a friend's house when he'd start yelling at her. Her bond with her mother remained strong, and she requested and cooperated with her in trying to get custody changed. Almost 3 years later, the same judge still hasn't been able to keep the set times to rehear the case. The child's therapist advises the father not to give up control, which, of course, fits with abusive men's need for power. Only the mother continues to advocate for the child's rights and needs.

Guidelines for the Courts

Some general guidelines exist to help the courts make adequate decisions in these cases. More detailed guidelines are in the preparation stage by the American Psychological Association. For example, "in the best interests of the child" must be individually defined for each case. It is not in the best interests of the child to be left in a home where physical, sexual, or psychological abuse takes place. Children need psychological support to cope with bitter and overlitigated situations. A therapist, school counselor, or advocate may need to be consulted, and therapy may be indicated. If children are afraid, supervised visitation is an alternative. Judges must educate themselves as to the psychological and legal issues in these cases, since they are community leaders who uphold the standards of the community.

Batterers need to be ordered into therapy if they are unwilling to seek it themselves. The data strongly indicate the likelihood that the batterer will go into another relationship. Since he has not learned how to deal with his anger, there is a high probability he will go on to batter another woman. Thus it is reasonable to assume the child will continue to witness violence. Perhaps he will batter the child as well.

When domestic violence is alleged, judges need to appoint evaluators who are skilled in such assessments. This specialization is as important as, for example, special skills when evaluating for alcohol abuse. There are clinicians and battered women's shelter workers who can perform such an evaluation. Judges can choose those who know the literature and are aware of the data that suggest that witnessing or experiencing family violence can have a profound effect on children.

Resources within the community can be tapped to develop adequate custody and visitation plans. It will be important to specify the access of each parent to the child, since that is often a litigated point. Payment of child support is another area of inconsistency. Large property awards in lieu of maintenance are a way to keep women financially solvent. Holding each person accountable for the success or failure of a custody recommendation might encourage more thought.

CUSTODY AND VISITATION: LEGAL AND CLINICAL ISSUES

Mediation as an Alternative

The frustration of the backlog of cases that courts must handle, along with the general dissatisfaction with how the adversarial process negatively affects all families, not just those where there is abuse, has created a new model of mediation as a way of achieving dispute resolution. Actually, mediation is not new; worldwide, community customs and religious groups have often designated an esteemed group member to resolve disputes. The mediator is thought to be a neutral facilitator, able to help each party reach a compromise and feel like a winner. In essence the judge, although obliged to follow the legal standards or formal rules to resolve the dispute, is supposed to be such a mediator. The American legal system assumes that by allowing each disputant to present formally his or her best position, the trier of fact will be able to find the best resolution. Mediation is an informal model of the formal system, with neither the limitations nor the benefits of the formal rules.

The essence of successful mediation is the spirit of compromise that allows the parties to conciliate their current dispute and govern their future behavior. But in the instance of risk of harm to minor children, there may be no room for compromise. The dispute often centers on what is best for the children; yet mediation deals with what is best for the parents. While the assumption is made that both parents will have the best interests of the child in mind, the psychological deficits of abusive men may prevent their being able to put their child's needs ahead of their own. Women, usually trained to be nurturers, are more likely to give in and compromise their own needs during mediation. Sometimes they give in and compromise their children's long-term needs to win them even temporary safety. They teach their children to placate their father and keep the situation as calm as possible so as to avoid precipitating a battering incident. Most importantly, however, the mediation-as-compromise model works only when disputants hold equal power.

The unequal power differential between battered women and their abusive partners dictates that mediation cannot be to the woman's advantage. Well-trained mediators believe their techniques can equalize the power differential, but battered women report that nothing can erase their terror that angering the man by not giving him what he wants is dangerous to themselves and their children. At the 1985 UN Decade for Women Conference in Nairobi, Kenya, women lawyers and judges from 36 developing countries reported on the progress women have made by using for protection the newly won formal laws that are replacing previously used custom and religious law. But they cited the difficulty in changing attitudes as a major stumbling block. Of course, we are aware that even formal law has not yet responded to the needs of battered women and children. Reverting to mediation can be a disastrous step backward as long as attitudes and knowledge about the impact of witnessed and experienced violence is so limited.

There are no formal training requirements for mediators, who, though allegedly neutral, will vary in competence. Some have previous legal or mental health training, but they can rarely be expected to have knowledge of domestic violence and its impact on children. Thus decisions are based on previously held ideas, often derived from training in "family systems" that are filled with sex-role bias against women and misinformation about the properties of battering relationships. Most common is the notion that children deserve to have equal access to both parents without regard for parent's ability to relate to the child. Joint or mutual custody is only effective when both parents can cooperate and put the child's needs ahead of their own

(Wallerstein & Kelly, 1980). Many batterers are unable to sustain cooperation with a former spouse due to their extreme hostility, denial, and acting-
out tendencies (see Sonkin, Chapter 10, for a more complete discussion).

Joint or Mutual Custody

Clinical experience suggests that children whose time is shared between a
battering father who is likely to be highly controlling and demanding of
compliance, and a mother who may be more spontaneous and less structured
in her parenting, suffer substantially from this discrepancy. They may be
confused as to what behavior is expected and appropriate; they may become
exploitive of each parent's weakness by testing the limits of what will be
allowed; or they may quite typically "erupt" while in the mother's care after
having to contain their impulses and feelings while with the father. Custody
evaluators may be impressed with the father's better "discipline," not understanding that the children are manifesting their frustration and anger in the
only place where it is safe to do so.

When these behaviors continue to be observed in children after custody
and visitation determinations have been made, psychological consultation is
often sought. If witnessing or experiencing abuse has been part of these
children's lives, therapeutic interventions to teach them positive control over
contingencies in their lives is most appropriate to reverse the negative psychological effects of victimization. The authors have devised techniques for
individual therapy with children and for parent/child therapy to move
toward this goal. The model is based on developing skills, mastery, and
competence, both in general social situations and situations specific to the
parent/child relationship. Children's perceptions are clarified and validated,
providing the cognitive stability necessary for further development. Strategies are evaluated for effectiveness in getting their needs met. Assertiveness
training is helpful in getting children to define their rights and select a
variety of behaviors that can predict success.

Abusive fathers who have voluntarily agreed to attend joint sessions with
their children are taught to listen to what their children request of them and
learn strategies to validate their children's feelings even though they may not
comply with the request.

The men become more aware of what makes them angry and how devastating displays of that anger can be to their children. They learn to share some
power with the children and are then able to relax and enjoy their children
without worrying about the need to use external sources of control. The
establishment of behavioral contingencies reinforces these new skills; in
some cases we have observed their transfer to other interpersonal relationships. Mandatory sessions with therapists as a part of supervised visitation
arrangements produce slower progress but have also been successful with

those men motivated enough to attend. It may be possible to design an educational therapeutic program that would be required of those abusive men who wish to retain a relationship with their children.

Adequate Custody Evaluation Procedures in Domestic Abuse

The authors' experiences have come from involvement in initial and second-opinion custody evaluations. We have had the opportunity to review a variety of styles and procedures in conducting such evaluations. To assure that certain information is routinely gathered, some structure seems necessary. At the same time, flexibility is also required so that people are not expected to be assessed in areas where no apparent problems reflecting on ability to parent exist. The outline below represents an initial attempt to formulate such a procedure:

A. Interview format
    1. Interview as many members of the family as is possible. Insist on *offering* to meet with those who are unwilling to participate. Even telephone interviews can give some information.
    2. Interview individuals at separate times so there is no possible intimidation in the waiting room or fear of being overheard.
    3. Interview family members together only if you determine that you can keep it safe and that the joint interview will yield important information. (Sometimes you can get information about the woman's anxiety and how she changes when the man is around, which is important to document. This is also true for the children.)
    4. Videotape joint interviews if possible—this helps keep the man on his best behavior.
    5. Follow this typical interview format:
        a. interview the woman
        b. interview the man
        c. interview the child or children alone
        d. interview the child and the mother
        e. interview the child and the father
        f. interview the child and both parents together (optional)
        g. interview both parents together (optional)
    6. Know which parent has had physical custody of the children immediately prior to interviewing them. Offer additional interviews if either parent feels the session does not reflect their relationship. Also, interview any significant others in the child's life; some can be done by telephone. This can include grandparents, other relatives, teachers, babysitters, doctors, former therapists, and clergy. Some custody evaluators ask to interview friends. Given the isolation, denial, and disturbance in interpersonal relationships so common in battering relationships, any information so obtained might not be reliable. But it might support allegations of abuse.

B. Questions to ask
    1. Is battering being alleged in this relationship? (Ask a variety of questions
        to go beyond initial denials. Generally, questions about how each parent
        responds to anger reveal possible abusive situations.) If so, obtain batter-
        ing history:
        a. How aware is each parent of how much violence the child has heard,
            seen, or knows about?
        b. How does each parent views the impact on children?
        c. How much does each parent depend on the child for emotional
            support?
        d. How does it affect her ability to parent?
        e. How does it affect his ability to parent?
        f. How does it impact on use of resources?
        g. How does it impact on ability to form support networks in commu-
            nity to help with parenting?
        h. How dangerous is it for the woman to be in charge of visitation
            exchange?
        i. How much risk is there that the mother will continue to be
            battered?
        j. How much risk is there that the child will be physically and/or
            psychologically battered?
        k. How much risk is there that the child will be sexually abused?
        l. How much risk is there for emotional incest?
    2. What is the current mental health of each parent and child?
        a. What does the current mental status and clinical interview show?
        b. What is each parent's mental health history?
        c. Cognitive and personality tests can be used if time is limited and a
            standardized sample of behavior is wanted. But tests are not always
            necessary or accurate, so the results must be interpreted carefully.
        d. How do these factors interact with parenting skills required? (This is
            the critical question, which often goes unanswered even when a full
            battery of tests is administered and a long, detailed social history is
            obtained.)
    3. What are the woman's and man's current parenting skills?
        a. In what behavioral and cognitive areas do they show agreement and
            disagreement with each other?
        b. On what values do they agree and disagree?
        c. How do they present areas of disagreement to the child?
        (Joint and individual structured and unstructured tasks can be used to
        answer this set of questions. Observations of solving a task can be partic-
        ularly significant, especially if designed to demonstrate if controlling
        behavior is revealed. Also, look for typical battering patterns, such as the
        woman's reacting with defensive strategies to the man's behavior, i.e.,
        compliance with or hostility to his control or hostility.)
        d. What is their knowledge of developmental expectations for children?
        e. How do they handle discipline?
        f. How do they promote the child's intellectual growth?
        g. How do they promote the child's emotional growth?

4. What is the family history for the woman and the man and how does it contribute to parenting skills?
    a. What factors in each parent's family of origin contribute to positive or negative parenting ability? Was there abuse witnessed or experienced in either home that places either at high risk? Be sure to check for sexual molestation or abuse in both parents' backgrounds.
    b. What are each parent's values about sex-role-stereotyped standards? Rigidity is often associated with battering behavior.
    c. Who, if anyone, has had primary responsibility for parenting the child until the separation? This includes caretaking, decision making, nurturing, and scheduling responsibilities.
    d. Have there been shifts in parental responsibility over time? Describe.
5. What is the developmental functioning for the child?
    a. Is it age appropriate?
    b. Cognitive area? (Individual intelligence tests can be used, especially if school performance is below expected level. Dispartiy in verbal ability in different situations can be a clue.)
    c. Affective area? (Structured and unstructured measurement can be compared with observations of how the child expresses feelings with each parent).
    d. Behavioral area? Does child demonstrate age-appropriate behavior? Does it change with each parent? With peers?
6. How do custody and visitation affect growth patterns?
    a. Are there differences in each parent's ability to provide parenting skills required at the different development ages of the children? (It is common for batterers to be nurturing when children are young and more controlling as they age.)
    b. Does the child have special needs? If so, how does each parent view them and cope with them? (Reviewing videotapes of interviews often helps to demonstrate the child's needs.)
7. What kind of information does the court need for its action?
    a. Ethics of protecing raw data and conflict with legislation requiring that material to be available (often translated as required).

Visitation Schedules

Although much of this chapter concerns custody issues, the question of visitation often follows from such evaluations. In other cases, agreements stipulated to by the parties are upheld by the court. It is rare that the court deny visitation, even when there is known physical and sexual abuse of the child. Most states have adopted the *Uniform Children's Code,* which specifies that the state will do everything to support the reunification of the family. The family assumes corporation-like status. Thus the rights of other family members usually take precedence over children's rights to safety. In extreme cases children have killed parents to escape abuse (Morris, 1985); others become mentally ill or simply find more or less pathological ways to adapt and cope.

Women who have finally taken action to free themselves from an abusive situation find that they perpetuate their own fears by sending their children to visit the man who both loved and hurt them. They soothe their children's fears and try to find ways to help smooth the process. But they are angry that the abuser has another chance to hurt them by harming their children. The history of violence creates memories too strong to allow parents to complement each other's strengths when co-parenting their children. For example, in one case the mother provided the nurturing and emotional spontaneity while the father provided intellectual stimulation. However, the anxiety created by the abuse made it impossible for the mother to encourage the child to relax and enjoy visits with the father. She was too busy teaching him ways to protect himself. And the father was so rigid in his disciplines that the child could not adjust his behavior from that tolerated in his mother's less structured environment. One parent was all this child could handle.

The batterer may continue to harass the woman in circumstances that surround the pick-up and return of the children. If the harassment involves abusive telephone calls, we advise clients to install an answering machine that can record the verbal abuse. Using a public place to exchange the child is another technique to lessen the probability of continual abuse. Frequent court hearings, which usually deplete the woman's finances before the man's, is another common tactic to continue the harassment. Refusal to pick up or return children at the specified time also occurs. Such tactics can create enormous anxiety in children, such that anxiety disorders are not uncommon in those as young as 2 years old.

In some cases, judges are willing to order supervised visitation with the abusive father. Good supervisors are difficult to find, and the cost may be prohibitive for the father who wants frequent contact with the child. Therapy with the father and child in place of one supervised visit per week, as discussed earlier, is aimed at reducing the child's fear by teaching assertion skills and simultaneously helping the father develop empathy and tolerance for the child's need for control during visits. Our clinical findings indicate that training in such parenting skills is more effective than didactic courses tha stress the application of intellectual understandings to a variety of situations. Videotapes of sessions can later be reviewed for further skill enhancement. So far, the major obstacle has been getting abusive fathers to seek such services without court order.

CONCLUSIONS

In summary, we have discussed the failure of the legal system, specifically the divorce courts, to adequately evaluate and provide for children who have lived in abusive homes. The theoretical and empirical literature complement the clinical findings that direct or indirect exposure to violence has a negative impact on the healthy development of children. In fact, witnessing violence is more likely than actually experiencing violence to result in the inter-generational transmission of violence. Aggression tends to be directed across gender lines in homes where there is violence. Despite these findings, courts and custody evaluators rarely pay much attention to domestic violence and do not see it as creating a risk for children who must continue to have contact with the abusive parent. Suggestions for appropriate custody evaluations in such cases have been made. Reasons for rejection of mediation as a way to resolve the disputes between battered women and their abusive partners were discussed, as was the inappropriateness of a recommendation for joint or mutual custody. There are difficulties with visitation for the child, as well as for the mother who continues to be battered or harassed. Supervised visita-tion might be an alternative, as might court-ordered therapy in parenting skills. It is to be hoped that as society becomes more sensitive to the issues of family violence, fewer children will grown up to repeat the horrible cycle.

REFERENCES

American Psychiatric Association. (1981). *The diagnostic and statistical manual of mental disorders (3rd ed.)*. Washington, DC: Author.

Bandura, A. (1977). Self-efficacy: Toward a unifying theory of behavioral change. *Psychological Reviews, 84*, 191–215.

Burgess, R. (1984, November). *Social incompetence as a precipitant to and consequence of child maltreatment*. Paper presented at the NATO Conference on Victimology, Lisbon, Portugal.

Cummings, E.M., Dannotti, R.J., & Zahn-Wexler, C. (1985). Influence of conflict between adults on the emotions and aggression of young children. *Developmental Psychology, 21*(3), 495–507.

Kalmuss, D. (1984). The intergenerational transmission of marital aggression. *Journal of Marriage and the Family, 51*(4), 11–19.

Martin, D. (1981). *Battered Wives*. San Francisco: Volcano Press.

Minuchin, S. (1984). *Family kaleidoscope*. Cambridge, MA: Harvard University Press.

Morris, G. (1985). *The kids next door*. New York: Morrow.

Patterson, G. (1982). *Coercive family processes*. Eugene, OR: Castaglia Press.

Peters, J., & McGovern, K. (in press). Guidelines for assessing sex offenders. In L.E.A. Walker (Ed.), *Handbook on sexual abuse of children: Assessment and treatment issues*. New York: Springer.

Reid, J., Taplin, P., & Lorber, R. (1981). A social interactional approach to the treatment of abusive families. In R.B. Sturat (Ed.), *Violent behavior: Social learning approaches to prediction management and treatment*. New York: Brunner/Mazel.

Rosewater, L.B., & Walker, L.E.A. (Eds.). (1985). *Handbook of feminist therapy:*

Psychotherapy issues with women. New York: Springer Publishing Co.

Russell, D.E.H. (1983). The incidence and prevalence of intrafamilial and extrafamilial sexual abuse of female children. *Child Abuse and Neglect, 7*, 133–146.

Seligman, M.E.P. (1979). *Helplessness: On depression, development, and death*. San Francisco: W.H. Freeman.

Sonkin, D.J., Martin, D., & Walker, L.E.A. (1985). *The male batterer: A treatment approach*. New York: Springer Publishing Co.

Straus, M.A., Gelles, R.A., & Steinmetz, S. (1980). *Behind closed doors: Violence in the American family*. New York: Doubleday.

Walker, L.E.A. (1979). *The battered woman*. New York: Harper and Row.

Walker, L.E.A. (1984). *The battered woman syndrome*. New York: Springer.

Wallerstein, J.S., & Kelly, J.B. (1980). *Surviving the breakup: How children and parents cope with divorce*. New York: Harper & Row.

Wolf, S., Conte, J., & Engle-Menig, M. (in press). Assessment and treatment of sex offenders in a community based setting. In L.E.A. Walker (Ed.), *Handbook on sexual abuse of children: Assessment and treatment issues*. New York: Springer Publishing Co.

PART IV
The Offender

9

Perpetrators of Domestic Violence: An Overview of Counseling the Court-Mandated Client

Anne L. Ganley

In September 1984 the Attorney General's Task Force on Family Violence issued a final report. This report, with its recommendations for law enforcement, prosecutors, and judges, calls national attention to a fact that victims and some communities have known for years—battering is a crime. It is a crime against an individual and it is a crime against the community. It is neither a private affair nor a family dispute. It is a crime that is destroying the bodies and spirits of its victims. It is a crime that is committed not by faceless strangers but by those closest to the victims. These perpetrators of violence are now being held accountable by their communities, and in increasing numbers some are becoming court-mandated clients in specialized counseling programs for those who batter.

Counseling the court-mandated client who batters is both the same as and different from counseling the noncourt-mandated client who batters. To understand these similarities and differences, one must understand the rationale for this intervention by the criminal justice system, the meaning of the term *court-mandated,* and the current thinking about the components of effective counseling for these clients. With this context established, the specific clinical and program issues of court-mandated clients can be addressed.

155

RATIONALES FOR COURT-MANDATED COUNSELING

Court-mandated treatment for batterers has developed over the past five years as one of the interventions designed to end domestic violence and protect victims from further abuse. There are four primary reasons that communities have begun to utilize the power of the judiciary, in combination with the resources of counseling systems, to mandate perpetrators of domestic violence into rehabilitative programs. These four different but not mutually exclusive rationales emerged from the understanding that domestic violence is a public rather than private problem. They reflect new learnings about battering being criminal behavior, about certain characteristics of the perpetrator, about the impact of the family context of the violence on the victim, and about the social causes and reinforcers of battering.

First, certain communities have been recognizing that domestic violence —or at least some of it—is a crime (Soler & Martin, 1982; Pence, 1985; Domestic Abuse Project, 1985) and as such is under the jurisdiction of the criminal justice system. Just as with crimes unrelated to domestic violence, the court's role is to hold the offender accountable and to determine the appropriate sentence. In sentencing, the court may mandate counseling in certain circumstances in order to rehabilitate the offender and in doing so prevent further commission of the crimes. Counseling or mental health treatment, such as alcohol/drug abuse treatment, inpatient psychiatric care, and outpatient care, has been mandated for such crimes as shoplifting, arson, driving to endanger, driving under the influence of alcohol, robbery, indecent exposure, and embezzlement. In recognizing the criminal behavior of those who batter adult intimates as being no different than those same crimes against strangers, the court has as options for sentencing the same rehabilitative possibilities it utilizes with other offenders. While battering is not a mental illness per se, the mental health and rehabilitative intervention systems offer possible avenues to assist some individuals in changing their violent behaviors as well as the attitudes and beliefs that support such behaviors.

Second, certain characteristics of those who batter suggest that court-mandated participation in a rehabilitative program may be necessary for change to occur. Several authors (Bern & Bern, 1984; Brown & Chato, 1984; Ganley, 1981; Saunders, 1984) discuss those who batter as having tendencies to minimize and deny their battering behavior and/or to attribute responsibility for their behavior to persons or events outside of themselves. Examples of such minimization or denial include "it only happened once" or "it was just a little argument" or "I just shoved her" when a careful history-taking reveals that the "shove" was down a flight of stairs and the "little argument" resulted in hospitalization of the victim or the "only once" is once per month in a three-year relationship. The attribution of responsibility to events or others outside of oneself, also called externalization, is expressed in "she bruises easily," "she knows how to push my buttons," "I am under a lot of pressure," "the police officer was just out to get me," and so forth. When individuals deny or minimize their behavior or attribute its responsibility to others, they are unlikely to change that behavior. Through both the criminal justice process and mandated counseling, the court cuts through some of the minimization, denial, and externalization by holding the individual responsible both for his battering behavior and for changing that behavior so that future violence will not occur.

Another aspect of the externalization is the offender's tendency to be motivated externally rather than internally. Even with noncourt-mandated clients, the motivation for seeking intervention is often external to themselves, as in "wanting to get her back" or "my minister told me I had a problem." In the initial stages of intervention the client may often be more externally than internally directed. Eventually to remain free of battering behavior, the individual needs to develop some internal motivation for controlling his behavior. Because this takes time, the client may benefit from having an external motivator for going through the change process. The community, through its courts' mandating clients to rehabilitation pro-grams, can become that external motivator.

Typically the victim has been expected to perform that role alone. But it is unrealistic to expect a person who is in crisis due to the violence of another to provide the consistent, external motivating force that those who batter need to make major changes. It would be like asking the victim of a mugging to take sole responsibility for influencing the mugger to change the mugging behavior while that victim is both recovering from the impact of the assault and is fearing another assault. It is the responsibility of the court, not the victims, to hold offenders accountable for their crimes and to require that the offenders complete the conditions of their sentences.

Third, due to the family context of the violence, victims of battering usually want somewhat different responses from the criminal justice system than do victims of crimes committed by strangers. While both sets of victims may want to be protected from further victimization and to have justice, they may define how to reach those goals somewhat differently. Victims of domestic violence crimes primarily seek an end to the battering through the rehabilitation of the offender rather than through revenge, punishment, or restitution. The victims of these crimes, unlike victims of crimes committed by strangers, have had or expect to have an ongoing relationship with their batterers. Regardless of whether they plan to continue the intimate relationship with the offender, they know that it is highly likely that they will continue to be in some kind of relationship with him because of shared children, relatives, property, history, or community. Victims of crimes committed by strangers are rarely confronted by such a continuance of the relationship. Victims of battering most often want the battering to stop and for the criminal justice system to accomplish that through rehabilitative measures rather than through punishment. Victims of violence committed by strangers usually want protection, restitution, and punishment. They are usually not interested in the rehabilitation of the offender or in keeping the offender in the community. In fact, they may look upon such efforts as being "soft on criminals." The intimate context of the crime of battering influences what the victims seek from the criminal justice system. Some communities have responded to that difference by developing a criminal justice response that emphasizes rehabilitation rather than punishment.

Fourth, because domestic violence is embedded in our social customs and institutions (Dobash & Dobash, 1979; Schecter, 1982; Straus, 1976) it has been generally viewed as normative and acceptable. Battering results not from the specific interactions of a dysfunctional relationship nor from the stressors in life, but from the offenders' previous learnings about the use of violence and power in relationships (Ganley, 1981). These learnings take place as the individuals interact with their families of origin, with society as a whole, and with specific personal experiences in their lives (Dutton, 1984a; Ganley, 1981). These learnings occur through observation and through actual experience (Bandura, 1973; Wiggins, 1983). Significant progress in preventing battering, and specifically the violence against women and children, can only be accomplished if customs and institutions also change their responses to domestic violence. Court mandating clients to counseling to end their abuse of partners is one way to reflect a new social custom of not tolerating violence against wives or female intimates. Such an approach also brings together two major social institutions, the criminal justice system and the counseling field, in a proactive effort to work against battering. In the past both have either ignored or misunderstood battering and in doing so they have reinforced and perpetuated the problem. Court-mandated counseling for the perpetrator of the violence then becomes one step in changing social customs and institutions that have supported domestic violence.

MEANING OF "COURT-MANDATED"

Counseling court-mandated clients raises certain issues for both those providing the counseling and those monitoring the offender. However, before those issues can be addressed, the meaning of "court-mandated" needs to be clarified and an overview of the specialized counseling approaches for the perpetrator of battering needs to be outlined. There seem to be several different popular understandings of the phrase "court-mandated," and the work with such clients may vary depending on what is meant by the term.

One definition—and probably the most commonly used one by criminal justice system personnel—is to be ordered or directed postconviction by the criminal court to follow through on certain conditions outlined in the sentence or the probation agreement. There are stated consequences if these court orders are not followed. For such court-mandated clients, counseling is then ordered as a condition of probation or as part of the sentence (sometimes combined with jail time, fines, restitution, community service time, ceasing contact with the victim, and prohibitions against further violent behaviors). Court-mandated directives may be monitored through an officer of the court or through a probation department.

A second understanding of "court mandated" stems from involvement in procedures that fall under civil court rather than criminal court jurisdiction. In these cases the orders or directives come from the civil court rather than from the criminal justice system. Protection orders, restraining orders, divorce, or custody determination are examples of procedures under the jurisdiction of the civil courts that may result in either requests or requirements for those who batter to complete counseling programs successfully.

A third category of so called court-mandated clients are those who are referred as part of a pretrial diversion process. In the diversion programs the individuals are given the opportunity to have all charges dismissed by completing all conditions of the program (no further offenses, successful completion of a counseling program, etc.). In these cases the court is not mandating the treatment since diversion is an alternative to going through the prosecutory process itself. In fact, if an individual does not successfully complete such a diversion program, then the prosecutorial process is to be reinstituted. Only at that point does the court become involved directly. There usually is some monitoring system associated with such programs. With diversion, there has been no admission or determination of responsibility for the battering.

A final uderstanding of "court-mandated" actually concerns a misunderstanding of the term. To some, "court-mandated" is misunderstood to be any recommendation or suggestion by a member of the law enforcement or legal system. Therefore, there are clients who say they are court mandated to treatment because the arresting officer told them "to get help for their problem," or because their lawyer in a criminal or civil case told them to go to a batterer's program "to be evaluated for not really being a batterer," or their lawyer told them to go to an anger-control class "to improve their chances in court." With such clients, the suggestion is just that—a suggestion rather than a mandate of a particular court. The misconception stems from the belief that any act by law enforcement or the legal system is synonymous with a court action. A large number of clients report being court mandated who are actually only referred by someone from law enforcement or the legal system. A crucial point in understanding this type of "court mandate" is that there are no legal consequences to the client for not following through with the suggestion.

SPECIALIZED COUNSELING APPROACHES FOR MEN WHO BATTER

Specialized programs for men who batter adult intimates began to appear in 1977–1978 in response to the need to end the violence while also ensuring the safety of the victims. A variety of programs utilizing a variety of staffing patterns, intervention techniques, recommended number of sessions, funding sources, and so forth began to appear. While a detailed review of these programs (Eddy & Meyers, 1984) is beyond the scope of this chapter, it is useful to describe generally the similarities of the approaches (Bern & Bern, 1984; Domestic Abuse Project, 1985; Edleson, Miller, & Stone, 1983; EMERGE, Inc., 1980; Frank & Houghton, 1983; Gondolf, 1985; Pence & Paymar, 1985b; Sonkin & Durphy, 1982). This will provide a descriptive context in which to consider the specific issues raised by working with court mandated clients.

Specialized programs for men who batter have some common characteristics (Genley, 1981). The stated primary goal of such programs is to eliminate the physical, sexual, and psychological battering used by the clients to control their intimate relationships. From this primary goal programs have developed lists of objectives such as, but not limited to, increasing clients' responsibility for their battering behavior, developing behavioral alternatives to battering, decreasing isolation by developing personal support systems, decreasing dependency on and control of person(s) they are abusing, increasing the appropriate identification and constructive expression of all emotions, increasing appropriate communication and problem-solving skills, and increasing their understanding of the societal and family facilitators of wife battering.

Client accountability for behaviors, emotions, and attitudes is central to the philosophy of counseling with these clients. Throughout the process, clients are held responsible for what they have done, felt, or believed as well as for what they are doing in the present and will be doing in the future. Client accountability is built into the counseling process in several ways: reports on behavior outside the counseling session; communication within the sessions, programs encouraging others to hold the client accountable; and measuring progress on what is observable, not on intentions or promises. Different programs will emphasize different dynamics as a way of assisting the clients in understanding their behavior, but all the specialized programs hold the client responsible for the battering behavior and responsible for changing that behavior.

Appropriate use of confrontation is crucial to altering the client's characteristics of minimization, denial, and externalization. It is difficult to change one's own behavior when one is not acknowledging it or is attributing responsibility for it to others. Programs take care in confronting the minimization, denial, externalization, and other self-destructive characteristics common in those who batter. This confrontation is done in a matter-of-fact way to educate the clients, rather than as a covert means of punishing them.

Psychoeducational therapeutic approaches are utilized by specialized programs for male batterers. This is due in part to the theoretical view that battering behavior results from learning rather than from biochemical genetic traits. Consequently, psychoeducational approaches can be used to alter those past learnings and to teach new behaviors and attitudes that will prevent further battering. Such psychoeducational approaches lend themselves to a structured format and a somewhat directive role for the counselor. They can accommodate a client population that includes a wide variety of personalities and life experiences more easily than can therapeutic approaches that rely on more homogenous groupings of clients. This is important since those who batter do not seem to have one specific personality profile. While no empirical research has at this date been completed to address that issue, clinical data support the hypothesis that battering is not associated exclusively with a particular personality structure. Furthermore, this client population includes those from various races, socioeconomic classes, educational levels, ages, religious affiliations, and occupations. Psychoeducational approaches that focus on changes in behavior, emotions, and belief systems have proven effective with this heterogeneous client population (for one outcome study, see Program Evaluation Resource Center, 1982).

Groups are utilized by specialized programs for men who batter as the major format for therapeutic intervention. The rationale for using this particular strategy ranges from the practical (it is a cost-effective response to such a large number of clients needing intervention) to the therapeutic (groups provide a laboratory for clients' changing behavior).

PROGRAM AND CLINICAL ISSUES

What is currently accepted as effective counseling for men who batter is applicable to the court-mandated client. One of the basic operating principles of the criminal justice system is that certain individuals must be held accountable for their acts against individuals and against the community. This process of accountability involves assessment (did the acts occur and under what circumstances?), adjudication, and consequences. Most simply put, the primary goal of the criminal justice system is to stop criminal behavior and to protect lives in the community. This is compatible with the

programs for counseling those who batter, where the goal is to stop all battering to ensure the lives of all who are involved.

While some programs only serve the court-mandated client (e.g., MEN,
INC. of Juneau, Alaska's program for the incarcerated offender; Duluth's
Domestic Abuse Intervention Project; Brown and Chato's project through
the Forensic Assessment Services of the Calgary General Hospital, Alberta),
many other specialized programs for men who batter accept both court-
mandated and noncourt-mandated clients. Whether or not the program is
designed solely for the court-mandated client, the staff and clients must
address certain issues. Some are unique to working with the court-mandated
client; e.g., collaborative roles of the counselor and the criminal justice
system, defining those roles to the client, information needed from the
criminal justice system, information to be given to that system, and responses to the racism and classism of the systems. Some that apply to all
clients who batter—e.g., victim safety, coordinating with victim services,
ongoing assessment of lethality, re-offenses while in the program, client
motivation for change, and evaluation of the program's effectiveness—must
be responded to in particular ways when the program also serves the court-
mandated client. Often there are no set prescriptions for responding to these
issues, since laws and resources vary so greatly from community to community. What is important in working with the court-mandated client is
that these issues be understood and addressed in order to increase the effectiveness of counseling and to meet the program's responsibilities to the community as a whole. Each issue will be raised separately, although in practice
they are intertwined.

Collaborative Roles

Defining the collaborative roles of the specialized counseling program for
those who batter and the criminal justice system is a matter of keeping clear
with whom one is working and for what purpose The previous sections outline some of the thinking that is necessary in working with the batterer,
regardless of whether one is the counselor, prosecutor, judge, or probation
officer. This section will now address the collaborative roles of the courts and
the mental health system in evaluations for determining whether an individual is responsible for a crime, for predicting dangerousness to a community,
and for determining the appropriateness of particular sentences. Much of that
material appears in the Chapter 10 of the text. One note: Evaluation for the
determination of responsibility or sentencing should always be kept separate
from the evaluation for the purpose of counseling. This section deals with the
collaborative roles in working with court-mandated clients postsentencing.

In the case of the convicted offender, the task of all is to hold the client
accountable for what he has done as well as for the process of changing that

behavior. Problems arise when the counselor or criminal justice system loses sight of that task or expects one system to be solely responsible for changing the offender.

Understanding each other's roles promotes collaboration. It is the responsibility of the criminal justice system to determine who is to be held accountable, to determine how that will be accomplished (e.g., jail, restitution, fines, community service, probation, rehabilitation programs), and to monitor that offender until he is no longer under the jurisdiction of the court. It is the responsibility of the counselor to determine which court-mandated clients would benefit from the specific counseling programs available, to provide that counseling as long as the clients use it effectively to stop the battering, and to provide specific information to assist the criminal justice system in its monitoring function. The criminal justice system may determine that a particular client is appropriate for rehabilitative programs according to its assessment of the offender and the criteria established for sentencing. Such a criminal justice system determination does not guarantee that there are rehabilitative programs available in the community that can provide counseling for all such clients. The counselor must retain control over who is admitted to the treatment phase of the program, since only the staff knows the program well enough to know what will be effective with which kind of client. Given the scarcity of rehabilitative programs and the abundance of clients, this creates some tension between such programs and the criminal justice system personnel.

Another source of tension between the two systems is the monitoring function of the criminal justice system and the interface of that role with the ongoing assessment role of the counselor. In terms of monitoring, the criminal justice system has legal access to more information pertinent to the monitoring function than a counselor does. For instance, the criminal justice system has access to police reports and to other community members who may have knowledge of the client, whereas the counselor's information about the client is based almost solely on the interactions of the client with the program. Sometimes the counselor will have information from the victim, but that varies from program to program. Counselors are legally prevented from gathering the kind of information that is necessary to carry out the monitoring function of the criminal justice system. Thus the court must remain responsible for that function and not expect the counseling program to become the monitor. Certain communities have delegated the monitoring of abusers to a specific agency that is part of neither the counseling program nor probation department (Pence & Paymar, 1985a). However, counselors do have some information that is pertinent to that overall monitoring function, and procedures must be developed for sharing that information. This sharing of pertinent information has to be recognized as ultimately being in the best interest of the client: his being held accountable for his progress is to his benefit. If it is not viewed by both systems in this light, then information may be withheld under the guise of client confidentiality. Suggestions of which information should be shared between the two systems will be given later in the chapter.

If an adversarial relationship develops between the specialized batterers' programs and the criminal justice system, it usually results from some confusion over who has what role with the client. Frequent communication between the two systems in a community clarifies the collaborative nature of their differing roles.

Specific Roles

It is important to define these collaborative roles of the counselor and the criminal justice system directly to the court-mandated client. In accepting court-mandated clients, specialized programs for men who batter are agreeing with the court that the client engaged in the battering behavior and that the client can change that behavior through participation in that program. If either is not the case, then it is best for the program to refuse to accept the client. The client needs to know how the two systems work together, what information will be shared and what will not shared, and which system is responsible for which decisions. The counseling program is responsible for decisions pertaining to admission to, participation in, and termination from the counseling process, while the court is responsible for those decisions involving legal proceedings. These decisions may overlap at times, but they are not always the same. For example, the program may decide to terminate a client because he is not motivated to participate in the program, as evidenced by uneven attendance or tardiness. This information is given to both the client and the court/probation department. It remains the responsibility of the court or probation department to determine the next course of action. The court may refer the client to another rehabilitative program, or change the terms of probation, or refer the client back to the court for reconsideration of the sentence. The counselor cannot and should not be making that decision for the court. These differences in roles, as well as the overlapping responsibilities, need to be explained to the client.

Legal Records

To work effectively with the court-mandated client, the counselor needs certain information from the criminal justice system. The counselor should have on record the name, contact address, and telephone number of the person/office monitoring the client for the court. In addition, the counselor should ask that officer of the court for information on the charges filed against the client, the charges the client was convicted for, the sentence, and all conditions of probation (no contact orders, restrictions on alcohol or drug use, fines, restitution, etc.) including the length of time the client is to be under the jurisdiction of the court. If possible, information from the police report, court records, and presentence evaluation should also be made available to the counselor. It is also important for the counselor to know how the monitor will be carrying out that function (regular meetings with the client, information gathering contacts with victims or employers, etc.). Each community's system is somewhat different; when counselors work with clients mandated from different courts, it is important not to assume that there is consistency among the various courts.

Due to the client's minimization, denial, or genuine confusion about the criminal justice system, the client is not the best source of these facts. After gathering such information, it is often useful to review it with the client. If the client has questions about matters regarding the courts, he should be referred back to that monitor. The purpose of the review is to establish an openness for dealing with all information relevant to the battering and the court mandate. Some programs have developed a check list wherein such information from the criminal justice departments is systematically recorded for easy access throughout the process. Once the client has started the process, the probation officer or court monitor should inform the counselor of re-offences or any significant changes in the client's legal status.

Counseling Records

At the outset of working with the court-mandated client, the counselor should establish with the monitor what and how information will be provided. For the most part, it is not appropriate for all the details disclosed by the client or gathered in the counseling process to be given to the court. Such details are often unnecessary to the monitoring function, although they are relevant to the counseling process. However, the criminal justice system does need certain kinds of information from the programs in order to make the evaluations necessary for the monitoring. The criminal justice system should be given a *brief* description of the intervention process: type of assessment, format of counseling, length of treatment recommended. In addition to this generic information about the program, the monitor will typically want to know attendance, re-offenses, and evaluation of progress.

There may have to be clarification between the court monitor and the counselor as to which re-offenses should be reported. A counseling definition of battering includes both behaviors that are illegal and some that would not be considered illegal. It is important that all re-offenses be reported to the monitor, even though when taken individually they may not be grounds for reinvolving the court. The reality is that battering is a pattern of behavior and the pattern can only be documented if there is a central place where the information is recorded. With court-mandated clients, that central place must be with the court monitor. Sometimes the counselor will hear of one seemingly minor event from the client, but information about it supports reports given to the probation officer by others not involved in the counseling. To work successfully with those who batter, one teaches accountability by not intervening between the offenders and the consequences of their behaviors. This means being willing to share information with those responsible for the monitoring. Just as in gathering the information, an efficient system for information exchange, complete with client-signed release-of-information forms, needs to be put in place. Since systems are useful only if used, the simple ones consisting of check lists or form letters or telephone calls are typically more productive. Regardless of the type, contacts between the criminal justice system and the specialized programs for men who batter should be documented in the client's records.

Racial and Class Issues

Working with court-mandated clients may bring the counselor into direct contact with the racism and classism of the criminal justice system. Like all other major social institutions in this country (including counseling systems), the criminal justice system too often reflects the racism and classism of this society. Its policies and procedures may discriminate against people solely on the basis of their class or race. In some communities, crimes will be differentially responded to by law enforcement, lawyers, judges, and corrections depending on the race and/or class of the individual. Court-mandated clients will bring their experiences of such discrimination into the counseling process. These experiences will affect how they view the rehabilitation program, which in their eyes may be merely an extension of the criminal justice system. In order to avoid perpetuating racism or classism, the rehabilitation program must ensure that its own policies and practices are not discriminatory. It must also be willing to acknowledge such racism and classism in the criminal justice system and work toward changing it by participating actively in community coalitions dealing with such problems.

In specific work with court-mandated clients, the program staff should be knowledgeable about the impact of cultural and class backgrounds on the experience of domestic violence, on the role of the criminal justice system, and ultimately on the counseling process. For some, their cultural background predisposes them to following the law of the land. For others, it increases initial resistance. The experience of racism or classism can be acknowledged without allowing it to become a justification for their battering their families. Understanding the impact of racism or classism, as well as knowing the cultural backgrounds of clients, makes change more possible. The focus of the counseling should remain on helping the perpetrators stop their violent behavior against intimates.

Victim Safety

The most important issue facing programs for men who batter, whether court mandated or not, is the issue of safety for the victims. Stated simply, the issue is one of how to implement effective intervention for those who batter without further victimizing or endangering the victims of the violence. Understanding domestic violence for what it is—a pattern of behavior, not isolated or individual events, that occurs in an intimate and usually ongoing relationship—means that ensuring the future safety of the victims is a complicated task. A priority of abusers' programs must be to support the development and maintenance of shelters and safe homes for victims of battering. Without such sanctuaries, it is impossible to perform the information gathering and confrontation necessary to work through the offenders' minimization and denial. The first-stage interventions may themselves be stressful. Initially such intervention may increase the clients' feelings of helplessness. For those who batter, such anxiety is too easily displaced by increasing their control over victims through further physical and psychological abuse. Yet to change, the offenders must confront those anxieties. During that stage victims and their children must have safe options in the community. Shelters are often the only means for that safety.

In addition to supporting services for victims, programs intervening with offenders need to monitor their own policies and procedures for their impact on the victims. The reality is that when we are counseling the violent offender, our client is not only that individual offender but also the family members and the community who have been his victims in the past and may be his victims again. Information from the victims is needed for accurate assessment and for appropriate monitoring. Respecting the confidentiality of the victim when getting her input is more than just a matter of respecting her individuality. It is often a necessity for protecting her life. Sharing information gained from the victim with the offender must only be done with her full consent and assessment of the possible consequences to her. A victim should be given accurate information about the intervention process in order for her to have realistic expectations about the offender's willingness to change or potential to re-offend. She should be encouraged but not coerced to participate in programs designed to increase her safety and her ability to take care of herself and her children.

Coordinating with Victim Services

In order to insure victim safety, programs for men who batter must be coordinated with services for victims. Victim services include but are not limited to shelters, legal advocacy, medical services, counseling, community-based suport groups, and advocacy and support projects for the children. In some communities (Pence & Paymar, 1985a; Gamache,

Edleson, & Schok, 1984) the coordination of these services with those working with offenders is accomplished through systematic programs with paid staff to carry out the coordinating and monitoring tasks. In other communities this is accomplished through coalition meetings and informal communications among those working to end spouse abuse. Ending spouse abuse requires the resources of social activists, medical and legal systems, counseling projects, shelters, law enforcement, and religious and educational groups. This kind of collaborative work requires intentional effort and a willingness to develop trust based not on traditional credentials or signs of status but on skills and knowledge about ending battering. Just because a program is working with court-mandated clients and by its structure is connected with the legal system, it is not necessarily connected with victim services. Those connections must be actively sought.

Lethality Assessment

Given the life-threatening nature of some battering behavior, there has to be ongoing assessment of the lethality of the abuse. Chapter 10 of this text discusses the issue of lethality as it pertains to decisions about the appropriateness of particular intervention programs for particular clients. The issue of assessing lethality remains even after someone has been evaluated and admitted to a rehabilitation program. To assess the risk of injury or death occurring at a particular point, the counselor must know the individual's past history—severity and frequency of the violence; the presence of any interactive effects of alcohol, drug, or psychiatric impairment (psychosis or organic brain syndrome) with the battering; suicide attempts or threats by any family member; and the sexual or physical abuse of the children. The counselor must also evaluate the current status of the offender—his access to the victim, the suicide potential of any family member, current presence of stressors that the offender would typically have handled by battering his spouse, and the quality of his participation in the counseling program. The risk of injury or death may be low, moderate, or high at any given point in the rehabilitative process. When it is moderate or high, crisis intervention strategies should be used to prevent further violence.

Client Accountability

Since holding the client accountable is central to working with a man who batters, it is crucial for rehabilitation programs to develop consistent responses to the problem of the man who re-offends while in the counseling program. Given that battering is a pattern of behavior covering a wide range of physical, sexual, and psychological assaults, it is predictable that battering will re-occur during the intervention process. The legal process and the initial stages of counseling may not be sufficient to end the battering behavior of all court-mandated clients. In fact, some counselors report that there is often an increase in psychological battering when the physical, sexual, or property battering stops.

When any battering occurs, the counselor must respond to it in order to avoid colluding with it or inadvertently reinforcing it. With court-mandated clients, this information about re-offenses needs to be given to the individual doing the monitoring. Some of the re-offenses include criminal behavior such as physical assault, sexual assault, kidnapping, menacing, harassment, or crimes of property. Such battering must be dealt with by both the counseling program and the legal system. The response by the counselor or the officer of the court wil vary according to the particulars of the re-offense. Responses may include confrontation and consequences: specified time out of the counseling program, changes in sentence, revoking of probation, charging and processing for new crimes, and so forth. For court-mandated clients, responses to the re-offense should be coordinated and not left the sole responsibility of one system or the other.

Client Motivation

Because of the minimization, denial, and externalization of those who batter, there is always the issue of increasing the client's motivation for change. Initially clients may not identify what they are doing as being a problem, or if they see it as a problem they may not assume the responsibility for changing it. There is often an assumption that so-called voluntary clients have already worked through this minimization and denial and therefore are more successful in treatment than the court-ordered client. The alcohol and drug abuse treatment field has already demonstrated that success in treatment cannnot be predicted by whether the client is court ordered or not. Some noncourt-ordered clients are very successful in making changes and some are not. The same is true for the court-ordered client.

With court-mandated clients, the issue of motivation for change is sometimes clouded by the particulars of how the client came to be identified as having a problem. The externalization typically found with those who batter may take the form of blaming the police, the prosecutor, the judge, or even the probation department for the problem. There may also be claims that the victim made the whole thing up. In states where there is domestic violence legislation, the blame may be put on the laws themselves. Having been through the criminal justice process, many of the clients approach the counselor with claims that they do not really have a problem. One way of responding to this is to clarify for the client that while he is court ordered into treatment, the program is not court ordered to treat him. Consequently, the client's role at this juncture in the process is to convince the counselor that he does indeed batter. Otherwise he will not be accepted into the program and will have to accept other consequences for his crime. Note that the program is not designed neither to work with those who totally deny the problem nor to evaluate whether someone is battering. This clarification will often redirect the client's efforts away from minimization and denial. Another way to increase motivation is to listen to the client's description of the events and to assist him in identifying how his battering behavior is costly to him: loss of intimacy, impact on his relationship with children, friends' fear of his "temper," court costs, loss of work time, damage to property, loss of self-esteem, and so forth. Each offender is affected differently, and motivation to change must be initially nurtured by pointing out how it is in his self-interest that he stop his violent behavior. Pointing out these negative consequences is most effectively done in a group where the client can hear the comments of the others and start to develop new group norms that support being nonabusive.

There are advantages to working with the court-mandated client. The staff person begins the intake interview knowing that the client is a batterer and has had legal difficulty due to the violence. Such a client, when redirected into convincing the counselor that he should be accepted into the program, may in the process work through some of his denial. Many court-mandated clients will attend the first sessions regularly, thus giving the counselor some opportunity to deal with other aspects of the minimization or externalization. Noncourt-ordered clients may come only when there is an emotional crisis and quickly terminate when there is a superficial resolution to it. Also, with the court-ordered client there have already been some community sanctions placed against his violence; this is an important message in a society that still gives out very mixed signals about violence in the family.

Success in increasing the internal motivation to change in the court-mandated client often rests with the skill and experience of the counselor. If the counselor believes that court-ordered clients are more resistant per se, then clients will conform to that expectation. There are pros and cons to working with both sets of clients. Programs for counseling those who batter need to keep in mind that increasing and maintaining motivation for change is an issue for all clients.

Program Effectiveness

Next to victim safety, the most important issue to be addressed by all programs for those who batter is that of evaluating the effectiveness of the intervention. Too often counseling is seen as a panacea. The reality is that it does not work for some clients, and at this point it is not clear with whom it might be successful. In this field, the success of an intervention must be evaluated in terms of the impact that intervention has on the battering behavior. Does the battering end, decrease, remain the same, or increase following the intervention? Since battering is a behavior problem that can become habituated, an additional question concerns how long the change lasts. To answer such questions, information first needs to be systematically gathered at intake in order to have baseline data about the physical, sexual, psychological, and property battering committed by the offender against family members and those in the community. Such information must be gathered from several sources, including the victims. These measures should be administered again during counseling, at termination, and in follow-up intervals of six months, one year, three years, and five years.

With limited funds and the large demand for the development and maintenance of intervention programs for the perpetrator, the systematic information gathering needed for outcome studies has often been overlooked. As curricula have been designed and intervention programs stabilized, more attention is being directed toward those basic outcome studies. The gathering of reliable and valid data is costly in staff time, especially in the initial stages of developing appropriate methodology. For programs that have not conducted outcome studies, it is better to start with simple designs that can be expanded upon rather than to an attempt an elaborate design with insufficient resources for carrying it out. Regardless of the size of the project, a crucial step is to put in place a system for gathering the intake data integral to outcome studies. This establishes the mechanism for conducting follow-up studies, when additional resources become available, on representative samples of clients participating in the program. With programs open to court-mandated clients, there is particular interest in the evaluation of rehabilitative counseling versus other consequences imposed by the legal system. As in all outcome studies, the information gathered can be used to improve the effectiveness of the intervention by providing the data needed for program monitoring.

BEYOND COUNSELING

Counseling the court-mandated client who batters represents a major shift in our understanding of the community role in addressing the problem of battering. Violence against intimates is no longer to be tolerated, and all the community's resources should be utilized to develop a wide variety of interventions for this problem. Intervention with the offender must include specialized counseling programs, but ultimately must not be limited to them. Counseling is always rehabilitation, and for prevention to occur attention must be given to how we socialize future generations to live in intimate relationships.

REFERENCES

Attorney General's Task Force on Family Violence, Final Report, September 1984. Washington, DC: U.S. Attorney General.

Bandura, A. (1973). *Aggression: A social learning analysis.* Englewood Cliffs, NJ: Prentice-Hall.

Bern, E., & Bern, L. (1984). A group program for men who commit violence towards thier wives. *Social Work With Groups,* 7(1), 63–76.

Brown, R.J., & Chato, F.L. (1984). Characteristics of wife batterers and practice principles for effective treatment. Calgary, Alberta: Forensic Services, Calgary General Hospital.

Dobash, R.E., & Dobash, R. (1979). *Violence against wives.* New York: Free Press.

Domestic Abuse Project. (1985). *Intervening in women abuse: A total systems approach.* Minneapolis, MN: Author.

Dutton, D.G. (1984a). A nested ecological theory of male violence towards intimates. In P. Caplan (Ed.), *Feminist Psychology In Transition.* Montreal: Eden Press.

Dutton, D.G. (1984b). Interventions into the problem of wife assault: Therapeutic, policy and research implications. *Canadian Journal of Behav. Sci./Rev. Canad. Sci. Comp.,* 16(4), 281–297.

Eddy, M.J., & Myers, T. (1984). *Helping men who batter: A profile of programs in the U.S.* Texas State Department of Human Resources.

Edleson, J., Miller, D., & Stone, G. (1983). Counseling men who batter: Group leader's handbook. Albany, NY: Men's Coalition Against Battering.

EMERGE, Inc. (1980). *Organizing and implementing services for men who batter.* Boston: Author.

Frank, P. & Houghton, B. (1983). *Confronting the batterer: A guidebook to creating the spouse abuse educational workshop.* New City, NY: Volunteer Counseling Service.

Gamache, D.J., Edleson, J.L., & Schok, M.D. (1984). *Coordinated police, judicial and social service response to woman battering: A multiple-baseline evaluation across three communities.* Minneapolis: Domestic Abuse Project.

Ganley, A. (1981). *Court-mandated counseling for men who batter: A three-day workshop for mental health professionals.* Washington. DC: Center for Women Policy Studies.

Gondolf, E. (1985). *Men who batter: An integrated approach for stopping wife abuse.* Holmes Beach, FL: Learning Publications.

Pence, E., & Paymar, M. (1985a). *Domestic abuse intervention project: Curriculum for men who batter.* Duluth: Domestic Abuse Intervention Project.

Pence, E., & Paymar, M. (1985b). *Criminal justice response to domestic assault cases: A guide for policy development.* Duluth: Domestic Abuse Intervention Project.

Program Evaluation Resource Center. (1982). *Exploratory evaluation of the domestic abuse project.* Minneapolis, MN: Author.

Saunders, D. (1984). Helping husbands who batter. *Social Casework: The Journal of Contemporary Social Work,* 347–353.

Schecter, S. (1982). *Women and male violence.* Boston: South End Press.

Soler, E., & Martin, S. (1982). *Domestic violence is a crime.* San Francisco: Family Violence Project.

Sonkin, D., & Durphey, M. (1982). *Learning to live without violence: A handbook for men.* San Francisco: Volcano Press.

Straus, M.A. (1976). Sexual inequality, cultural norms, and wife beating. *Victimology, 1,* 54–76.

Wiggins, J.A. (1983). Family violence as a case of interpersonal aggression: A situational analysis. *Social Forces, 62*(1), 102–123.

10

The Assessment of Court-Mandated Male Batterers

Daniel Jay Sonkin

A thorough assessment of any person seeking mental health services is a necessary prerequisite to a successful counseling outcome. When treating clients who have a high risk of acting out, e.g., men who batter women, an accurate assessment is critical in order to protect the safety of intended and unintended victims (Sonkin, Martin, & Walker, 1985; Ganley, 1981). In addition, the potential of a legal suit being brought against a counselor is always present when an offender commits violence during the course of counseling (Sonkin, 1986; Pesner, 1985).

With the proliferation of domestic violence diversion programs as an alternative to prosecution and the increased use of probation with counseling as an alternative to incarceration (Martin, Chapter 1 of this text; Ganley, Chapter 9 of this text; 1981; Sonkin, Martin, & Walker, 1985), counselors are called upon by probation departments and the courts to assess whether particular defendants are suitable for counseling within the context of these criminal justice options. Although many probation officers now have training and experience with domestic violence cases, they will frequently utilize the counselor as a second opinion before writing presentencing reports or diversion eligibility and suitability reports. In addition, some men may be intimidated by an officer of the court and may be more likely to share details with an individual who appears to be neutral. The degree of neutrality varies from counselor to counselor; however, our experience has shown that the most successful counseling outcomes are the result of the counselor and probation officer working in concert (Sonkin, Martin, & Walker, 1985; Pesner, 1985; Ganley & Harris, 1978; Ganley; 1981).

This chapter will discuss the assessment procedures utilized by the author when evaluating male batterens. This discussion will also include some of the legal and ethical issues inherent in the assessment of court-mandated clients and will recommend spicific procedures in reponse to these issues.

THE ASSESSMENT PROCESS

Although there is not necessarily a clear delineation between assessment and treatment processes, this discussion will consider the assessment process as that period of time during which the counselor collects data from the client and from collateral contacts to determine the counseling plan. This time period can last from four to eight sessions, depending on the client and the complexity of the situation. The delineation between assessment and treatment may be further defined by the court process whereby a period of time may elapse between the initial referral and final disposition; that is, suspended sentence with probation and counseling rather than incarceration. Because many batterers do not demonstrate overt psychopathological features, the clinician must become aware of more subtle psychological and behavioral characteristics and patterns during the assessment process. Clarifing the goals of the assessment can be helpful to this end:

1. Determination of dangerousness of client
2. Determination of motivation for change
3. Determination of victim/other family members' needs
4. Determination of counscling plan
5. Submission of presentencing/dispositional report

FRAMING THE ASSESSMENT PROCESS

Many men who enter counseling are not familiar with the counseling process (Sonkin, Martin, & Walker, 1985; Murphy, 1985). Therapy may be an unkown quantity that leaves them feeling anxious, fearful, or withdrawn. It is important for the counselor to realize that the primary motivating reason for the court-mandated offender's appearing at the door to the office is that he is being told by somebody else to attend. This fact can be advantageous or detrimental to the therapy process; the degree of each may be determined in part by the manner in which the counselor structures the theraputic interventions. Although specific treatment techniques were addressed in Chapter 9, the discussion here will include some specific procedures that may enhance the assessment process.

Before the court-mandated client makes his appointment with our program, we will usually have had phone contact with his probation officer. Although we do not usually receive specific details of the crime committed, we will be told the status of his case and the probation officer's need regarding the referral. For example, a probation officer may call to inform us that a particular client has been granted domestic violence diversion and referred to our program. The officer may also request to be informed by a certain date about whether the client called us. The officer may also want to be told whether the client showed up for his scheduled appointment (Pesner, 1985).

A probation officer may also call to let us know that a client is being assessed for diversion and to request a second opinion as to his appropriateness for counseling and, if so, a tentative treatment plan. Likewise, another client may be in the process of evaluation for presentencing and a counselor's opinion may enhance a report to the court.

In this way, the counselor may already know some of the facts of a case and why the client is being asked to attend the session. When the client apears for his appointment it is important for the therapist to address directly the reason for the client's attendance. An initial interchange may go as follows:

THERAPIST: Can you tell me why you are seeking conunseling at this time?
CLIENT: The probation officer told me to see you.
THERAPIST: Can you tell me what specifically happened that got you involved with the courts?
CLIENT: Two weeks ago . . .

or

THERAPIST: I spoke with your probation officer the other day and I understand that you are being considered for domestic violence diversion. Can you tell me how you got involved with the courts in the first place.
CLIENT: My wife called the police.
THERAPIST: What specifically happened that led your wife to call the police?

The focus of the session thus becomes the client's relationship to the criminal justice system and the reason for that involvement; that is, his violence (Ganley & Harris, 1978). When the counselor addresses these issues immediately, the client receives the implicit or explicit message that his violent behavior will be the primary focus of the assessment. Although other issues may be relevant to his violent behavior—such as his low self-esteem, his relationship with his parents, or communication difficulties in his relationship—the counselor must be clear that the reason for his involvment with the courts is his violent behavior (Ganley, 1981). In addition, because of the high probability for continued violence, the safety of the client and the victim must be a primary concern. Finally, the liability is great for counselors working with this population, given the frequent need to violate confidentiality in order to protect intended and unintended victims from danger (Sonkin, 1986).

A portion of the first session is reserved to discuss the parameters of the assessment procedure. For many men, this may be their first visit to a therapist. I may ask them several questions regarding their experience with and expectations about counseling:

1. Have you ever been to counseling?
2. If so, what was your experience? What did you like about it? What didn't you like?
3. How can you benefit from counseling? How so?
4. If you don't think you can benefit from counseling, why not?
5. What do you expect counseling to be like?

In addition to giving the counselor information about the client's preconceived notions about the counseling process, these questions may help to assess the client's motivation for treatment. A clear explanation of the assessment process may alleviate the anxiety of not knowing just what it is. Frequently, therapists lose sight of the fact that not everyone is comfortable discussing the details of their private lives. Batterers in particular experience a great deal of embarrassment, guilt, or shame regarding their violent behavior (Ceasar, 1985). Subsequently, they may be reluctant to discuss their violence and other problems in their relationship. This anxiety may cause them to minimize or deny the extent of their problem (Ganley, 1981; Walker, 1979, 1984). This minimizing may also be a function of their wanting to escape criminal responsibility. To address this issue, the counselor needs to set clear limits with regard to confidentiality. Confidentiality is always a concern for individuals seeking counseling. However, the counselor who treats male batterers must realize the limits of confidentiality when the safety of a victim (or the client) is a concern (Sonkin, 1986).

This is done in the first session. Our procedure involves the client's reading and signing a confidentiality policy (see appendix of Sonkin, Martin, & Walker, 1985). The policy outlines several areas involving the need to receive and share information with others:

1. The need to exchange information with regard to the assessment with the probation department
2. The need to have contact with other counselors involved with the family
3. The need to have immediate contact with the victim of violence
4. The reporting of child abuse

5. The reporting of threats made by the client during treatment
6. The reporting of any crimes committed by the client during treatment
7. The disclosure of our assessment that the client is a danger to himself or others

The policy discusses our need to have regular contact with the victim to determine whether the client has re-offended or is utilizing the treatment material. It also discusses our need to report all re-offenses, as well as poor participation in treatment, to his probation officer. It explains our need to violate confidentiality in cases of child abuse, commission of illegal acts, specific threats of harm to another person, and assessment that the client is a danger to himself or others. This policy creates an understanding between the client and counselor that if there comes a time when he cannot control his actions, we will act in his behalf.

This policy also precludes the client's tendency to minimize and deny his violence. He is well aware that his behavior is being closely monitored. When the limits of confidentiality are clearly defined from the beginning of the assessment, there is less likelihood that the client will continue his violence or mislead the therapist. It may also alleviate concerns the client may have about his privacy in counseling: The policy clearly articulates the boundaries of that privacy. This policy is directly related to our concern about the dangerous nature of domestic violence (Browne, 1986; Sonkin, 1986; Ganley, 1981). Because of this continuing danger, the most important goal of the assessment is the determination of potential lethality. The following section will discuss this issue in detail.

DETERMINING DANGEROUSNESS

Much of the current psychological and legal literature is concerned with the therapist's ability to predict dangerous behavior (Monahan, 1981; California State Psychological Association, 1985; Sonkin, 1986; McNeill, Chapter 11 of this text). Although there is much controversy as to the accuracy with which such predictions can be made, it would be valuable for the reader to note several facts. When examining the literature on predictability of violent behavior, one finds that much of the research has utilized subjects incarcerated for criminal behavior or individuals hospitalized for either criminal behavior or severe psychological impairment (Menzies, Webster, & Sepejak, 1985; Monahan, 1981; Werner, Rose, & Yesavage, 1983). Although it may be argued that prediction with these particular populations is important, it is interesting to note that no studies on dangerousness have been conducted on male batterers. In addition, false positives and false negatives (Hamilton & Freeman, 1982; Hinton, 1983; Kozol, 1975;

Steadman, 1977; Steadman & Cocozza, 1974) are high in prediction situations. A false positive is when violence is clinically predicted but not perpetrated (Monahan, 1981); a false negative, when violence is not clinically predicted but *is* perpetrated. Another flaw of many prediction studies is that clients' violent behaviors can only be measured by additional involvements with the criminal justice system. In other words, a client who is predicted as nonviolent and assessed in this manner as being nonviolent (that is, no further police involvement) may be acting violently in the community but not being detected by the criminal justice system. This may be called an undetected false negative.

Second, the supreme and appellate court decisions that have mandated psychotherapists to warn victims in potentially dangerous situations were cases that involved persons known to each other. In these cases, the risk for future violence was assessed to be present by the therapist involved, the victim was easily identifiable, and the therapist was negligent in protecting the identifiable victim from harm (McNeill, Chapter 11 of this text; Sonkin, 1986; Sonkin, Martin, & Walker, 1985).

The issue of duty to warn is of most concern in cases where an assessment has indicated that the lethality risk is greatest. Studies examining family homicides suggest that in most cases a history of physical abuse preceded these final acts of violence (Boudouris, 1971; Browne, 1983, 1986; Chimbos, 1978; Thyfault, 1984). A recent study of family violence homicide, in which a battered woman killed an abusive partner, showed that a positive relationship does exist between lethality and a number of factors common in adult relationships controlled by a violent man (Browne, 1983, 1986). In comparing relationships in which women killed their abusers with those in which women were battered but did not perpetrate violence against the abusive mate (assault-only cases), Browne found the following variables discriminated between the two groups:

1. Frequency of violent incidents
2. Severity of injuries sustained by the woman from these incidents
3. Man's threats to kill
4. Woman's suicide threats
5. Man's drug use
6. Man's frequency of intoxication
7. Forced/threatened sexual acts by the man

Although a similar study has not been conducted on men, the results could guide our assessment procedures and shed some light on when a counselor must act to protect a potential victim (Sonkin, 1986).

In determining dangerousness a clinician needs to take a number of factors into consideration. The most important of these is adequately operationalizing the concepts of violence and dangerousness (Ganley, 1981; Monahan, 1981). Definitions of violence and dangerous behavior may differ between evaluators. For example, one person might not consider slapping to be either violent or dangerous, whereas another might view such an act as violent but not dangerous. Still a third person might define a slap as both violent and potentially dangerous. Studies describing populations of battered women show a high incidence of beatings requiring medical care or hospitalization (Rounsaville & Weissman, 1977; San Francisco Family Violence Project, 1982; Walker, 1984). Theories regarding the cycle of violence (Walker, 1979; 1984) indicate that although a single slap may not in itself pose serious harm to a victim, it is likely to escalate to more life-threatening behaviors. Ganley (1981) describes four types of violence found in her work with male batterers: physical, sexual, property, and psychological. A thorough assessment of dangerousness would involve obtaining a complete inventory of all violent acts perpetrated by the offender.

Upon intake, the client is asked to complete a violence inventory (see appendix of Sonkin, Martin, & Walker, 1985) that lists all the violent acts perpetrated by the client in his current or last relationship. This inventory, similar to ones utilized by other clinicians and researchers (Straus, Gelles, & Steinmetz, 1980; Walker, 1984), describes acts of physical, sexual, property, and psychological violence, the number of times each act has been perpetrated, and the victim involved. The client immediately becomes aware of the scope of violent behavior, as well as the focus of treatment intervention.

The violence inventory includes the physically violent acts of slapping, grabbing, punching, choking, pulling hair, and so forth. Sexual violence includes forced sexual intercourse and other forced sexual acts. Property violence includes the throwing and breaking of objects or personal effects. Psychological violence includes threats of violence, threats to kill, pathological jealousy, mental degradation, controlling behaviors, and intimidation.

In addition to this general inventory, clients are asked to describe four incidents of violence that they perpetrated in their past relationship (Walker, 1984). These acts are the last episode, the first episode, the most violent or dangerous episode, and the episode that was most frightening to the victim. In this way the counselor begins to develop a fair idea of the scope of violent behaviors and the current level of danger.

At the end of the first interview, the client is asked to complete a psycho-social-violence assessment form (see appendix of Sonkin, Martin & Walker, 1985). This form asks the client to supply information in a number of other areas including the following:

Violence in family of origin. It is estimated that over half of all male batterers were either physically or sexually abused as children or viewed violence between their parents (Fagan, Stewart, & Hansen, 1983; San Francisco Family Violence Project, 1982; Straus et al., 1980; Walker, 1984). This information certainly sheds light on the transmission of violent behavior, as well as suggesting areas needing theraputic intervention. Recent data suggest that batterers who were either physically or sexually abused as children may experience more anger than batterers who were not abused (Sonkin, 1985). In addition to experiencing and witnessing violence, almost 25% of a small and select sample of batterers in treatment indicated that they had attacked one of their parents (Sonkin, Martin, & Walker, 1985).

Past violent behavior. Men who are in their late twenties and older and who have had previous intimate relationships are likely to have battered a previous partner (San Francisco Family Violence Project, 1982). This information can assist the counselor in predicting the risk and degree of seriousness of future violence. Knowing how serious the violence became in past relationships may indicate the potential for similar or more lethal violence with a current victim. This information may also be useful in helping the batterer who blames his partner or the relationship for his violence. Discussing his acts of violence in prior relationships forces him to see his independently established pattern of violent behavior. It may also motivate a client if he is reminded of previous marriages/relationships that may have ended in divorce or separation because of this violence.

Current relationship. A thorough assessment includes establisment of the frequency and cycle of violence (Walker, 1979), an inventory of injuries sustained by the victim, and a detailed description of four incidents of violence (described above). When the client describes these four incidents of violence we ask him to complete a violence inventory for each incident. The client also completes an inventory for all violent acts perpetrated during the course of the relationship. Other areas explored include areas of stress in the relationship, assessment of physical and sexual abuse of children, the witnessing of violence by children, assessment for abuse of the elderly, family support systems, and the current living arangements (e.g., separated or together). It is important that the counselor obtain corroborating data through collateral contacts with the victim, children, and other family members. Batterers will tend to minimize and deny the extent of their violent behaviors, which can subsequently mislead the counselor in his or her assessment. We inform the client that treatment is contingent on our receiving his permission to have this contact with his partner (or other sources of information).

Alcohol and other drug use/abuse. Researchers and clinicians have indicated a high correlation of alcohol/drug abuse and domestic violence (Browne, 1986; Ganley, 1981; Gelles, 1974; Rosenbaum, 1979; San Francisco Family Violence Project, 1982; Sonkin, Martin, & Walker, 1985; Straus et al., 1980; Walker, 1984). Each client is administered an alcohol screening test and asked to answer questions regarding his alcohol and drug history. We are noting increasing evidence that suggests that men who are already predisposed to violence are more likely to become violent when under the influence of alcohol or drugs (Sonkin, 1986). Likewise, when a batterer is under the influence of alcohol or other drugs, he is likely to cause more severe injuries due to his lack of control (Browne, 1986).

Violence outside the home. The violence assessment also includes information on such violent and illegal activities outside the family as previous criminal history and activities; violence involving friends, relatives, neighbors, and strangers; military experience; and occupational violence. The counselor needs to assess how much violence is integrated into the client's life. The counselor may need to obtain this information through collateral contacts with the victim, other family members, the probation departments, or other therapists involved in the case. Excepting occupational violence, it is usually a goal of treatment for the client to stop his violence outside the home as well. It is recommended that counselors set strict limits with the client who has established violent patterns outside the home, so as not to give him double messages. The batterer must realize that all violence, outside of self-defense, is against the law. Re-offenses of this type of violence are also reported to the probation department.

Attitudes toward violence. A good predictor of success in treatment relates to the batterer's attitudes toward his violence. Many men will externalize the causes of their violence, that is, they justify their behavior because of "her provocation" (Ganley & Harris, 1978). However, most men will also admit that they feel remorse about their violent behavior and would like to change. Additionally, most male batterers do not perceive themselves as being violent individuals. From the first contact, the counselor must address these issues in order effectively to prevent further violence (Ganley, Chapter 9 of this text). The male batterer must realize that he is in control of his behavior and that the victim does not make him violent. Although his remorse may be a good first step toward stopping his violence, there also needs to be some active process of change that will require his time and energy (Fortune, epilogue of this text). It is also important that a man who batters view himself as a person with violence problems. This fact must always be in his mind. He needs to monitor his anger continually so as to avoid a violent reaction (Ganley, 1981). If a client recognizes that he has a predisposition toward a particular behavior, he is in a much better position to prevent it's recurrence.

In addition to his attitudes toward violence, it is equally important to assess a client's attitudes toward women, men, marriage, and relationships (Adams McCormick, 1982; Schechter, 1982). Utilizing the hostility towards women scale (Check & Malamuth, 1983), we have found that over half of our military clients have generalized hostility toward women. We also found that those clients with high hostility toward women were more likely to assault their partner sexually, more likely to have been abused as children, and more likely to manifest general anger (Sonkin, 1985). Many programs for batterers focus intensely on this factor as a treatment issue (Adams & McCormick, 1982; Garnet & Moss, 1982; Saunders, 1982).

Mental and physical assessment. Each client is required to complete the Minnesota Multiphasic Personality Inventory (MMPI) (Hathaway & Meehl, 1951) to determine serious psychological impairment as well as articulate general personality traits. The MMPI has described our clients' defensive patterns, such as denial, intellectualization, hostility, and withdrawal. Many batterers test as depressed and angry and more than half as feeling anxious about their situation. Their profiles are descriptive of persons with problems in impulse control and chronic acting out. Few see themselves in a positive light, and many may be characterized as having low ego strength, experiencing extreme stress, and feeling out of control of their lives. Many of the scores corroborate our assessments for alcohol abuse.

In addition to formal testing, each client is given a differential diagnosis as described by the *Diagnostic Manual of Mental Disorders* (DSM-III) (American Psychiatric Association, 1980). The five-axis system of categorizing clients helps the clinician develop an appropriate treatment plan, as well as predicting and measuring success in treatment.

The DSM-III five-axis system allows the clinician to separate the clinical syndromes, personality and developmental disorders, and physiological disorders on separate axes. Axes four and five measure the severity of psychosocial stressors and level of adaptive functioning, respectively, in the last year.

On axis one, batterers may be diagnosed with an impulse disorder such as intermittent explosive disorder (312.34) and/or a substance abuse disorder, such as alcohol dependence (303.9x). A Vietnam veteran may be suffering from post-traumatic stress disorder (309.81).

On axis two, a batterer may be suffering from a borderline (301.83), antisocial (301.70), passive-aggressive (301.84), or paranoid (301.00) personality disorder. There is no research to date that suggests that batterers represent any one particular type of personality disorder. Each client needs to be assessed for his own particular characteristics.

Axis four describes the degree of stress the client has experienced in the past year. Axis five describes his adaptive functioning in social relations, occupation, and leisure activities. It is expected that the client will cope better or experience less stress over time. It is also expected that the client will function better in his family and that this improvement will spill over into the other areas of his life.

As it is important to assess for general mental functioning, it is also important to assess for general health. Axis three of the DSM-III diagnosis describes physical disorders that may or may not be related to a client's violent behavior. An assessment in this area would include the client's history of serious illness and accidents, past and current medications, and current health condition. If the counselor has any concerns that a client may have an organic problem, it is recommended that the client seek a medical examination and consultation. A thorough medical examination could provide valuable treatment information for the therapist, especially in cases where a client may be suffering from a chronic condition such as epilepsy, other neurological disorders, hypoglycemia and/or cardiovascular disease. Unusual violence patterns, such as spontaneous explosions out of context or memory losses, may indicate a physiological disorder.

Experience has shown that past behavior is the best predictor of future behavior (Monahan, 1981) and that not all clients benefit from treatment (Ganley, 1981; Sonkin, Martin, & Walker, 1985). For these reasons it is reasonable for the counselor treating male batterers to assume that some clients will continue to be violent while they are in treatment. Therefore, the risk of danger is high for victims and others in close proximity to the batterer. In addition, the liability is high for the counselor who refuses to take "reasonable care to protect the intended (and unintended) victims against such danger." We will routinely warn the victim that general danger exists to herself and others and that her safety is not guaranteed because her partner is now in counseling. We also issue a warning and act to protect at times of high risk for the client.

Because dangerousness or risk is a matter of degree and not a black and white phenomenon, it is recommended that the therapist consider a duty to warn and protect in the following high risk situations:

1. When the violence is escalating, either in frequency or severity, during the course of treatment
2. When explicit or implicit threats are made during the course of treatment
3. When the client is in crisis and is unable to assure the therapist of his self-control (depending on the situation, even with such assurances from the client it may be necessary to issue such a warning)
4. When the victim(s) express(es) fear for her own or others' safety
5. When there is an escalation in the use of drugs and/or alcohol by the client
6. When the client refuses to cooperate with the treatment plan (e.g., attend counseling sessions, attend alcohol/drug treatment sessions, utilize treatment material, etc.)
7. When it is discovered that the client has omitted telling the therapist about specific acts of violence committed while in therapy
8. When it is discovered during the treatment process that prior to

entering treatment the offender has committed life-threatening violence or has made specific threats to kill

Any one or a combination of these factors could imply an extremely high violence potential and therefore may dictate a particular course of action. Protecting an intended or unintended victim may involve warning the victim, calling the police, hospitalizing the victim or the offender, informing the probation officer, recommending revocation of probation, sheltering the victim, or informating other family members or friends. One must take into consideration the state mind of the offender, that of the victim, the proximity of the victim and the offender, and the victim's perception of the dangerousness of her situation.

It is recommended that counselors regularly consult with colleagues regarding case management and treatment (Ganley, 1981; Sonkin, 1986; Walker, 1979). In this way, when a crisis arises, there may already be an associate or supervisor familar with a particular case. In addition to consultation, counselors are encouraged to keep accurate assessment notes and document all conversations regarding a particular incidence of duty to warn and protect. Even if the above factors are not present, the counselor should not be lulled into a false sense of security. The client must get the clear impression that the counselor takes all forms of violence seriously and realizes that even the least severe forms, such as a slap or a push, could lead to serious injury.

DETERMINING MOTIVATION FOR CHANGE

Historically, mental health professionals believed that the most important decision a client makes before entering treatment is that he or she needs help. The client who is most likely to benefit from counseling is the person who on some conscious level realizes that the difficulties in his or her life are unmanageable and that counseling may help. However, our experience has shown that this is not necessarily a prerequisite to a successful treatment outcome.

Counselors working with men who batter often become distressed about the high rate of attrition of this clinical population. It is frequently stated that "These men are not motivated." Yet many of these men appear to feel genuinely upset about their behaviors. Perhaps motivation is not the underlying issue.

The male batterer who minimizes the seriousness of his violence and externalizes the causes is not likely to see himself as needing help. In his view, violence is not that serious a problem, and if it were, it is his wife who is the problem (makes him violent), so it is she who needs the help. He is not likely to seek treatment on his own accord. Therefore, external forces are needed to encourage his participation in a rehabilitation program. It should become the focus of this program to help the client take his violence seriously and see that *his violence* is *his problem* and that he has the ability within himself to control his behaviors. Through this process it is also hoped that the client will subsequently recognize his need for counseling, and therefore his attendance will become increasingly a function of his desire to change rather than simply "his having to be there."

For most men, the counseling process is not an experience with which they are familiar or comfortable. Traditional counseling requires a willingness on behalf of the client to examine and communicate inner thoughts and feelings as well as a desire to engage in the type of intimate relationship that may lead to feelings of vulnerability. These are skills that are neither encouraged nor developed in most men, which is why it is women who most frequently request mental health services. Expecting the typical male to feel comfortable with the therapeutic process would be similar to expecting an individual to be feel comfortable with skiing without developing the physical stamina and skills necessary for that particular activity.

Men need to value the skills necessary for a successful counseling experience—reflection, communication of inner thoughts and feelings, and valuation of interpersonal relationships. Motivation for counseling is heavily determined by how much a person values those skills necessary to engage in the process and may not necessarily be a reflection of how bad they feel about their behavior or how defensive they may be about their feelings.

But not all men who batter are greatly distressed about their violence. For many men, violence is a viable response to their problems because "it works." It brings about a quick end to an uncomfortable situation. The tension leaves their body and they have taken control over that (their spouse) which they perceive as the source of their problem. Violent problem-solving alternatives become perpetuated when the community as a whole fails to protect the victim and inform the perpetrator that family violence is a crime. As a result of this societal neglect, many men have never seriously considered the need to seek assistance in stopping their violent behavior. Even if they were to consider the violence a serious problem, asking for help is antithetical to the male ideal. The obstacles are compounded when the individual is ignorant of the counseling process, thinking only crazy persons seek mental health services.

In spite of these social and psychological obstacles, there are increasing numbers of men who are seeking mental health services for their violence problems. They are distressed by their behaviors and are concerned about its affects on their spouse, themselves, and their children. Asking for help may not be unreasonable or awkward for these individuals. Perhaps they have had other successful counseling experiences or for other reasons possess the interpersonal skills necessary for the process. It may be that they are adventurous enough to take a leap of faith that this process can be beneficial, or they may have simply reached bottom and are desparate for help.

With these thoughts in mind, what can the therapist do to assess adequately the motivation of a particular client? The following are guidelines for such as assessment:

1. What is the client's emotional state of mind regarding his violence? Most men will display some embarrassment, regret, or sadness about their violent behavior. The degree to which they find their behavior personally distressing will dictate their motivation for change.

2. How does the client attribute the causes of his violence? The client who externalizes the most will be the least motivated for personal change. He will not see the violence as *his* problem but will attribute its occurrence to her problems, in that she must change for him to stop being violent. Some men may already know that their violence is a longstanding problem, stemming from childhood, and that they are responsible for their behavior.

3. Does the client want to change any of his behaviors? For some clients, insight may follow a substantial change in behavior. The client who wants to change a particular behavior will demonstrate a level of motivation that may indicate a good prognosis for treatment.

4. To what extent does the client realize his behavior is against the law? For some men, avoiding the consequences of criminal justice intervention will motivate this change in behavior. They may see that they have more to lose by remaining violent than by changing.

In addition to these questions, a counselor may observe commonsense behaviors that may indicate degree of motivation:

1. Does the client show up for counseling sessions?
2. Does he show up on time?
3. Does he appear to be making a genuine effort to examine his problem?
4. Does he cooperate with the counseling plan?
5. Does he talk about his problems at home, work, and so forth?
6. Is he willing to discuss the violence in the sessions?
7. Does he acknowledge that he could benefit from counseling?

Through collateral contacts with the probation department and the victim, the counselor may discover that the client has minimized or denied his violent behaviors (Ganley, 1981). The degree of this denial may shed light on the client's motivation for change. In addition, his response to confrontation may also indicate the degree to motivation.

At the end of the first session we will usually prescribe homework for the client to complete by the second session. This consists of completing an extensive assessment form, testing material, and a specific reading assignment in the workbook we utilize in the program (Sonkin & Durphy, 1982). The degree to which this work is completed can also be an indicator of motivation. The quality of the client's responses to the assessment questionnaire may indicate his adaptability to a particular counseling approach or intervention.

Motivation is a dynamic phenomenon, in that it waxes and wanes during the course of therapy. The counselor's attitudes about the client can either embue hope and trust, thereby increasing motivation, or they can cause a client to distrust the counselor and the process involved in change. The decision to change is ultimately within the control of the client, and the counselor is simply a guide to that end. If the client suspects that the counselor is trying to control him, he may believe that entering into this relationship means abdicating power (Searle, 1985). This is a senstive issue for many batterers. Many battering men experienced or witnessed violence in their children (Ceasar, 1985; Fagan et al., 1983; Sonkin, Martin, & Walker, 1985; Straus et al., 1980; Walker, 1984) and as a result felt powerless. For many men, their abuse is an attempt to overcome that childhood powerlessness by taking on the power of the abuser (Finkelhor, 1984). The issues of control and power are central to the treatment process. Therefore, the counselor's attitudes play an integral role in the assessment process (Ganley, 1981).

DETERMINING VICTIM'S AND OTHER FAMILY MEMBERS' NEEDS

Although the counseling, health, legal, and housing needs of the victim and other family members are not directly related to the assessment process of the offender, we have found that many victims have only talked with criminal justice personnel and have little information about the services available to them in the community. During our collateral contact with the woman, we will routinely assess her personal needs and make the appropriate referrals (Ganley, 1981).

The woman often appears apologetic, anticipating that her batterer's counselor may believe she has contributed to his violent behavior (Douglas, Chapter 3 of this text; Walker, 1979; 1984). We directly emphasize to her that his violence is his responsibility and that she did not provoke or otherwise cause him to be violent. We strongly believe that counselors must actively take the onus off the victim for being responsible for changing his behavior. In addition, we give her an informational handout that explains that his being in counseling is no guarantee that he will stop beating her and that if she chooses to stay with him, she may be in continued danger (Sonkin, 1986). Included is a description of the behaviors she should look for to determine if he is benefiting from treatment (Sonkin, Martin, & Walker, 1985). Referrals for counseling are made to the local shelter or domestic violence program. We encourage women to utilize shelters, police, and the probation officer for the protection and safety of her and her children.

We have also found it helpful to discuss with the woman her past relationships and her family of origin. We ,like others, have found that many women in battering relationships were sexually abused as children (Russell, 1984; Thyfault, 1980; Walker, 1984). If this is the case, we will refer her to a sexual abuse program that helps survivors overcome the issues related to victimization.

Like the adult woman victim of violence, children are frequently victimized or traumatized by viewing the violence (Goodman and Rosenberg, Chapter 7 of this text; Martin, 1981; Walker, 1979, 1984). Therefore it is necessary that they be assessed for mental and physical health needs. It may become known or suspected through the interview with a child that physical or sexual abuse is simultaneously occurring. In this case, child protective services must be immediately notified to conduct further investigation.

Through these collateral contacts, the woman may reveal information that she would like to remain confidential. This can obviously put the counselor in a difficult position. We decide as a team if the release of that information is necessary for our counseling the offender. If so, we will go back to the woman and discuss with her the possible implications of withholding and releasing the information before confronting the offender. If the information relates to acts of violence he has perpetrated, we may wait to see if the client discusses those facts himself. If he does not reveal the information, we will discuss with the woman the fact that her fearfulness and his denial may be an indication of the high lethality of the situation. We discuss her legal alternatives and the possibility of her utilizing a battered woman's shelter to assure her own and her children's safety. If a woman is adamant about our not confronting her partner for fear of her safety, we will treat that situation as we would any "duty to warn and protect crisis," that is, warn both her and the police and work with her to create an environment of safety (e.g., sending her to a battered woman's shelter, hospitalizing her or the offender, etc.) (Sonkin, 1986). In addition, we will consult with probation and examine our alternatives for dealing with the defendant.

Although these collateral contacts may create conflicts of allegiance, the helpful information gleaned from the majority of cases far outweighs the drawbacks of such a practice. When these "conflicts" manifest, it is an indication of the seriousness of the problem as well as illustrative of the distrust and manipulation that results from domestic violence.

DETERMINING A TREATMENT PLAN

Treatment planning depends heavily on one's theoretical orientation. The rationale for one successful approach was discussed more thoroughly in Chapter 9 of this text. The discussion here will address the various types of treatment plans and the relationship of the counselor to probation.

Through our experience we have found that a counseling plan that involves only one particular modality is rarely as effective as a multidimensional approach. Almost one-half of our clients have scored positively on an alcohol screening inventory, indicating a potential need for alcohol counseling (Sonkin, Martin, & Walker, 1985). We have found it extremely helpful to utilize Alcoholics Anonymous and/or outpaitent (and in some cases inpatient) alcohol counseling programs as an adjunct to our particular counseling service.

In order to accommodate the number of clients referred, we offer each client group counseling. This counseling focuses on ceasing violent behavior through development of anger management skills and exploration of beliefs and attitudes about violence, men, women, and relationships (Sonkin & Durphy, 1982). Such an approach is the most effective means to bring an immediate stop to the violent behavior and to engage the client in the therapeutic process. Each counseling plan includes this component either on a group or individual basis.

In cases where it appears that a client may not have sufficient motivation for group therapy, may feel extremely fearful of being in a group, or has completed prior group counseling, or is ready and interested, we will see that person on an individual basis. Some of the less motivated clients could benefit from a period of time in individual counseling before entering the group. For many men the lengthy assessment process serves as an acclimation period. The counselor's flexibility in this regard is a key factor to success.

Some counseling plans may include couples counseling as an adjunct to individual or group work. We will usually wait for a period of time before recommending this in order to determine how well the client is incorporating the counseling techniques into his relationship. Couples counseling can be very helpful in those cases where the violence is relatively less severe and the man is utilizing anger-management techniques on a regular basis. Couples counseling could exacerbate the stress between the couple and subsequently increase his risk for violence. Couples counseling may also give the victim (and the offender) the implicit message that her behavior is related to the batterer's violence (Ganley, 1981; Sonkin, Martin, & Walker, 1985).

Some men may need hospitalization. This may be required with alcoholics, drug abusers, or those individuals with severe psychological impairment. We will wait until their release from their inpatient program before considering acceptance into our group. Furthermore, many inpatient programs ask that their clients not particiapte in other forms of counseling while they are inpatients.

Some men have found it extremely helpful to be in both individual and group counseling during the initial stages. A two-hour group with eight clients does not allow much time to discuss every man's difficulties during the previous week. In individual counseling the man could discuss issues tangential to his violence.

Frequently the probation officer or the client will ask the counselor, "How long does counseling last?" This question can put the counselor in a position of power over the client's freedom, which can be an important issue to be discussed in treamtment. The counselor's degree of involvement in the decision-making process for each client may vary. However, if a counselor treats a court-mandated client, he or she is going to have some influence over the disposition of the case (Pesner, 1985). There are three basic approaches to this issue. One is on a case-by-case basis. The second involves a blanket policy. We have tried both and have had trouble either way. When deciding on a case-by-case basis, the clients are very sensitive to inconsistencies in decision making and fairness. With the blanket policy, one is usually accused of inflexibility. A third approach can leave it up to the probation department; however, the client and probation department can accuse the counselor of being too neutral and/or indecisive. Probation officers will tell the counselor, "You know the client best and therefore you are in the best position to assess his progress." In addition, some probation officers may terminate a client too early, which may subsequently increase the risk for the victim.

Our current approach combines the first two alternatives. We recommend that the offender be on probation or diversion for the complete term and that the length of counseling be contingent on his progress. We go on to say that it is our recommendation that most clients need to be in counseling for the duration of probation or diversion but in some cases it may be appropriate to terminate counseling (not diversion or probation) early. The type of counseling may vary during the course of probation or diversion; this will depend on the original treatment plan and periodic reevaluations.

From our experience, clients are less likely to act out if they continue on diversion or probation to the maximum length of time prescribed by law. Although this alone will not stop all persons from being violent, it does have some deterrent effect and is therefore useful (Boffey, 1983; Martin, Chapter 1 of this text; San Francisco Family Violence Project, 1982).

It is of the utmost importance that the therapist and probation officer work closely together in monitoring the court-mandated client. Miscommunications and acting out by the client are common and therefore need to be frequently addressed. Monthly or bimonthly communication between the therapist and the probation officer regarding the client's participation and response to treatment can prevent or readily resolve crises that might arise.

SUBMISSION OF PRESENTENCING OR OTHER DISPOSITIONAL REPORTS

After the intial evaluation we will submit a written report to the probation department with our assessment and recommendations. Our recommendations to the probation department are first discussed with the client and his partner, if she is available. This report includes the following information:

1. The number of hours of the evaluation
2. Assessment of dangerousness and the basis for that assessment
3. Assessment of motivation and the basis for that assessment
4. Any warnings issued to intended and unintended victims
5. Recommendations made to the victim and other family members
6. Treatment plan for the offender, including length of time before first evaluation (three to six months) and length of treatment
7. Recommendations regarding client's supervision needs

When working with new probation staff, we will often include our recommendations of what we need from the probation department to facilitate our providing effective counseling services for the offender. This includes follow-up with the victim, regular contact with the defendant, a clear message to the offender that any re-offense or nonparticipation with his counseling program is grounds for revocation of diversion or probation and that any re-offense, no matter how serious, is to be reported to probation. The probation department's support of the treatment plan minimizes the risk of the client's acting out. Open lines of communication and cooperation between all professionals involved in the case also minimize this possibility.

When a client is subsequently referred for continued counseling while on probation or diversion, we will send the probation officer a monthly report on his progress and recommended actions with regard to therapy (Sonkin, Martin, & Walker, 1985). Similarly, at the completion of treatment a termination report describes our final assessment of the client's progress in treatment and any needed follow-up. Therapists are encouraged to thoroughly document and explicitly communicate their assessment, treatment plan, and the client's progress with criminal justice personnel, such as probation officers, to assure successful treatment results.

IN SUMMARY

The thorough assessment of court-referred domestic violence cases is necessary for a successful treatment outcome. The counselor needs to take his or her time in obtaining minute details that shed light on the pattern of abuse by the offender, the effects of the violence on the victim and other family members, and the dynamics of the family separate from the violence. In doing so, the clinician will discover that domestic violence is a complex issue that demands equally complex and well-thought-out solutions.

The counselor is encouraged to utilize the various types of counseling and education services available in the community, such as alcohol and drug treatment, vocational rehabilitation services, and couple or family counseling services. Assessing the dangerousness of the client is a necessary first step to a thorough clinical assessment. This is following by an assessment of motivation and the development of a comprehensive treatment plan. Given the high lethality of domestic violence, the counselor has to assess whether there is a need to warn and protect an intended or unintended victim of violence.

Counselors working with male batterers are encouraged to work as a team with other service providers involved in a case, such as probation staff, colleagues, and so forth. Seeking consultation from colleagues can be of great value when making decisions about dangerousness and duty to warn. Given the fact that there still exists a significant possibility that the client will re-offend while in treatment, a "better safe than sorry" policy is usually appropriate in such situations.

Therapists are also encouraged to utilize the entire duration of probation as a guideline for determining the length of treatment. With the early termination of counseling as a option, the counselor can help the client focus on what is occurring in treatment rather than when such treatment will end. In addition, the extensive length of treatment indicates to the client, court, probation, and victim that domestic violence is a serious problem that must be thoroughly addressed by the offender to assure the safety of those around him. The offender also needs to be reminded that treatment is an alternative to the more severe criminal justice sanctions, such as prison, and that two or three years of financial and time inconvenience is a more desirable alternative than loss of personal freedom.

REFERENCES

Adams, D.C., & McCormick, A.J. (1982). Men unlearning violence: A group approach. Based on the collective model. In M. Roy (Ed.), *The abusing partner:*

An analysis of domestic battering. New York: Van Nostrand Reinhold.

American Psychiatric Association (1980). *Diagnostic and statistical manual of mental disorders* (3rd ed.). Washington, DC: Author.

Boffey, P.M. (1983, April 6). Arrests advised in domestic disputes. *Oakland Tribune*.

Boudouris, J. (1971). Homicide in the family. *Journal of Marriage and the Family, 33*, 667–676.

Browne, A. (1983). *When battered women kill*. Unpublished doctoral dissertation, University of Experimenting Colleges and Universities, Cincinnati, OH.

Browne, A. (1986). Assault and homicide at home: When battered women kill. In M.J. Sakes & L. Saxe (Eds.), *Advances in Applied Social Psychology: Vol. 3.* Hillsdale, NJ: Erlbaum.

California State Psychological Association (1985). Research discouraging on clinical predictions. *California State Psychologist, 20*(1), 1.

Ceasar, P. (1985). *The male batterer: Personality, and psychosocial characteristics*. Unpublished doctoral dissertation, California School of Professional Psychology, Berkeley, CA.

Check, J.V.P., & Malamuth, N.M. (1983, August). *The hostility towards women scale*. Paper presented at the 91st Annual Convention of the American Psychological Association, Anaheim, CA.

Chimbos, P.D. (1978). *Marital violence: A study of interspousal homicide*. San Francisco: R & E Research Associates.

Fagan, J.A., Stewart, D.K., & Hansen, K.V. (1983). Violent men or violent husbands? In D. Finkelhor, R.J. Gelles, G.T. Hotaling, & M.A. Straus (Eds.), *The dark side of families: Current family violence research*. Beverly Hills: Sage.

Finkelhor, D. (1984). *Child sexual abuse: New theory and research*. New York: Free Press.

Ganley, A.L. (1981). *Court mandated counseling for men who batter (participants' and trainer's manuals)*. Washington, DC: Center for Women's Policy Studies.

Ganley, A.L., & Harris, L. (1978, August). Domestic violence: Issues in designing and implementing programs for male batterers. Paper presented at the 86th Annual Convention of the American Psychological Association, Toronto, Canada.

Garnet, S., & Moss, D. (1982). How to set up a counseling program for self-referred batterers: The AWAIC model. In M. Roy (Ed.), *The abusive partner: An analysis of domestic battering*. New York: Van Nostrand Reinhold.

Gelles, R.J. (1974). *The violent home*. Beverly Hills: Sage Publications.

Hamilton, J.R., & Freeman, H. (Eds.). (1982). *Dangerousness: Psychiatric assessment and management*. Oxford, England: Alden.

Hathaway, S.R., & Meehl, P.E. (1951). *An atlas for the clinical use of the MMPI*. Minneapolis: University of Minnesota Press.

Hinton, J.W. (Ed.). (1983). *Dangerousness: Problems of assessment and prediction*. Winchester, MA: Allen and Unwin.

Hollon, S.D., & Beck, A.T. (1979). Cognitive therapy of depression. In P.C. Kendall & S.D. Hollon (Eds.), *Cognitive behavioral interventions: Theory, research and procedures*. New York: Academic Press.

Kozol, H. (1975). The diagnosis of dangerousness. In S. Pasternak (Ed.), *Violence and victims*. New York: Spectrum.

Lazarus, R.S., & Folkman, S. (1984). *Stress, appraisal and coping*. New York: Springer Publishing.

Martin, D. (1981). *Battered wives (rev. ed.)*. San Francisco: Volcano Press.

Menzies, R.J., Webster, C.D., & Sepejak, D.S. (1985). The dimensions of dangerousness. *Law and Human Behavior*, 9(1), 49–70.

Monahan, J. (1981). *Predicting violent behavior: An assessment of clinical techniques*. Beverly Hills: Sage Publications.

Murphy, W. (1985, August). The male batterer: Working with anger and violence. Paper presented at the 93rd Annual Convention of the American Psychological Association, Los Angeles, CA.

Pesner, J. (1985, August). *Psychologist as cop*. Paper presented at the 93rd Annual Convention of the American Psychological Association, Los Angeles, CA.

Rosenbaum, A. (1979). Wife abuse: Characteristics of the participants and etiological considerations (Doctoral dissertation). Dissertation Abstracts International, 40, 1383–1388.

Rosewater, L.B. (1985). Schizophrenic, borderline or battered. In L.B. Rosewater & L.E. Walker (Eds.), *Handbook of feminist therapy: Women's issues in psychotherapy*. New York: Springer Publishing.

Rounsaville, B.J., & Weissman, M.M. (1977). Battered women: A medical problem requiring detection. *International Journal of Psychiatry*, 8, 191–202.

Russell, D.E.H. (1984). *Sexual exploitation: Rape, child sexual abuse and workplace harassment*. Beverly Hills: Sage.

San Francisco Family Violence Project. (1982). Domestic violence is a crime. San Francisco: Author.

Saunders, D. (1982). Counseling the violent husband. In P.A. Keller & L.G. Ritt (Eds.), *Innovations in clinical practice: A source book:* Vol. 1. Sarasota, FL: Professional Resource Exchange.

Schechter, S. (1982). *Women and male violence*. Boston: South End.

Searle, M. (1985). Introduction. In D.J. Sonkin, D. Martin, & L.E.A. Walker, *The male batterer: A treatment approach*. New York: Springer Publishing Co.

Sonkin, D.J. (1986). Clairvoyance vs. common sense: Therapist's duty to warn and protect. *Violence and Victims*, 1(1) 7–21.

Sonkin, D.J. (1985). Final report: Domestic violence treatment program. Oak Knoll Naval Hospital, Family Advocacy Program, Oakland, CA.

Sonkin, D., & Durphy, M. (1982). *Learning to live without violence: A handbook for men*. San Francisco: Volcano.

Sonkin, D.J., Martin, D., & Walker, L.E.A. (1985). *The male batterer: A treatment approach*. New York: Springer Publishing Co.

Steadman, H. (1977). A new look at recidivism among Patuxent inmates. *The Bulletin of the American Academy of Psychiatry and the Law*, 5, 200–209.

Steadman, H., & Cocozza, J. (1974). *Careers of the criminally insane*. Lexington, MA: Lexington Books.

Straus, M.A., Gelles, R.J., & Steinmetz, S.K. (1980). *Behind closed doors: Violence in the American family*. New York: Anchor-Doubleday.

Thyfault, R. (1984). Self-defense: Battered women on trial. *California Law Review*,

20, 485–510.

Thyfault, R. (1980, October). *Childhood sexual abuse, marital rape and battered women: Implications for mental health workers.* Paper presented at the Annual Meeting of the Colorado Mental Health Conference, Keystone, CO.

Walker, L.E.A. (1979). *The battered woman.* New York: Harper & Row.

Walker, L.E.A. (1984). *The battered woman syndrome.* New York: Springer Publishing Co.

Walker, L.E.A. (1985). Feminist forensic psychology. In L.B. Rosewater and L.E.A. Walker (Eds.), *Handbook of feminist therapy: Women's Issues in Psychotherapy.* New York: Springer Publishing.

Werner, P.D., Rose, T.L., & Yesavage, J.A. (1983). Reliability, accuracy and decision making strategy in clinical predictions of imminent dangerousness. *Journal of Counsulting and Clinical Psychology, 51*(6), 815–825.

11

Domestic Violence: The Skeleton in *Tarasoff's* Closet*

Mary McNeill

News accounts of random street attacks and televised depictions of brutal slayings continually remind us of imminent violence. Ironically, they also divert our attention from the arena in which deadly assaults are most likely to occur—the family home. Contrary to popular belief, homicide statistics nationwide reflect that lethal assaults are far more likely to be perpetrated by intimates than by strangers. While we have spent considerable energy focusing on, if not solving, random street violence, we have historically turned our backs on the chronic, foreseeable violence inflicted by "loved ones."

Mounting community pressure and lawsuits have recently forced law enforcement and social service agencies to change their response to violence in the home. Interestingly enough, one lawsuit, which was directed at the psychotheraputic community that has given rise to such change, has affected the problem of spousal abuse without ever having intended to. It seems poetically fitting that a major salve for the hidden problem of domestic violence should itself be hidden in a case in which domestic violence was never mentioned.

THE *TARASOFF* CASE

In a 1976 landmark case, *Tarasoff* v. *Regents of the University of California* (*Tarasoff II*), the parents of a young college student sued the University of

---

* I would like to thank Catherine Campbell for her help in organizing the original draft of this paper and for her tireless support throughout. I am also indebted to Jack Orrock for his generous technical assistance and Professors Leo O'Brien and D. Kelly Weisberg of Hastings College of the Law for their guidance and suggestions.

California, including its campus police and mental health departments, over the death of their daughter, Tatiana Tarasoff. They claimed that the student who murdered their daughter had told campus authorities beforehand about his plans to kill her and that the campus authorities should have warned them or Tatiana about her danger. After a lengthy legal battle that involved the issuance of two separate decisions, the California Supreme Court agreed with the parents. It ruled that psychotherapists who have reason to believe that a patient poses a hazard to a foreseeable victim owe a duty of care to protect that victim. Toward that end, the court noted that psychotherapists may be required to take "one or more of various steps, depending upon the nature of the case. [It] may call for them to warn the intended victim of the danger, to notify the police, or to take whatever other steps are reasonably necessary under the circumstances" (*Tarasoff II*: 431). "Psychotherapist" is defined in California Evidence Code, section 1010, as:

(a) A person authorized, or reasonably believed by the patient to be authorized, to practice medicine in any state or nation who devotes . . . a substantial portion of his or her time to the practice of psychiatry;

(b) A person licensed as a psychologist;

(c) A person licensed as a clinical social worker . . . when he or she is engaged in applied psychotherapy of a nonmedical nature;

(d) A person who is serving as a school psychologist and holds a [state issued] credential;

(e) A person licensed as a marriage, family and child counselor.

It is noteworthy, however, that the *Tarasoff* court's imposition of a duty on the psychotherapeutic community to protect foreseeable victims turned on the *special relationship* created between the psychotherapist and the patient. *Special relationships* have been found to arise in other contexts between hospitals and patients, innkeepers and guests, common carriers and their passengers, teachers and students, jailors and their prisoners, and parents and their children, among others. Hence, it appears that the logic of the *Tarasoff* decision could easily be extended to other actors who stand in a special relationship to another or who have the inherent ability to control another's conduct.

Although the *Tarasoff* case was decided in California and is binding only on that state's psychotherapists, it met a nationwide response. This may have been due to concerns that other states might adopt the decision's requirements or that the duty to protect foreseeable victims might be extended to other individuals. In its aftermath, critics from both legal and mental health professions anticipated the decision's impact on the future of psychotherapy. Most predicted that it would spell the demise of the profession. They argued that clients would abandon therapy if informed that their candid statements therein could be transmitted to police or potential victims, and they suggested that therapists would refuse to take on potentially violent clients for fear of liability. Only a few commentators believed that the decision would have minor impact.

Now, a decade after the *Tarasoff* decision was issued, it appears that the critics' gloomy prognoses were unfounded. While *Tarasoff* may have affected treatment practices, that impact, as discussed below, may well be interpreted as positive by many in the field. What is of interest, however, is that after ten years' time and the publication of scores of law review articles analyzing the decision, a vital aspect of *Tarasoff* remains unmentioned. Though virtually every case that the California Supreme Court relied on in deciding *Tarasoff* involved domestic violence, and nearly every case where psychotherapists have been found liable for failing to protect readily identifiable victims based upon *Tarasoff*'s rationale have involved domestic violence, those facts are consistently unmentioned in the commentaries.

The nexus between domestic violence and a therapist's liability for failure to protect foreseeable victims is critical for two reasons. First, understanding that link may affect our view of *Tarasoff*'s merits and its rationale. Second, the decision takes on a completely different practical import when its relationship to domestic violence, a problem of enormous lethality and prevalence, is seen. This is particularly true in light of recent nationwide policy changes in the field of domestic violence.

In the discussion that follows, *Tarasoff*'s facts will be reviewed and related cases that have been decided in its wake will be described. Critics' concerns about *Tarasoff* will then be examined with an eye toward identifying areas where practicing therapists should direct their attention. At that point, an alternative analysis of *Tarasoff* and its role in the management of potentially volatile clients will be offered, along with practical strategies for handling such cases. Clarifying the meaning of the case, identifying its vital link to the problem of domestic violence, discussing its likely relation to new nationwide policies on domestic violence, and offering practical strategies for avoiding *Tarasoff* liability may help therapists begin to see the decision as a tool in handling volatile clients rather than a Sword of Damocles dangling over them.

BACKGROUND ON THE *TARASOFF* CASE

In 1969, Prosenjit Poddar, a graduate student from Bengal, India, was undergoing outpatient therapy at Berkeley's campus hospital. Poddar was distraught with unrequited love and informed his therapist that he planned to kill an unnamed girl, who was readily identifiable as Tatiana Tarasoff, when she returned home from spending the summer in Brazil. In October, after Tatiana had returned, Poddar stopped attending therapy. At that point his therapist, a Dr. Moore, conferred with two other doctors, and the three agreed that Poddar should be committed for observation in a mental hospital. Campus police assisted in taking Poddar into custody, but after obtaining his promise to stay away from Tatiana, released him, satisfied that he was rational. Thereafter, a Dr. Powelson, Moore's superior who had been absent during these events, asked the police to return or destroy all writings in their possession pertaining to Poddar and to take no further action. Shortly thereafter, Poddar went to Tatiana's home, found her there alone, and stabbed her to death.

Poddar was tried, eventually convicted of voluntary manslaughter, and served time in Vacaville, a state medical/penal facility. Following the criminal proceedings, Tatiana's parents brought a civil suit, charging that the Regents of the University, the therapists involved, and the police were negligent in failing to commit Poddar and warn them of their daughter's peril. The trial court dismissed the complaint, holding that there was no legal basis under California law to sustain a claim against the defendants. The court of appeal affirmed the dismissal [at 108 Cal. Rptr. 878, 33 Cal. App. 3d 275 (1973)], and the parents appealed to the California Supreme Court.

In the first of the two *Tarasoff* decisions ultimately handed down by the court (*Tarasoff I*), the Supreme Court noted that where therapists had determined that the medical or psychological condition of their patient might give rise to danger, they incurred a *duty to warn* the victim or others who could have been expected to warn him/her of the peril. This result was well publicized by many mental health organizations, leading to widespread familiarity with the "duty to warn" requirement.

Unfortunately, when the court granted a rehearing and changed the standard of care that psychotherapists were expected to exercise, the second version was less publicized. In *Tarasoff II*, the court backed away from a strict *duty to warn* and broadened the options that a psychotherapist might exercise when faced with a client who was in danger of losing control. As noted above, the new duty owed to a foreseeable victim under the final *Tarasoff* decision was a *duty of care to protect that victim*. While the difference may seem like hair splitting to some, it does afford more flexibility to the therapist who might consider calling the police, detaining the client for observation, or taking other steps where appropriate.

INTERPRETING *TARASOFF*

Critics charged that the California Supreme Court in issuing the *Tarasoff* decision was expecting psychotherapists to be telepathic. This concern was echoed by many prestigious mental health organizations that submitted briefs to the court arguing against such abilities. The court responded by saying that the prediction of violence is unnecessary for avoiding liability for a client's unforeseen violent acts. What the court does expect of psychotherapists based upon *Tarasoff*, however, is a two step process:

1. They must exercise a reasonable degree of skill, knowledge and care ordinarily possessed and exercised by members of their profession.
2. Having exercised such a reasonable degree of skill, therapists who find that a patient poses a serious danger of violence to others bear a duty to exercise reasonable care to protect the foreseeable victim of such danger. (*Tarasoff II*, 438–439.)

What these requirements suggest on a practical level is that in order to exercise a reasonable degree of care, therapists will have to begin to inquire about a patient's violent propensities. If there is any reason to believe that a client may be prone to violence, that issue should be raised at an initial interview with the client. Conscientious (or cautious) therapists will likely inquire routinely into the client's past or potential violence at the onset of the theraputic relationship, whether indications of violent tendencies are presented or not. Fundamental as one's assaultive behavior may seem to the question of mental health, it appears from the literature that many therapists are actually loathe to approach the subject.

If therapists, upon raising the issue of violence, find that a client has violent propensities, they must begin to monitor those propensities in the course of regular contact with the client. Indicators for assessing the likelihood of a violent episode must be identified and considered. Perhaps the most obvious indicator of probable violence would be seen where a client has a history of repeated violent acts or has been incarcerated for violent behavior. The following indicators should be considered as well:

- The extent to which the client appears to have a plan as distinguished from a fantasy;
- Whether the client has the present ability to carry out the plan;
- The specificity with which the client describes the plan;
- Whether the client has targeted a victim or a victim is reasonably foreseeable in light of knowledge in the therapist's possession;
- Whether triggering events are attached to the plan that will cause the client to activate it upon the occurrence of some condition;
- Whether a dramatic or sudden change in the client's circumstance has occurred, such as divorce, loss of job, infidelity of a spouse, romantic rejection, failure in an educational setting, humiliation caused by a known person, or death of a loved one;
- Whether any steps have been taken to execute that plan, such as purchasing weapon or other dangerous materials, buying an airline ticket to visit the intended victim, saving money toward the objective,

sending threats to the victim directly or through third parties, or performing minor acts as a prelude to the intended grand finale.

Assuming that the therapist does identify indicators of potential violence, those indicators are, alone, insufficient to trigger a *Tarasoff* duty to exercise reasonable care to protect a victim. Before such a duty will arise, the victim must be *foreseeable*. That does not mean that the victim must be *named*; as noted in *Tarasoff*, the fact that the victim was readily identifiable to the therapist based upon his past contact with the client was sufficient. Nevertheless, in post-*Tarasoff* decisions the court has clarified that therapists will not be held liable for harm to a victim who has not been targeted.

One example of the court's requirement of foreseeability was a 1980 case, *Thompson* v. *County of Alameda*, 27 Cal. 3d 741 (1980). There, the court refused to impose liability on a county institution for releasing a juvenile offender without a warning. The county knew that the juvenile had "latent, extremely dangerous and violent propensities regarding young children and that sexual assaults upon young children and violence connected therewith were a likely result of releasing [him] into the community" (*Thompson*, 746). Moreover, the juvenile had informed the county that if released he would take the life of a young child in his neighborhood. Despite these facts, the juvenile was released for a temporary leave into his mother's custody with no warning to his mother or to the neighborhood; less than 24 hours later, he killed a 5-year-old child. Finding that the 5-year-old boy was not a foreseeable victim, the court refused to find the county liable for failing to issue warnings. By denying liability in the face of such unsympathetic facts, the court sent out a loud message that it does not intend to impose *Tarasoff* liability for generalized threats. This result should assuage the fears of *Tarasoff* critics dismayed by the prospect of issuing wholesale warnings over their clients' threats.

The court has limited the instances in which it will impose *Tarasoff* liability on therapists by confining it to foreseeable victims and by requiring only the exercise of a reasonable degree of care, skill, or knowledge possessed by professional peers in the detection of potential violence. Still, there are ways in which potential liability has been extended for therapists by virtue of the fact that other bodies of law have an impact on *Tarasoff*. A cursory glance at two decisions that have had the effect of expanding *Tarasoff* follows, so that their requirements may also be kept in mind.

CASES EXTENDING *TARASOFF* DUTY

In *Tarasoff*'s aftermath, two domestic violence cases resulted in decisions that have extended the *Tarasoff* duty to exercise care to protect foreseeable victims.

The first of those cases in *Hedlund* v. *Superior Court*, 34 Cal. 3d 695 (1983), involving an unmarried couple, La Nita and Steven Wilson, who shared a last name by coincidence. During the course of the Wilsons' therapy with the defense psychologists, Stephen, in La Nita's absence, informed his therapists that he intended to commit serious bodily injury upon her. Thereafter, while La Nita was seated next to her 3-year-old boy, Darryl, Stephen shot her with a shotgun. La Nita threw herself over her child, thereby saving his life.

In a suit against the psychologists, La Nita and Darryl argued that the defense psychologists were professionally negligent in failing to diagnose Stephen's dangerousness and warn La Nita of her peril. Further, they urged that Darryl should recover by virtue of his close relationship to his mother, which made his harm foreseeable as well. The California Supreme Court agreed. It found that the psychologists were liable for La Nita's harm by failing to meet the two-step requirements of *Tarasoff*: the duty to diagnose Stephen's violent tendencies using a reasonable degree of skill, knowledge, and care ordinarily possessed by other members of their profession; and the duty to exercise reasonable care to protect La Nita from that potential violence.

Liability for Darryl's harm was based on different legal reasoning, however. Because Stephen had never threatened to harm Darryl, Darryl was not a foreseeable victim as defined by *Tarasoff*. Other existing areas of personal injury tort law provided precedent for finding Darryl foreseeable, however. In a growing body of cases unrelated to *Tarasoff*, the court has, in recent years, consistently allowed family members or those in a very close relationship to a victim to recover for the severe emotional trauma that they suffer when their loved one is harmed by another's negligence. In *Dillon* v. *Legg*, 68 Cal. 3d 728 (1968), one of the best known of these cases, the court allowed an emotionally traumatized mother to recover money damages from a negligent driver after she saw the driver run over and kill her toddler son. Relying on the logic of the *Dillon* case, the court similarly found that Darryl should recover for the trauma he experienced when witnessing his mother's shooting.

Some have argued that the result of the *Hedlund* and *Dillon* cases is that once a duty to one individual is breached (as, for instance, the duty to La Nita was breached by the psychologists after Stephen identified her as his intended victim), defendants may be liable to the whole world for the results of their negligence (Laughran & Bakken, 1984, p. 6). Such assertions are unfounded and serve only to alarm and paralyze the psychotheraputic community. As explained above, the court will impose liability only where the harm is *foreseeable*, and that liability will extend to others only if they are family members or have close ties to the victim such that they, too, are foreseeably harmed by the suffering of a loved one. The Court's refusal in *Thompson* to create a duty to respond to generalized threats makes this quite clear:

We are skeptical of any new benefit which might flow from a duty to issue a generalized warning of the probationary release of offenders. In our view, the generalized warnings sought to be required here would do little to increase the precautions of any particular members of the public who already have become conditioned to locking their doors, avoiding dark and deserted streets, instructing their children to beware of strangers and taking other precautions. (*Thompson*: 755)

The second case that expanded upon *Tarasoff*'s reach was *Jablonski by Pahls* v. *United States,* 712 F2d 391 (1983). In *Jablonski*, the U.S. Court of Appeals, Ninth Circuit, applied California law and found psychiatrists of Loma Linda Veterans Administration Hospital liable for harm to a victim despite the fact that their patient never made specific threats toward the victim. While such liability may seem outrageous at first blush, a look at the facts of *Jablonski* shows that the case does not really change *Tarasoff*. In fact, the psychiatrists were found liable for failing to meet the first step of *Tarasoff*'s requirements: the duty to diagnose violent tendencies using the reasonable degree of care, knowledge, and skill possessed by other members of the profession.

The psychiatrists in *Jablonski* knew that their patient, Phillip Jablonski, was referred to them by the police department and that he had an extensive prior criminal record. Upon interviewing Jablonski, they learned that he had served a five-year prison term for raping his former wife and that he had previously been treated for psychiatric problems. He admitted that he had a chronic problem with violent reactions, but he was vague as to his prior treatment and refused to commit himself voluntarily for inpatient treatment. Both doctors concluded that Jablonski was dangerous and that his case was an emergency, but found no basis for involuntarily committing him; nor did they seek his prior medical records. Instead, they scheduled him for more tests and gave him Valium.

During the course of several visits to the hospital, Jablonski's companion, Melissa Kimball, expressed her fear of him to his psychiatrists. Though they suggested that perhaps she should live apart from him if she were fearful, the psychiatrists' advice was never posed in the form of a warning, nor did the psychiatrists take other steps to secure her safety. Kimball finally did move out Jablonski's apartment at the urging of her priest, but upon returning there to retrieve baby diapers she was met by Jablonski, who attacked and murdered her.

As it turns out, had Jablonski's psychiatrists obtained his medical records, which were readily available by phone from another Veterans Administration Hospital, they would have had ample grounds for involuntarily committing him for observation. His records revealed that he had a history of extensive treatment at an army hospital, that he had a "homicidal ideation toward his wife, whom he had tried to kill on several occasions," that he "had probably suffered a psychotic break and the possibility of future violent behavior was a distinct probability," that he was "demonstrating some masculine identification in beating his wife as his father did frequently to his mother," and that he had a "schizophrenic reaction, undifferentiated type, chronic, moderate; manifested by homicidal behavior toward his wife." (*Jablonski*: 393–94.)

Following the murder, Kimball's daughter, Meghan, sued Jablonski's doctors for malpractice, which she argued was responsible for her mother's death. The court agreed that Meghan had proven claims of malpractice for (1) failing to record and transmit information provided to them by the police regarding Phillip's dangerousness, (2) failing to obtain past medical records, and (3) failing to adequately warn Kimball pursuant to *Tarasoff's* requirements.

Some commentators have suggested that "the acts of malpractice [in *Jablonski*] appear to be fairly remote under the circumstances, and none explain how Kimball could have been more adequately warned." (Laughran & Bakken, 1984, p. 26.) Such comments raise the question of just what the therapist's responsibility is when s/he is aware that a client has a history of violence. Here, Jablonski's psychiatrists knew that he was referred by the police department, that he had served a five-year prison term for rape, and that he was, by his own admission, a veteran who had a chronic problem with violent reactions. The doctors observed that Jablonski was being vague about his prior treatment, and they concluded that he was dangerous. In light of these facts, their irresponsibility in failing to obtain his prior medical records, which were available by phone from their own organization, does not seem a "remote" instance of malpractice. Treatment of manifestly violent patients requires a vigilant posture; offering Valium and a future appointment would appear to fall short of vigilance.

With regard to the "warning" issue, to discharge their *Tarasoff* responsibility, the doctors were required to take steps to protect Kimball. True, Jablonski had not verbally targeted her, but his medical records would have immediately alerted the doctors to her danger. As the *Tarasoff* case itself noted, the victim need not be named so long as s/he is foreseeable. Here, Kimball indicated her fear of Jablonski to the doctors. Although they mentioned staying away from Jablonski as one option, it does not appear that they squarely approached her with cautionary information; rather, their suggestion that she relocate was a casual response to her reports of fear. It is noteworthy that when she was squarely admonished about Jablonski's danger by her priest, she did move out of the house that she had been sharing with him. Perhaps without receiving a direct assessment of Jablonski's status from his doctors, she was unclear about what definite steps she should take.

Some suggest that it was Kimball's fault for not withdrawing when she was admittedly fearful of Jablonski. Unfortunately, that suggestion is at odds with the natural tendencies of family members or intimates when faced with the crisis of a loved one. In the absence of contrary guidance, many will try to lend support to the troubled individual. Therapists are in a unique position to protect those well-intentioned associates of their clients by using the knowledge that they alone may be privy to and taking steps to avert probable harm.

EVALUATING CRITICISM OF *TARASOFF* DUTY

The psychotherapist's duty to assist in averting harm to foreseeable victims has been repeatedly attacked by many in the mental health and legal communities. They argue that such a duty would "imperil the therapeutic alliance and destroy the patients' expectation of confidentiality, thereby thwarting effective treatment" and "diminish the ability and motivation of therapists to treat effectively mentally disturbed and potentially dangerous people" (Stone, 1976, pp. 368, 373). While one commentator felt that *Tarasoff* would not "drastically affect the psychiatrist as it has long been the general practice to discreetly warn appropriate individuals or law enforcement authorities when a patient presents a distinct and immediate threat to someone," he offered a minority viewpoint (Slovenko, 1975, pp. 392–393).

To evaluate *Tarasoff*'s merits, it is necessary to look beyond critics' contentions, for their views of the duty to protect foreseeable victims are likely influenced by factors of which they may not be consciously aware. One of those factors, it may be argued, is a legal tradition in our society that frees people from any responsibility to aid others who are in peril. While 22 different countries have statutes requiring citizens to aid people who are endangered (Feldbrugge, 1966, pp. 655–657), only three states—Vermont, Minnesota, and Rhode Island—have statutes requiring such assistance (Prosser & Keeton, 1984, p. 375, n.21). Our legal history is replete with instances in which people have stood by and watched while a friend beats a baby to death, a woman is raped, or a man is drowning while life preservers are readily available; yet no crimes are charged as a result. That is simply because in all but three states it is not against the law to be an indifferent bystander, no matter how heinous the crime, so long as there is no formal relation between the bystander and the victim (e.g., parent–child, doctor–patient, student–teacher, etc.). This legal tradition no doubt affects the views of many when faced with the need to protect another from peril.

The second factor that may influence our views of *Tarasoff* duty is public perception of domestic violence. Though the cases giving rise to *Tarasoff*, *Tarasoff* itself, *Hedlund*, and *Jablonski* have all involved domestic violence, that fact has gone unmentioned by virtually all of the commentators. The failure to notice that all of these cases involve violence committed against intimates is consistent with patterns generally attending the problem of battering. Typically, the offender denies and minimizes his violence, the victim colludes in covering it up due to her embarrassment, and those victims who do come forward to seek help are disregarded by a society that views the family home as an arena beyond scrutiny. In all, it is as if the problem does not exist.

When our societal reluctance to intervene on behalf of others and our tendency to ignore or minimize the existence of domestic violence are viewed in tandem, the hidden sources of resistance to *Tarasoff's* requirements are uncovered. This uncovering helps to explain why some criticisms actually lodged against the decision have seemed inadequate when measured against the degree of condemnation that it has received. The following are examples of criticisms or reactions frequently expressed.

Moral Dilemma for the Psychotherapist

Critics argue that the duty to disclose a patient's imminent violence poses a personal, moral dilemma for therapists who may feel that they are betraying the client.

A recent nationwide study of 3,000 mental health professionals suggests that this claim is unfounded. Between 75 and 85% of all those surveyed felt that *Tarasoff's* requirement of exercising reasonable care to protect foreseeable victims applied as a matter of personal ethics—whether or not the law so provided (Givelber, Bowers, & Blitch, 1984, pp. 474–475).

Deterrent to Taking on Potentially Dangerous Clients

Refuted by the same study was the claim that *Tarasoff's* existence and the fear of liability among mental health professionals would make them more reluctant to accept volatile clients and more willing to "dump" violent clients, once identified. In fact, among psychiatrists, the opposite was true. Those who believed that they were legally bound by *Tarasoff's* requirements showed a great willingness to treat dangerous patients and less willingness to terminate them once they were identified as dangerous.

Burden on Theraputic Community to Predict Violence

Responding to *Tarasoff's* opponents, who urged that the decision burdened the therapeutic community with the impossible task of predicting violence, the survey asked therapists about their abilities in that regard. Of those responding, only 5% felt that it was impossible to predict violence. Over 75% felt that they could make a prediction ranging from "probable" to "certain"

(Givelber et al., 1984, p. 463). The therapists queried were also fairly confident that their peers would agree with their assessment of their client's dangerousness. Seventy percent believed that 90–100% of their colleagues would agree with their conclusions. Whether or not such assessment abilities exist, the researchers noted that "Therapists appear to believe that there are objective professional standards for evaluating dangerousness . . . . If therapists believe there are common professional standards or practices, it is difficult to fault a court for believing so also" (Givelber et al., 1984, p. 464).

In addressing this concern about prediction, critics may be understating the abilities of most therapists by suggesting that they are incapable of distinguishing between amorphous fantasies and imminent threats. Most observers would readily see a difference between "God, I feel so bad; I wish I could disappear" and "I can't take this anymore; I bought a gun today and I'm gonna use it." Similarly, the difference between "I hate that bitch! If she doesn't wanna be with me, she's not gonna be with anybody. I'm gonna fix her so that nobody'll wanna have her" versus "She makes me so mad I could ring her neck" can also be seen. There are bound to be threats that fall in a gray area, but to avoid a malpractice claim the therapist need only exercise reasonable care, not forecasting abilities.

Concern That Clients Will Avoid Therapy

Critics argue that *Tarasoff* requirements may discourage clients from participating in therapy when they learn that their therapist may reveal information gained in the course of a therapy session. Yet little evidence has been offered to show that clients inquire about confidentiality and its exceptions or that they would refrain from beginning therapy if they knew that their therapists were obliged to protect a potential victim. Until recently, most states have not acknowledged a psychotherapist/patient privilege that acts to preserve the confidentiality of a client's disclosures in therapy in the event that the therapist is asked to testify. This absence of privilege has not prevented a tremendous increase in the use of therapy. As one judge noted, "[W]e cannot blind ourselves to the fact that the practice of psychotherapy has grown, indeed flourished, in an environment of non-absolute privilege" [*In re Lifschutz*, 2 Cal. 3d 426 (1970)]. It is entirely possible that, if polled, clients might support a policy requiring their therapists to intervene should harm appear imminent.

Concern That *Tarasoff* Will Undermine Psychotherapeutic Practices

According to critics, the duty to divulge or act on a client's threats will undermine the entire process of psychotherapy. In an early study conducted approximately one year after *Tarasoff II*, which took a very critical view of the case, the researchers were forced to concede that *"Tarasoff* did not mandate a radical change in therapeutic practice . . ."* (Stanford Study, 1978, p. 190). Among the deleterious effects attributed to the decision, the authors noted that:

> Many therapists now devote added time and attention to the problem of their patients' propensities to violence, both by talking more with their patients about violence and by concentrating their clinical energies on minor threats uttered by their patients. [Footnote omitted.] Therapists also report spending more time in therapy discussing with their patients the general issue of confidentiality and the specific circumstances under which they may feel legally compelled to breach it. (p. 187)

Why these effects are characterized as negative is unclear. Delving into a patient's violent propensities may be constructive; patients may seek out therapy to address such problems. Where commission of violent acts is destructive both to the victim and the offender who may face criminal sanctions, it appears that it may be in the patient's interest to explore these issues where symptoms of potentially violent behavior arise.

It is also interesting that the authors of the Stanford Study suggest that spending time on minor threats uttered by clients is a waste of time. It would seem that threats, no matter how minor, are symptomatic of the larger issues presented by a client. Those threats could provide useful starting points for exploring issues of anger, guilt, and rejection and for developing methods for coping with those feelings.

Concerns about Confidentiality Generally

The author of the Stanford Study notes a "strong reluctance among therapists to discuss confidentiality with their patients . . ." and adds,

> Therapists may therefore fear that any legal duty they have to divulge private communication may . . . harm the therapeutic relationship by disabusing patients of their comforting illusion of absolute confidentiality. If the therapists' apparent preference for not discussing the issue of confidentiality . . . reflects a clinical principle that patients make more complete disclosures . . . crucial to successful treatment when . . . ignorant of possible breaches of confidentiality, then *Tarasoff* may harm therapy by removing the illusion of absolute confidentiality. (Stanford Study, 1978, p. 184)

This conjecture suggests that therapists know what their patients think about confidentiality, when the authors admit that there is a strong reluctance even to bring up the subject. In their paternalistic effort to avoid exposing patients to the truth, some therapists may be obscuring their own discomfort in openly broaching the topic of confidentiality. Yet these assertions are offered as "clinical principles." Like the suicide-prone patient who asks for help by forewarning others of his intentions, the patient who utters specific threats in the presence of his therapist may also be hoping that the therapist will set limits. This suggestion does not appear to have been considered.

Just as raising the issue of violence may be constructive for the therapeutic relatonship, so may raising the issue of confidentiality be similarly positive. A candid discussion about confidentiality at the inception of a therapeutic relationship, if handled sensitively, may serve to build trust, create important limits, and define parameters of the relationship between the therapist and client.

Confidentiality as Overriding

The belief that confidentiality must always override other concerns is an issue that critics raise, yet inadequately address. Perhaps part of the problem is that some therapists have avoided the issue of their clients' violence altogether, and as a result are unaware of the harm that they inflict. When the activities occurring outside of therapy are seen as beyond the clinician's responsibility, it is not surprising that divulging a client's harmful plans would seem inappropriate.

A policy of more active monitoring of violence is important for many reasons. The first is that initiating a therapeutic relationship can actually trigger a violent episode due to the predictable anxieties that accompany seeing a therapist for the first time. This is especially true if the client is participating in therapy "involuntarily," due to coercion from a partner or a court's mandate. Involutary clients may be more resistant to therapy, more distrustful of therapists, and more susceptible to the anxiety that discussing problems with a therapist-stranger can sometimes induce.

A second consideration is that it may *not* be in clients' best interest to avoid responding to their threats. Where unchecked threats materialize into lethal acts, both the victim and the client are harmed. The disastrous effects of committing a homicide or burning a house down weigh heavily on a client whose bleak future may include incarceration, ostracism, loss of self-esteem, and alienation—not to mention unemployability.

Some experts reject the idea that clients who are rapidly losing control do not want their therapists to intervene. Slovenko writes, "Trust—not absolute confidentiality—is the cornerstone of psychotherapy. Talking about a patient or writing about him without his knowledge and consent would be a breach of trust. But imposing self-control where self-control breaks down is not a breach of trust when it is not deceptive" (1975, p. 395.) John R. Lion maintains that "violent patients are frightened of their own hostile urges and desperately seek help in preventing a loss of control." He adds that:

[V]iolent patients are very much afraid of their own impulses. The homicidal patient ... wants control furnished so that he will not kill. Therefore, ... the psychiatrist should assure him that he will not be allowed to act upon his feelings .... [T]he psychiatrist elicits the emotions and some of the accompanying fantasy, but firmly conveys to the patient that he will be prevented from any violent act. The latter statement is usually most reassuring to the patient. (Slovenko, 1975, p. 393)

Consistent with this view are the thoughts of Dr. Emanuel Tanay, an expert on homicide:

A patient in treatment has the right to expect from his therapist a rescue intervention in the face of realistic danger. *To be the perpetrator of a homicide is one of the most self-destructive actions one can take.* The therapist as a human being also has an obligation to an innocent victim and, last but not least, he has a duty to his own human dignity .... There are many areas where the law has intervened unnecessarily into the practice of mental health professionals. [The *Tarasoff* case] is not such a situation. The decision does not require a therapist to report a fantasy .... It simply means that when he is realistically convinced that a homicide is in the making, it is his duty to act like a human being and not a robot. (Slovenko, 1975, p. 393)

The conscientious therapist who monitors clients' violent tendencies and intervenes when harm is imminent faces in admittedly difficult situation. Unfortunately, those difficulties have been misrepresented and, in many instances, magnified by critics. Such misrepresentation has caused many therapists to thwart *Tarasoff's* requirements rather than embrace them. In spite of the challenges that *Tarasoff* may offer to therapists, the value of the decision must be kept in mind. The court was attempting to address vital problems through the decision and those problems must be kept in mind:

Our current crowded and computerized society compels the interdependence of its members. In this risk infested society we can hardly tolerate the further exposure to danger that would result from a concealed knowledge of the therapist that his patient was lethal. If the exercise of reasonable care to protect the threatened victim requires the therapist to warn the endangered party or those who can reasonably be expected to notify him, we see no sufficient societal interest that would protect and justify concealment. The containment of such risks lies in the public interest. (*Tarasoff II:* 422.)

REDEFINING *TARASOFF*

The criticisms of *Tarasoff* noted above have at times been short-sighted and unfairly lodged. More troubling, however, is the failure of commentators to recognize the thrust of the decision and the arena in which it is likely to be applied. *Tarasoff* requires therapists to act to protect potential victims only where they are foreseeable or targeted. As a result, it is extremely likely that liability for failing to protect a foreseeable victim will be imposed in domestic violence settings, for it is there that victims are most frequently targeted and the potential for violence is greatest. Thus far, nearly every case in which a therapist has been found liable for failing to protect a victim has involved spouses or intimates.

Harm perpetrated against "loved ones" is foreseeable because of the dynamics of battering. The parties involved live in close proximity. They see each other constantly. Their emotional ties bind them to situations that may be destructive and dangerous, yet those same ties continually offer them hope for improvement. As improvement eludes the parties, they become embroiled in a vicious cycle of violence that escalates over time in frequency and severity. This cycle, as documented by psychologist Lenore Walker, is marked by three distinct phases and is self-replicating at intervals that vary from one couple to the next. While assaults may initially be of a minor nature and occur infrequently, Walker points out that over time they may become lethal (Walker, 1979).

The statistics on domestic violence demonstrate its profound lethality and longevity. During 1885 to 1905 in England and Wales, almost 50% of all murder victims were women killed by a spouse or sweetheart (MacDonald, cited in Dobash & Dobash, 1979, pp. 15–16). Fifty-five years later in Philadelphia, the criminologist Marvin Wolfgang reported that 41% of all female murder victims were women killed by their husbands, and one in ten male murder victims was killed by his wife (1958, pp. 213–214). The rates in California are strikingly similar. In 1979, 53% of all female murder victims in the state were killed by a family member. The bulk of these deaths are attributable to the spouse; in a few, the female was killed by a son or daughter (State of California, 1979, 1982).

These homicides were not the result of random, unexpected attacks. In the vast majority of murders the killing was preceded by a protracted history of assaults. In one study, 109 victims were interviewed at shelters for battered women. Forty percent of those victims reported that they had sought medical attention on five separate occasions before coming to the shelter; over 50% reported that they had been beaten more than twice a week (Dobash & Dobash, 1979, p. 109). The Family Violence Project (1982–1984) of San Francisco's District Attorney's Office reports that 63% of victims responded to by their victim services unit required medical treatment for injuries sustained in their most recent assault; and 10% of those victims had been beaten so severely during pregnancy that they miscarried. The escalating nature of these assaults was demonstrated in a Kansas City Police Department study conducted in 1971. There, in 85% of all family homicides, police had been called to the house at least once before; in 50% of the homicides, police had been summoned to intervene five or more times prior to the murder (State of California, 1978, p. 119).

These findings portray the chronic and lethal nature of domestic violence. Still, they do not begin to convey the prevalence of the problem. According to F.B.I. reports, domestic violence is the most underreported crime in the nation and as many as 37% of all families have experienced the problem at one time or another (State of California, 1979, p. 119). In San Francisco, 41% of all incoming assault-related calls to the police department are domestic violence calls (approximately 400 calls per week). The emergency room staff at San Francisco General Hospital reports that 150–200 acutely battered women are treated each month in their facility (which is only one of a dozen or more hospitals in the city proper) (Family Violence Project, 1982–1984).

These figures indicate that domestic violence is a problem of enormous dimensions. Moreover, in light of recent lawsuits and legislative changes, it appears that the problem may become even more prominent. In a recent spate of civil suits across the country, battered women individually and as members of a class have challenged the policy of arrest avoidance practiced by police departments across the country. These suits are leading to the development of policies that seek to put alleged crimes of domestic violence on equal footing with other kinds of crimes (Gee, 1983, p. 554).

These statistics mean two things for therapists concerned about *Tarasoff* malpractice liability. First, regarding the incidence of domestic violence generally, unless therapists are working a very aberrant caseload, they must begin to expect that the some of their clients are either battering or being battered. Keeping in mind that *Tarasoff* liability (via the *Jablonski* case) can arise when a therapist fails adequately to *inquire* about a client's violence (by obtaining medical records, etc.), it will not be enough simply to avoid the issue. Only by confronting and assessing the question of the client's violent propensities, by looking for the problem in medical records, and by broaching the issue with the client can the duty to protect foreseeable victims be discharged.

Second, because of changes in police department policies nationwide, more and more offenders are likely to be identified and arrested and thereby placed in the pool of future potential clients. In states that have diversion programs, such as California's Penal Code Section 1000.6 (better known as Domestic Violence Diversion), many of those offenders who have committed lesser assaults will be allowed to participate in court-ordered counseling instead of facing fines or jail time. This means that therapists who have never before been aware of having batterers in their caseload will be much more likely to see the problem in a manifest way. If a client is sent to therapy specifically to address his or her violent propensities, therapists will have to begin developing skills to reach those clients and pursue such problems.

CONFIDENTIALITY AND THE VOLATILE CLIENT

Given the difficulty of managing a caseload populated by batterers, therapists should consider implementing a confidentiality policy and therapy plan that reflects the potential dangerousness of clients. If outlined at the beginning of therapy rather than invoked midstream, the plan is more likely to gain acceptance from the client.

The requirements of *Tarasoff* make it clear that having a well-articulated confidentiality policy is essential. Some clinicians use a written document that explains clients' rights and the extent to which confidentiality can be assured (Sonkin, Martin, & Walker, 1985). It then details the requirements of *Tarasoff* in layman's terms and explains the therapist's role in averting potential violence. While other therapists choose to explain the policy verbally, it seems that some basic, written statements can be a useful tool for initiating a discussion about confidentiality. Using the reasoning of *Tarasoff*, the therapist can create hypothetical fact patterns illustrating the circumstances under which a disclosure of information obtained in the course of therapy might become necessary.

It is important to reassure clients that a breach of confidentiality would be the rare exception; that absent danger signals they can expect complete confidentiality. Moreover, in the event that a disclosure were warranted, clients should be reassured that only a limited amount of information, sufficient to protect a would-be victim, would be disclosed. Finally, it should be pointed out that a policy of intervention in the face of violence is likely to benefit both clients and their potential victims in the long run. Showing clients that their therapist is concerned about their overall well-being and future stability can serve to build trust into the therapeutic relationship at its inception.

Programs specializing in the treatment of batterers often incorporate contact with the client's spouse into the therapeutic process. Where there is reason to believe that the spouse may be in continued danger, some therapists make it a standard policy to contact the spouse regularly to see if s/he reports assaults that the client failed to mention in therapy. Futher, where clients are referred via court order, the therapist may be required as a condition of therapy to notify the client's probation officer or the court in the event that assaults occur during the course of therapy. If such is the case, these requirements should be discussed with the client at the initial therapy session. While such practices do erode the client's confidentiality in the purest sense, they may also provide important limits that volatile clients need in order to contain assaultive behavior.

Setting limits and clarifying goals, basic as they may seem, are fundamental to the successful treatment of batterers. Therapists who have not worked with violent offenders may fall prey to a therapy mode that is based more on esoteric principles than on practical concepts that deter violence. By identifying realistic goals with the client, explaining in what ways the therapist can facilitate those goals, and incorporating a *Tarasoff* conscious intervention policy that will provide important limits for the client, the therapist will begin to move toward more successful and responsible treatment.

BEYOND THE THREAT OF LIABILITY: OTHER FACTORS SUPPORTING *TARASOFF* DUTY

The need to protect foreseeable victims, to respond to severe and chronic violence, and to act in recognition of the qualitatively different dynamics of psychotherapy that volatile clients create are all factors that justify requiring therapists to disclose their clients' serious threats. Still, there are other reasons of supporting such a duty.

The psychotherapeutic community currently enjoys broad powers. Mental health professionals can involuntarily commit patients to facilities for evaluation; they can offer expert testimony testimony before courts and parole boards regarding the likelihood of an offender's future commission of crimes; and their expert opinions regarding a defendant's or victim's state of mind can mean the difference in a criminal case between a defendant's conviction and outright acquittal. In spite of the claims of *Tarasoff*'s critics, who maintain that they are unable to predict violence, we have long given their views on such subjects considerable weight in courts of law and in mental health inquiries.

Dr. Lee Coleman, in a letter to the California Supreme Court regarding the *Tarasoff* decision, pointed out the irony in the debate over whether therapists should have a duty to victims: "It is hard for me to understand how the psychiatric community can have it both ways—to be free of an obligation to warn on the basis of inability to predict dangerousness, and yet to have the authority to incarcerate patients on the basis of an ability to predict dangerousness." (Coleman, 1975, cited in Ayres & Holbrook, p. 686).

In light of national response trends to domestic violence and the increased pool of volatile clients now being referred by the courts for counseling, therapists are more likely than ever to find explosive clients in their midst. These clients present obvious dangers to partners and to therapists who are unprepared to treat them. Absent a duty to exercise care on behalf of likely victims and to implement corresponding plans for managing violent clients, therapists may find themselves faced with disastrous consequences—for the victims and for themselves. A plan designed to avert harm must incorporate steps for protecting the safety of both victim and therapist. This may include scheduling known violent offenders when other persons are available to step in should problems arise, having prepared lists of reference numbers for easy access (e.g., police, fire, clients' homes, and perhaps even workplace numbers for clients' partners), and even arranging office furniture so that the therapist has an easy means of escape should that become necessary.

The problem with these suggestions and with the general duty to protect victims is that they change the character of many therapists' work. Those who envisioned themselves being armchair observers trained to survey the landscape of clients' thoughts are suddenly faced with requirements leading to intervention. Like police officers who apply for the job expecting to pursue bank robbers and later find that half of their time is spent responding to violent homes, therapists may experience similar grave disappointment in their revised job descriptions. The question becomes whether we shift our orientations so that they coincide with the needs before us or cling to the vision of what we wish our jobs would look like.

The history of battering is long and tragic, with a death toll that climbs daily. While there may be no simple cure for domestic violence, we can attack the extent to which it thrives by disavowing our tolerance of battering and by encouraging intervention. Allowing those with phsycial strength to ventilate in the privacy of their homes the rage amassed from everyday living—with no fear of legal or social repercussions—has resulted in a perverse arrogance among many offenders who honestly believe that they are entitled to beat their partners. That arrogance can only be stripped away by a consistent response from every corner that condemns battering. The buddy who stands by when his friend slaps his wife, the neighbor who ignores the screams from next door, the police who respond to a victim's call but refuse to interfere, and the therapist who fails to respond to a client's pointed threats are all participants in a coverup—a lethal one. They see the potential danger, but they cling to the myth that just beyond this crisis is a family who can work out its own problems. Sadly, that resolution comes for many in the form of death.

The *Tarasoff* case has imposed a duty on therapists to respond to the hidden violence that we have all learned to ignore. Understandably, therapists feel singled out; yet the information they may be privy to can make the difference between life and death. Although *Tarasoff* requires intervention only from those who stand in a formal relationship to the violent party, it might foreshadow a recognition on all our parts that we, too, have a duty to respond to the real and potential violence in our midst.

REFERENCES

Coleman, L. Letter to California Supreme Court, March 11, 1975, quoted in Ayres & Holbrook, Law, psychotherapy, and the duty to warn: A tragic triology? *Baylor Law Review, 27,* 667, 686.

Dillon v. Legg, 68 Cal. 3d 728 (1968).

Dobash, R.E. & Dobash, R. (1979). *Violence against wives: A case against the patriarchy*. New York: Free Press.

Family violence project. (1982–1984). San Francisco: District Attorney's Office.

Feldbrugge. S.J.M. (1966). Good and Bad Samaritans. *American Journal of Comparative Law, 14*, 655–657. (The countries include Albania, Belgium, Bulgaria, Czechoslovakia, Denmark, Ethiopia, Finland, France, Germany, Greece, Hungary, Iceland, Italy, the Netherlands, Norway, Poland, Rumania, Russia, Spain, Turkey, the Ukraine, and Yugoslavia.)

Gee, P. (1983). Ensuring police protection for battered women: The *Scott v. Hart* suit. *Signs, 8*(3), 554. [Copies of the pleadings of *Scott v. Hart* (C–76–2395 N.D. Cal.) are on file with the National Clearinghouse for Legal Services, 500 N. Michigan Ave., Suite 2220, Chicago, IL 60611.]

Givelber, D.J., Bowers, W.J., & Blitch, C.L. (1984). *Tarasoff*, myth and reality: An empirical study of private law in action. *Wisconsin Law Review, 2*, 443.

Hedlund v. Superior Court, 34 Cal.3d 695 (1983).

In re Lifschutz, 2 Cal. 3d 415 (1970).

Jablonski by Pahls v. United States, 712 F.2d 391 (1983).

Laughran, C., & Bakken, G. (1984). The psychotherapist's responsibility toward third parties under current California law. *Western State University Law Reviews, 12*(1).

Prosser, W. & Keetown. (1984). *Torts* (5th ed.). St. Paul, MN: West Publishing.

Slovenko, R. (1975). Psychotherapy and confidentiality. *Cleveland State Law Review, 24*, 375.

Sonkin, D.J., Martin, D., & Walker, L.E.A. (1985). *The male batterer: A treatment approach*. New York: Springer Publishing Co.

Stanford Study. (1978). Where the public peril begins: A survey of psychotherapists to determine the effects of *Tarasoff*. *Stanford Law Review, 31*, 165,166.

State of California, Bureau of Criminal Statistics. (1979). *Homicide in California*. 11, 12, 16. Sacramento, CA: Author.

State of California, Bureau of Criminal Statistics. (1982). *Homicide in California*. 12, 17. Sacramento, CA: Author.

State of California, Senate Subcommittee on Administration of Justice. 1978. *Domestic Violence*. 119. Sacramento, CA: Author.

Stone. A. (1976). The *Tarasoff* decisions: Suing psychotherapists to safeguard society. *Harvard Law Review, 90*, 358.

Tarasoff v. Regents of the University of California, 118 Cal. Rptr. 129, 529 P. 2d 553 (1974). (cited as *Tarasoff I*)

Tarasoff v. Regents of the University of California, 17 Cal. 3d 425 (1976). (cited as *Tarasoff II*)

Thompson v. County of Alameda, 27 Cal. 3d 741 (1980).

Walker, L.E.A. (1979). *The battered woman*. New York: Harper & Row.

Wolfgang, M. (1958). *Patterns in criminal homicide*. New York: Wiley.

12

Domestic Violence Expert Testimony in the Prosecution of Male Batterers

Daniel Jay Sonkin
William Fazio

Prosecuting attorneys have recently begun to utilize domestic violence expert testimony in cases involving male batterers who have seriously assaulted or killed the women they have previously battered. Given the extent of family violence in this society (Gelles, 1974; Straus, Gelles, & Steinmetz, 1980) and the likelihood assaults may escalate to homicides (Boudouris, 1971; Browne, 1986; Chimbos, 1978; National District Attorneys Association, 1978; Walker, 1985), prosecuting attorneys need to familiarize themselves with the dynamics of family violence in order to try such cases effectively. This chapter will discuss how expert testimony can be utilized in the prosecution of highly lethal domestic violence cases. The discussion will include common defenses utilized by attorneys representing male batterers and an example of one case in which expert testimony was successfully incorporated into the trial strategy. By understanding the effects of violence on women and the psychological characteristics of male batterers, the district attorney is able to incorporate valuable expert testimony in the prosecution of domestic violence cases.

EXPERT TESTIMONY IN DOMESTIC VIOLENCE CASES

During the past six years expert testimony has been primarily utilized by defense attorneys in cases in which battered women have killed or assaulted their partners in self-defense (Bende, 1980; Bochnak, 1981; Thyfault, 1984;

218

Thyfault, Bennett, & Hischhorn, Chapter 4 of this text; Thyfault, Browne, & Walker, Chapter 5 of this text; Walker, 1984). More recently, because of the increased number of domestic violence programs across the country that are actively involved in reforming the criminal justice process, prosecutors are responding to this problem more aggressively (Attorney General's Task Force, 1984). Attorneys are developing an understanding of this issue and the skills necessary for the adequate prosecution of domestic violence cases. Many deaths could be averted if early intervention in domestic violence situations is aggressively pursued (Stephens, 1977).

In misdemeanor cases the threat of prosecution may be an adequate motivating force for a defendant to stop his violent behavior and participate in a pretrial diversionary treatment program (Boffey, 1983). For felony cases, probation (post-trial) with treatment may be necessary to motivate a person sufficiently to change his behavior. A plea bargain is an attractive alternative to a conviction that is likely to result in a jail term. However, dispositions are not easily secured in the more serious assault and homicide cases where the defendant denies his guilt. The defense is not as ready to bargain and the prosecution may not have much evidence to bargain with. Frequently in domestic violence cases the only witness is the victim, resulting in her word against his. In addition, many battered women make poor witnesses because of the effect of battering on their self-esteem and confidence (Douglas, Chapter 3 of this text; Walker, 1979, 1984). They may be afraid to testify for fear of retribution from the batterer. An expert witness could be utilized by the prosecution in the following domestic violence cases:

1. When a reluctant assault victim can be assisted by the expert in co-operating with the prosecution;
2. When the expert can provide additional testimony corroborating an assault victim's testimony of her victimization or rebut a defendant's erroneous claims;
3. When the expert witness has had previous contact with a homicide victim;
4. When the expert has not had previous contact with a homicide victim; examine the evidence and the state's witnesses to corroborate the existence of domestic violence;

THE RELUCTANT VICTIM

Why would a victim of family violence be reluctant to testify against her spouse? Battered women and children who are physically or sexually abused are the only victims of violent crime who live with their offender. Frequently, a victim may be subjected to threats, intimidation, or constant pleading by the batterer to not testify against him. Her desire to protect herself from further assaults may be complicated by her concurrent desire to remain married or in her relationship. She may not want to break up the family or be the cause of his losing his job. Her love for him may equal her anger and fear. Her motivation to testify against her partner may wane as a result of his contrition for his violent behavior (Walker, 1979). Given these realities it should be commonplace to expect a victim of family violence to experience a certain amount of reluctance to cooperate with the prosecution.

One way to minimize the possiblity that a victim will refuse to cooperate with the prosecution is to develop structures within the system that support her throughout the criminal justice process. The San Francisco Family Violence Project (1982; Soler, Chapter 2 in this text) developed the victim services unit to address this specific issue. It was found that women were more likely to cooperate with the prosecution when given infomation and support from both the attorneys and office staff from case identification all the way through final disposition and sentencing.

When a specific family violence project does not exist within the prosecutor's office, the attorney must turn to other resources in the community. Battered women's shelters have the staff and expertise to assist women through the criminal justice process. This may include offering the woman counseling, shelter, and assistance in procuring financial assistance for her and her family. Shelter staff may also assist in the transportation to court and be available to offer the needed emotional support during the preceedings.

Shelter staff may also be available to testify in an expert capacity. Testimony explaining to the judge and jury why a victim is reluctant to discuss the details of the violence or why she appears timid or unsure could alleviate their doubts that the victim is telling the truth. Mental health professionals in the community can also serve this purpose, while at the same time appearing to be more neutral since they may not be concurrently advocating for the victim or counseling her.

Specialists in the areas of spouse abuse and child physical and sexual abuse are developing techniques that facilitate the prosecution process while minimizing subsequent trauma to the victim (Thyfault, Browne & Walker, Chapter 5 of this text; Goodman & Rosenberg, Chapter 7 of this text; Walker & Edwall, Chapter 8 of this text). Attorneys need to familiarize themselves with these techniques in order to solicit the victim's cooperation; they also need to know who in their commumity can provide the necessary support to the battered woman during the criminal justice process.

THE MALE BATTERER

Understanding the male batterer is as important as understanding the victim. The attorney must be prepared to rebut a number of accusations and utilize certain of the defendant's behaviors to strengthen the state's case.

Men who batter come from all socioeconomic, occupational, racial, and religious backgrounds (Star, 1979; Straus, Gelles, & Steinmetz, 1980; Giles-Sims, 1983; Walker, 1984). Although race and socioeconomic factors put unique stresses on an individual, studies to date have not indicated the effects these factors have on violence rates. It is known, however, that lower socioeconomic groups are more likely to turn to the criminal justice system, county hospital emergency rooms, and social service programs, where this problem is more likely to be identified and documented; persons of higher socioeconomic status are more likely to utilize private resources, where documentation and/or identification is less likely to occur (Sonkin, Martin, & Walker, 1985).

Male batterers typically minimize and deny their violent behavior (Ganley, 1981; Murphy, 1985; Pesner, 1985; Purdy & Nickle, 1981). The batterer may be so convinced that his story is correct that he may appear to be a very credible witness to a person unfamiliar with this problem. Psychological testing indicates that batterers frequently utilize denial and intellectualization as defense mechanisms (Sonkin, Martin, & Walker, 1985). The denial and minimization may be a result of his embarrassment or shame; it may be a result of confabulation subsequent to an alcoholic- or drug-related incident; it may simply be a result of his desire to escape criminal culpability. Batterers who became violent while in a state of rage may genuinely not remember the details of their acts later. The victim, on the other hand, is likely to remember details because she must be extremely vigilant during a battering incident in order to minimize injury to her or children involved. In describing a violent incident a batterer may seem controlled, calm, and quite believable. On the other hand, the victim may be agitated, defensive, depressed, timid, or inconsistent, rendering her testimony somewhat questionable.

Male batterers externalize their behaviors (Ganley, 1981; Pesner, 1985; Saunders, 1982; Sonkin, Martin, & Walker, 1985). They will attribute the cause of their actions to the victim's provocation. This is evident when a defendant is asked to describe a violent incident. Typically, he will describe what the victim did rather than what he did to her. In his testimony he will portray himself as an innocent bystander who was forced to overreact because of her provocation. A male batterer will frequently tell his partner that she is the cause of his anger and subsequent violence. His partner will accept the blame and believe that she has somehow caused his violence. The prosecuting attorney has to direct the defendant's testimony in such a way that he is forced to describe what *he* did during the incident in question.

The concept of provocation is a sensitive issue to discuss in court because many people have biases about the nagging, provocative wife who deserves to be slapped around. It is essential that jurors in particular realize that even if a woman displays undesirable behaviors, she does not deserve to be victimized.

In addition, those undesirable behaviors may be a direct result of his violence (Rosewater, 1985, Chapter 6 of this text).

Alcohol and drug abuse are frequently found in concert with domestic violence (Browne, 1983; Gelles, 1974; Rosenbaum, 1979; Sonkin, 1985; Straus et al., 1980; Walker, 1984). Male batterers may utilize alcohol or other drugs as a way to manage the emotional stress that they are unable to control otherwise. Some men are only violent while under the influence, while others may be violent both while under the influence and when sober (Ganley, 1981; Sonkin, Martin, & Walker, 1985). Alcohol and/or drug use may be utilized by the defense as a mitigating factor in murder (Gutheil & Applebaum, 1982) or as a means to deny intent in general-intent crimes. However, such information may also be utilized by the prosecution as corroborating evidence that a defendant may in fact be characteristic of men who batter. In California, the Victim's Bill of Rights was enacted into law in 1983. This law removed the diminished capacity defense from the penal code (Calfornia Penal Code, Section 28.). The new law stated:

> The defense of diminished capacity is hereby abolished. In a criminal action, as well as any juvenile court proceeding, evidence concerning an accused person's intoxication, trauma, mental illness, disease, or defect shall not be admissible to show or negate capacity to form the particular purpose, intent, motive, malice aforethought, knowledge, or other mental state required for the commission of the crime charged. (California Penal Code, Section 25a)

However, one can still cite diminished capacity as a mitigating circumstance during sentencing (California Penal Code, Section 25c).

Some men will claim that they were in a black-out at the time of the incident. Alcoholic black-outs are difficult to disprove or substantiate. Extensive psychological and medical testing could possibly document the degree of body damage as a result of alcoholism, thereby suggesting that black-outs are possible. This fact will be further examined when discussing intent.

Research has shown a correlation of battering with a history of violence in childhood (Cesear, 1985; San Francisco Family Violence Project, 1982; Straus, Gelles, & Steinmetz, 1980; Walker, 1984). A defendant's history of violence in his childhood or in previous relationships can be further evidence that corroborates his current battering behavior. Social learning theorists (Bandura, 1973) note that a child who observes or directly experiences violence is more likely to incorporate those behaviors into his repertoire than the child who has not had these experiences. Psychologists studying the prediction of violence agree that the best predictor of future violence is past behavior (Monahan, 1981). Therefore, a person who has an already established pattern of woman beating or child abuse is likely to continue such abuse unless there is some intervention, such as criminal justice sanctions and/or treatment. These interventions, however, do not preclude the man from re-offending. Informal studies indicate as many as 25 percent of men in treatment for their violence will re-offend during the course of that treatment (Halpern, 1983; McNeill, Chapter 11 of this text; Sonkin, 1985, 1986).

Many batterers are dependent on their partner. Battered women interviewed describe their partners as being extremely possessive and jealous (Walker, 1979, 1984). Many battered women describe their partners as suspicious to the point of severely curtailing their freedom to participate in out-of-home activities. Although the men see these characteristics as signs of caring and love, the victims experience them as controlling, intimidating, and abusive.

Many batterers hold traditional sex-role attitudes (Adams & McCormick, 1982; Martin, 1981; Walker, 1984), have poor communication skills (Sonkin & Durphy, 1982), experience withdrawal during times of emotional stress (Sonkin, Chapter 10 of this text), demonstrate extremes of kindness and cruelty (Walker, 1979), are socially isolated (Murphy, 1985; Pesner, 1985; Searle, 1985), and are impulsive (Ganley, 1981). Attribution of these characteristics may be elicited from the victim, other family members, or other prosecution or defense witnesses. Typically the expert witness can interview a particular victim or other witness to piece together the characteristics of the defendant. In a homicide case, an evaluation of the available records as well as interviews with witnesses are necessary to conduct a psychological autopsy of the victim. Although these characteristics alone do not necessrily prove a particular defendant to be a murderer, they can, in conjunction with other evidence, strengthen the prosecution's case.

THE DOMESTIC VIOLENCE ASSAULT CASE

In most felony assault cases the issue of general intent puts the burden of proof on the state to prove that the offense charged was committed by the defendant. Frequently the defendant will deny the charge, leaving it up to the victim to give a convincing rendition of the incident and to the district attorney to present convincing evidence supporting the victim's claims. An expert witness can assist in several areas of such a case.

Unlike the district attorney's staff, the expert can spend considerable time with the victim discussing the details of her situation with her partner. During this interview the victim can become more comfortable discussing the facts of the case; this will subsequently increase her credibility on the witness stand. The expert can acquire additional information that may be helpful in the development of a case, such as the names of other persons who were aware of the violence and information about broken items, injuries from the current or previous battering incidents, and specific previous acts of violence and threats to kill. In addition, the victim can describe her assailant thus allowing the expert to testify as to whether the defendant fits the profile of the male batterer. The expert can also interview family members and any other witnesses to assist them in articulating information related to the defendant's violence and the victim's history of victimization and psychological characteristics. Essentially the expert, in his or her assessment, is determining whether the facts of the cases are consistent with the battered woman syndrome and the dynamics of battering relationships.

Case law varies from state to state as to when this testimony is permissible. The California Supreme Court has stated that in cases of sexual assault expert testmony is not admissible as evidence that a particular victim was suffering from rape trauma syndrome and therefore was raped [*People* v. *Bledsoe*, 366 3d. 236 (1984)]. Although the court did not deal specifically with the battered woman syndrome, that ruling may be generalized to include battered women. Depending on case law in each state, the expert may need to testify on rebuttal to address the defenses described below.

TYPICAL DEFENSES

Frequently the defense will portray the victim as being an evil, domineering and castrating woman. If done in a nonexaggerated manner, this powerful defense tactic will play into most people's personal biases against women in general and battered women in particular, eliciting a sympathetic response to the defendant from jurors and the bench. The expert needs to use this testimony as corroborating the battered woman syndrome assessment. For example, a defendant who describes his partner as an angry and depressed woman who does not contribute to the upkeep of the home is actually describing some of the most common characteristics of battered woman syndrome. The expert can thoroughly discuss how the woman develops these characteristics as a result of continuous battering.

In some cases the defense will assert that the defendant was a battered husband and was acting in self-defense. To date little research has been conducted on the battered husband. Although women do hit men, it is done more frequently in self-defense than when men assault women (Bende, 1980; Crimes of Violence, 1969; Jones, 1980). In addition, the injuries are much less serious than when women are victimized by men (Berk, Berk, Loseke, & Rauma, 1983). When women do assault men, unless it is done with a dangerous weapon, men will usually not experience the kind of fear that a woman will experience as a victim. If one were to determine that a man was, in fact, a battered husband, we would expect to find in him the same kind of characteristics present in the battered woman syndrome—the most important being fear, depression, post-traumatic stress syndrome (American Psychiatric Association, 1980), physical and psychological injuries, and learned helplessness (Seligman, 1975). A defense attorney could utilize this denfense quite successfully by playing upon the biases of the average juror (Thyfault, Bennett, & Hirschhorn, Chapter 4 of this text) mentioned earlier.

This type of defense may bring the victim's proclivity toward violence into question. As with other claims asserted by the defense, her violence may also corroborate with the battered woman syndrome. The expert who is familiar with the manifestations of this syndrome could present a cogent argument that the defendant's claims can be supportive of the state's case. In addition to expert testimony, the jury must use common sense to take into account the size and strength differential between the defendant and the victim to determine whether the defendant utilized reasonable force and or had the opportunity to retreat. Frequently, medical testimony can shed further light on the feasibility of self defense.

Some men who batter will initially claim that their violence was an accident. Specialists in the treatment of male batterers have observed that men are violent as a result of their need to control their partner (Ganley, 1981; Martin, 1981; Purdy & Nickle, 1981; Schechter, 1982; Sonkin, Martin, & Walker, 1985; Walker, 1979) and not as a result of lack of control. Accidents do happen and are most likely to occur when a particular act is novel to a person's experience or repertoire of behavioral responses. Like the alcoholic, drug abuser or career criminal, the batterer has developed a pattern of behaviors that he is aware of and may even feel remorse about, but he chooses to ignore this until he is ultimately forced to face the consequences via the criminal justice system.

In some situations, the defense may claim that the defendant was insane at the time of the offense. The burden of proof varies from state to state as to prove sanity or insanity (see California Penal Code, Section 1026). Both researchers and clinicians seem to agree that although male batterers have a variety of emotional or behavioral problems they could not be described as insane or unable to appreciate the consequences of their behaviors (Ganley, 1981, Chapter 9 of this text; Sonkin, Chapter 10 of this text; Straus et al., 1980; Walker, 1979, 1984). The primary cause of woman battering is a result of social conditioning (Straus, Gelles, & Steinmetz, 1980) and a learned response to anger, stress, and frustration (Ganley, 1981).

A defendant, in assault cases in particular, will often deny committing the charged offense. Like any not-guilty plea, the development of the case depends heavily on the credibility of the witness and the physical evidence. Utilizing an expert to conduct a thorough examination of the victim can be a first step in developing a convincing case for the state.

BATTERED WOMAN EVALUATION

A thorough battered woman assessment will include the use of psychological testing; examination of all available documents and reports; interviews with family members, friends, and probation officers; and an in-depth behavioral assessment of the victim. In assault cases, in which the victim is available, the strength of the testimony is greater than in homicide cases, in which the expert has to put together bits and pieces of interviews, evidence, and documents to create a coherent psychological and behavioral autopsy of the victim. When interviewing assault victims, the expert needs to operate on a number of levels at once. Most important, are the facts and her behavior consistent with battered woman syndrome? When taking a comprehensive history of violence, one is eliciting affect as well as related to victimization. Intense emotional outbursts may not be the way some battered women respond to relating their stories. Some women may be numb from the violence and relate their story in a monotone. While collecting data on the violence, one is also collecting, through behavioral observations, data on the woman's state of mind. One example of this was clearly illustrated during an interview with a battered woman who had shot and killed her husband. The defendant related stories of how the batterer would break down the doors in the house during battering incidents. After discussing a violent episode, someone walked into the attorney's office where I was conducting the interview without knocking on the door. The client quickly turned around and almost jumped off her seat when the door was abruptly opened. This is an example of the "exaggerated startle response" commonly found with persons suffering from post-traumatic stress disorder. Battered women show many of the characteristics of this disorder as a result of their traumatic victimization (Walker, 1984).

During the course of the interview the victim will be asked to relate the charged offense several times in order to establish consistency as well as additional details. Victims are not encouraged to confabulate or exaggerate the events. It is explained that lack of memory is common with women who have been battered (Walker, 1984). The interview may last anywhere from 6 to 10 hours. After an interview this long, a trained clinician will be easily able to detect inconsistencies in her story that indicate malingering. One common bias about the battered woman is that she is fabricating her story as retribution toward a husband who is threatening to leave her for another woman or who wants custody of the children. The jurors may not believe her because, if her story were true, how could she have stayed in the relationship? It is crucial to the expert's testimony to discuss how he or she assessed for malingering during the course of the assessment.

The information collected during the interview includes such content areas as alcohol and other drug use, history and types of violence, frequency of violence, history of injuries, previous criminal history, assaults on other family members, threats to kill, threats with weapons, use of weapons, suicide history (attempts and contemplations), violence outside the home, attitudes toward violence, life stresses and general physical and mental health. As each issue is elucidated the expert must be prepared to resond to each fact in a case, no matter how much it may appear to be initially incriminating. Even the most damaging evidence can be used to support the notion of the victim's being a battered woman, the defendant's being a batterer, and his guilt in the pending case.

As mentioned earlier, a thorough interview will include interviews with other family members, witnesses to violence, and other professionals involved with a case. Because of the time and expense involved in examining witnesses and giving court testimony, it may not be practical for the district attorney to use an expert witness in most misdemeanor and the less serious felony cases. Attorneys may want to use this option only in the most serious felonies or in cases in which the victim is either unavailable or reluctant to testify because of her fear of the defendant or injuries that impede her ability to articulate her experience clearly.

DOMESTIC VIOLENCE HOMICIDE CASES

The homicide case is complicated by two important factors. First, the element of specific intent frequently becomes of greater importance than the fact of whether the batterer actually killed his partner. Second, the victim is not available to elaborate on the domestic violence issue as it relates to the batterer's state of mind and intent. With regard to this second factor, the prosecution needs to determine immediately whether there are any mental health professionals or shelter workers who may have had discussions with the victim regarding past incidences of violence. Such a person may be a valuable asset to the prosecution. The role of the expert in a homicide case may be to address one or both of these issues and/or to rebut any assertion articulated by the defense, such as insanity, battered husband syndrome, and so forth.

The majority of men we have treated for domestic violence have stated that their assault was conscious and intended. Men will frequently state that they became violent in order to stop their partners from doing or saying something or as retribution or punishment for current or past acts. In few cases men have described themselves as "blacking-out" or "just seeing red." In the cases of alleged black-outs, the batterer was frequently under the influence of large amounts of alcohol and usually had a history of alcoholic blackouts. In a true alcoholic black-out, the memory is not likely to be retrieved; however the differential diagnosis of an alcoholic black-out and a person's repressing or denying the memory may be difficult to assess without the expert's directly interviewing the defendant.

Psychogenic amnesia (American Psychiatric Association, 1980) is the inability to recall important personal information, an inability not due to an organic mental disorder (e.g., alcoholic black-out). The defense may attempt to use a dissociation theory to prove innocence or as mitigating factor to the murder. Psychogenic amnesia may be localized, that is, the failure to recall all events occurring during a circumscribed period of time. Less common is selective amnesia, which is a failure to recall some but not all of the events during a circumscribed period of time. Least common are generalized amnesia, which is the inability to remember events during the entire course of one's life, and continuous amnesia, where the person cannot recall events subsequent to the traumatic event up to and including the present. Psychogenic amnesia does not imply that the person (at the time of the traumatic event) was not aware of his actions. The client could have had the ability to form the intent to commit the murder. As a result of committing the act, he may have experienced a sufficient amount of stress to cause a psychogenic amnesia. Memory loss is common for persons experiencing a stressful event. Hence, battered women frequently experience memory losses as a result of or subsequent to their victimization. Likewise, men who kill are likely to want to forget their actions but in time will retrieve such lost memories when the amnesia is not a result of organic factors.

As with premeditation, proof of malice may be equally difficult. As with their intention to be violent, most batterers have stated that they also intended to harm their partners. However, would a reasonable person expect that the violence committed could lead to an eventual death? Whether a person actually thinks of this possible consequence at the time of the murder is debatable. Many men who finally kill have made previous threats to kill and have been cognizant that they had the ability to commit such an act should they desire. At the least, they are aware that their violence could cause serious injuries. This awareness is similar to the alcoholic's ability to admit to himself, between drunks, how dangerous his drinking is to himself and others, but at the same time to do nothing to alter his drinking patterns. Men who batter are aware of the dangerousness of their violent behavior and its psychological impact on the victims. This knowledge is evident in the remorse that follows their violent outbursts as will as their ability in counseling to discuss the effects of their violence on their family.

The issue of control frequently arises within the context of treatment for male batterers. Some men will say that they were out of control as an attempt to deny responsibility for their violent behavior. However, when a man is asked why he did not kill his victim or why he stopped his violence during a particular incident, he will usually reply, "I wouldn't want to seriously hurt her or kill her." This statment implies that the batterer is aware of his violence at the time he is inflicting it and therefore has control of how and when he manifests it. Studies have shown that battered women are frequently beaten during pregnancy (Gelles, 1974) and that men will often deliberately direct their violence toward the unborn child (Walker, 1984). Victims of violence often state that a batterer will direct his violence toward unexposed parts of the body so that public detection is less likely to occur (Martin, 1981; Walker, 1979, 1984). The consistency of these statements with clinical observations lead one to believe that men do exercise control when they are violent toward their partners. The fact that men are culturally pre-scribed to fight (Bochnak, 1981; Martin, 1981; Sonkin & Durphy, 1982) is additional evidence that men are likely to use physical force as a result of a conscious intention to inflict injury onto another person.

When trying to prove malice aforethought, one must present other types of evidence in addition to expert testimony. History of battering (e.g., wit-nesses to violence, persons aware of the violence, etc.), insurance policies, property and child-custody settlements, sexual jealousy, separation, and divorce could all be indicators that a man would premeditate and malicious-ly murder his wife or lover.

A defense attorney may argue that a client killed in the heat of passion that resulted from an extremely stressful situation. Such a defense is more likely to be succesful in cases where the act is novel to a person's repertoire of be-havioral responses. For a man who has killed his partner and already has a history of violence, that violence can be said to be characteristic for him. This dynamic is different from that of the individual who has never been violent and who reaches a "breaking point" during a passionate moment. Likewise, the chronic alcoholic with a history of drunk driving or other alcohol-related offenses cannot claim that the alcohol was responsible for his actions. A manslaughter argument is perhaps more feasible in cases involving a defen-dant who has perpetrated no prior violence, given the discrepancy between the killing and past behavior.

Some theorists believe that the difference between the batterer who kills his partner and the one who only assaults is that the killer may be less famil-iar with violence or less aware of his own capabilities to cause harm either because of his lack of experience or being under the influence of alcohol or other drugs (Sonkin, Martin, & Walker, 1985). Involuntary manslaughter, or killing as a result of gross negligence, may be asserted by the defense in such a case. Life voluntary manslaughter, involuntary manslaughter may be likely in a case where the defendant has had less experience with violence. However, the experienced batterer is frequently responding to a conflict situation between him and his partner and will use his violence as a response to his inability to control her. In addition, in California, involuntary manslaughter occurs during the commission of either an unlawful act (not a felony) or a lawful act that may produce death in an unlawful manner or without due caution or circumspection. In most domestic violence homicides, the violence prior to the actual homicide is of a serious nature—that is, illegal and felonious—and therefore an involuntary manslaughter conviction may not be applicable to a particular case.

Certainly the issue of specific intent brings into focus complicated questions that must be addressed and answered in the determination of guilt. Given the fact that each case is ultimately decided by a jury based on the evidence presented, the prosecution has a duty to raise and respond to the issues relevant to domestic violence. The following section describes in detail a domestic violence homicide case where expert testimony was utilized by the prosecution. In this example (*State* v. *Dambouradjian*) the first author served as an expert witness and the second author tried the case as a deputy district attorney for the San Francisco District Attorney's Officer.

STATE V. DAMBOURADJIAN

The victim was married to the defendant for 14 years, during which time the defendant physically, sexually, and psychologically abused the victim. Approximately two years prior to the homicide, the victim separated from the defendant and filed for a divorce. It was discovered by her civil attorney that the victim had been forced to sign a quick claim deed to certain property and business assets during the course of the marriage. This quick claim deed gave those assets to the defendant upon divorce. During the separation the defendant was not violent toward the victim while he lived in an apartment below hers in the same building. The victim's 13-year-old daughter lived with her in the upper unit. A domestic violence expert was hired by the civil attorney to assess the relationship between the victim's being a battered woman and her signing this quick claim deed. It was determined during the course of the interview that the victim did sign this deed under duress and the undue influence of her husband. The expert was to testify in the property settlement hearing as to the dynamics of battered woman syndrome and its application to this case. Four weeks prior to the civil hearing the victim told a friend that the defendant told her that she would never live to see any of his property. Two weeks later, the victim brought some items over to his apartment, an argument ensued, and the defendant shot the victim. The daughter, who was in the upstairs apartment at the time, heard her mother yell and then the gun discharge. The police were called by the daughter; when they arrived they found the defendant standing over the victim's body stating he had killed his wife.

This case was actually tried twice. The first trial ended in a hung jury, with 10 of the 12 jurors voting for first-degree murder and 2 holding out for second-degree murder. In the first trial, no expert testimony regarding battered woman syndrome was elicited.

The second trial began much as the first; the prosecution stated its case, establishing time and cause of death and circumstances surrounding both. The victim had been repeatedly struck on the back of the head with what was believed to be the murder weapon, a 7.65 mm Barretta automatic pistol. She was then shot twelve times. It was necessary for the defendant to reload the pistol to continue shooting the victim. The defendant's statement of killing his wife, lack of any demonstrable remorse, absence of alcohol or other drugs in his system, and development of a motive all made up the prosescution's case.

Upon the resting of the direct evidence, the defense commenced its case. The defense case included elements of self-defense, black-out, and an irrational act committed in the heat of passion. The defendant again testified, but relied more on a theory of anger (heat of passion) and black-out that he did in the first trial. To this end, expert testimony of psychiatrists was brought forth. This included opinion testimony that the victim was a batterer and that the defendant suffered as a battered husband. This was totally inconsistent with the facts at hand and was the first time the prosecution has heard of such opinions.

The rebuttal case presented by the prosecution consisted entirely in educating the jurors about battered woman syndrome and in demonstrating the fact that the victim had been systematically battered by her husband, the defendant. Said evidence was elicited through the testimony of the first author.

Among other arguments brought forth by the defense was the objection to the expert's testimony, since he had no personal knowledge of the facts leading to the killing, and a general attack on the foundation of the battered woman syndrome.

It is totally unnecessary for an expert witness to have personal knowledge as a preliminary fact before that expert may offer an opinion on a subject beyond the common experience of the jurors. In California, under Evidence Code Section 801(b), expert opinion testimony may be based on matters perceived by or personally known to the witness or made known to him at or before the hearing. The California Supreme Court expressly held in *People v. Bassett*, 69 Cal.2d, 122 fn. 22 at 146 that expert psychiatric opinion is not inadmissible merely because the expert had not made personal examination of the defendant.

Note in this regard that all three defense psychiatrists offered opinions about the victim's mental state at the time she was shot, based on 12-year-old hospital records, without ever having personally interviewed her in order to make a psychiatric diagnosis. Any deficiency caused by not having interviewed the defendant went to the weight of the doctor's opinion, not its admissibility.

Next, the defense's claim concerning the lack of foundation for the battered woman syndrome raised a false issue. There was no dispute at trial as to the existence of this syndrome. Indeed, an expert witness called by the defense testified as to its existence and characteristics. This syndrome, it was testified to, has been known and used within the psychiatric community since at least 1977. The defense psychiatrist was familiar with some of the extensive literature on the subject. There having been no conflict in the facts about the existence of the battered woman syndrome, the defense was hardly in a position to contend that there was some question about the admissibility of testimony on this subject.

The admission of expert testimony rests within the sound discretion of the trial court. Such expert testimony is not inadmissible merely because it coincides with the ultimate issue of fact that the jury must determine. The expert's qualifications as a psychologist specializing in the area of treatment battered women, male batterers, and battered children were fully explored. As a practicing psychotherapist, his primary focus was spousal abuse. He had written a book for men who batter and was in the process of co-authoring another book for therapists who treat this problem. Contrary to the impression sought to be conveyed by the defense that the expert had no experience in dealing with men who batter, this was one of the doctor's specific areas of expertise. Most importantly to this case and his testimony, he had consulted with the victim on a professional basis related to her pending civil case. The claim that this expert witness could not offer an opinion about the mental state of the victim's husband because he lacked sufficient expertise was devoid of merit. In this context, it must be remembered that the victim had predicted her own killing by the defendant by means of a gun, in her interview with the expert, some five months before he actually shot her. The foundation for the conclusion that the defendant premeditated the killing was thus firmly established by the evidence upon which the doctor relied.

The expert testified in rebuttal to the defense psychiatric expert testimony that the defendant was suffering from battered husband syndrome, feeling emotionally abused by a violent, mentally disturbed, castrating wife. The testimony essentially articulated that the victim was a battered woman and the defendant was a batterer. The expert described battered woman syndrome and the psychological characteristics of male batterers and offered the opinion that the victim was suffering from this syndrome at the time of his interview with her five months prior to her death. He also testified that the defendant was a batterer and had made prior threats to kill the victim; one in particular when he pointed a loaded gun at her and verbally threatened to kill her should she leave his presence at that time. Included in his testimony were a description of a number of prior violent acts perpetrated by the defendant toward the victim during the course of their marriage.

Psychiatric records admitted into evidence by the defense described the victim as a schizophrenic. The defense attempted to utilize these records to support its claims that the victim was mentally disturbed and abusive toward the defendant. In an examination of the records the expert was able to determine that no assessment was made at the time of her admission to the hospital as to whether she was a battered woman. This hospital admission was made during the mid- to late 1960s when the issue of domestic violence was not being addressed by the mental health community; therefore many battered women were misdiagnosed as being psychotic when in fact the origin of their psychological disturbance was not endogenous but a direct result of their being battered by their partner. The expert was able to explain this phenomenon in light of what is now known about the battered woman syndrome. The expert was also able to point out specific entries in the patient's record that were suggestive of her suffering from battered woman syndrome and not schizophrenia.

The thrust of the expert's testimony was to utilize what the defense had testified as to the victim's character and use those opinions, descriptions, and characterizations to support the notion that the victim was a battered woman, the defendant a batterer, and that woman battering in its least and most serious forms is frequently a premeditated and malicious act perpetrated by male batterers.

The defendant was found guilty of first-degree murder and sentenced to 25 years to life. The case was later appealed on several grounds but for the purposes of this chapter we limit our discussion to issues of the expert testimony.

Appellant attacked the expert testimony under the theory that (1) the expert was not qualified, (2) the expert lacked a proper foundational basis to conclude that the defendant was a batterer, and (3) the expert improperly concluded that the killing was premeditated.

The appelate court sumarily rejected all of the above arguments. It found ample evidence within the record of the expert's educational expertise in the field of domestic violence generally and "battered wife syndrome" specifically.

The court also concluded that the doctor had ample evidence to support his conclusion that the defendant was a batterer and that the killing was premeditated. Even though he never interviewed the defendant, his familiarity with the victim, his knowledge of the field of domestic violence, and his review of the defense psychiatric reports all contributed to his ability to render an opinion. The court concluded:

> given [the expert's] extensive experience treating perpetrators of domestic violence, his familiarity with [the victim], and his familiarity with the testimony and reports of defense psychiatrists, we conclude that [the expert] was qualified to render an opinion on appellant's mental state of mind as it existed at the time of the killing, and that this opinion was based on adequate factual foundation. Any deficiency in the foundation for [the expert's] opinion went to the weight of his testimony, not its admissibility.

IN CONCLUSION

Although the evidence presented by the state and the defendant's testimony weighed heavily in the jury's ultimate decision, the expert testimony did play a crucial role in the rebuttal of defense expert testimony. Likewise in other cases such as *State of Kansas* v. *Harmon* (Pigg, 1984) and *State of New Hampshire* v. *Baker*, N.H. 424 Atlantic Rep., 2d Series 171, an expert was utilized to rebut a denial of domestic violence and an accident theory in the former and the assertion of insanity in the latter.

Today, very few prosecutors are utilizing the expert witness to assure the prosecution of men who assault or kill their partner. This is in part a result of the attitudes of many prosecuting attorneys that domestic violence is not as serious an offense as other types of crimes, as well as their lack of knowledge as to the dynamics of domestic violence situations. This lack of understanding makes it more difficult effectively to try a case involving family violence. Prosecuting attorneys are now receiving training on how to respond effectively to the unique intricacies of sexual assault, child physical abuse, and child sexual abuse cases. Likewise, special prosecution teams are being developed in district attorney's offices across the country (San Francisco Family Violence Project, 1982; Soler, Chapter 2 of this text) to address the specific needs of victims of woman battering.

The general public still lacks a thorough understandig of the issue of domestic violence. Although the public is experiencing greater exposure to this issue through newspapers, magazines, television, and the movies, there still exist misconceptions and biases that would affect jurors in making an informed decision regarding the guilt of a particular defendant. Until such time that the issue of domestic violence is a part of the general public's awareness and understanding, there will continue to be a need for such expert testimony in the criminal prosecution of men who batter.

REFERENCES

Adams, D.C., & McCormick, A.J. (1982). Men unlearning violence: A group approach. Based on the collective model. In M. Roy (Ed.), *The abusing partner: An analysis of domestic battering*. New York: Van Nostrand Reinhold.

American Psychiatric Association (1980). *Diagnostic and statistical manual of mental disorders* (3rd ed.). Washington, DC: Author.

Attorney General's Task Force on Family Violence. (1984). *Final report*. Washington, DC: Department of Justice.

Bandura, A. (1973). *Aggression: A social learning analysis*. Englewood Cliffs, NJ: Prentice-Hall.

Bende, P.D. (1980). Prosecuting women who use force in self-defense: Investigative considerations. Peace Officers Law Report (Newsletter), California Department of Justice, December, 8–14.

Berk, R., Berk, S.F., Loeske, D., & Rauma, D. (1983). Mutual combat and other family violence myths. In D. Finkelhor, R. Gelles, G. Hotaling, & M. Straus (Eds.), *The dark side of families*. Beverly Hills: Sage Publications.

Bochnak, E. (1981). *Women's self-defense cases: Theory and practice*. Charlottesville, VA: The Michie Company Law Publishers.

Boffey, P.M. (1983, April 6). Arrests advised in domestic disputes. *Oakland Tribune*.

Boudouis, J. (1971). Homicide in the family. *Journal of Marriage and the Family, 33*, 667–676.

Browne, A (1983). *When battered women kill*. Unpublished doctoral dissertation, University of Experimentaing Colleges and Universities, Cincinnati, OH.

Browne, A. (1986). Assault and homicide at home: When battered women kill. In M.J. Sakes & L. Saxe (Eds.), *Advances in Applied Social Psychology: Vol. 3*. Hillsdale, NJ: Erlbaum.

Ceasar, P. (1986). *The wife beater: Personality and psychosocial characteristics*. Unpublished doctoral dissertation. California School of Professional Psychology, Berkeley, CA.

Chimbos, P.D. (1978). *Marital violence: A study of interspousal homicide*. San Francisco: R & E Research Associates.

Crimes of violence. (1969). A staff report to the National Commission on the Causes and Prevention of Violence. Washington, DC: U.S. Government Printing Office.

Deerings California Penal Code (1983). San Francisco: Bancroft-Whitney.

Fagan, J.A., Stewart, D.K., & Hansen, K.V. (1983). Violent men or violent husbands? In D. Finkelhor, R.J. Gelles, G.T. Hotaling, & M.A. Straus (Eds.), *The dark side of families: Current family violence research*. Beverly Hills: Sage.

Ganley, A.L. (1981). *Court mandated counseling for men who batter (participants' and trainer's manuals)*. Washington, DC: Center for Women's Policy Studies.

Gelles, R.J. (1974). *The violent home*. Beverly Hills: Sage Publications.

Giles-Sims, J. (1983). *Wife battering: A systems theory approach*. New York: Guilford.

Gutheil, T.G., & Appelbaum, P.S. (1982). *Clinical handbook of psychiatry and the law*. New York: McGraw-Hill.

Halpern, M. (1983, August). *The male batterer: The BWA program*. Paper presented as the 91st Annual Convention of the American Psychological Association, Anaheim, CA.

Jones, A. (1980). *Women who kill*. New York: Holt, Rinehart & Winston.

Martin, D. (1981) (rev. ed.). *Battered wives*. San Francisco: Volcano Press.

Monahan, J. (1981). *Predicting violent behavior: An assessment of clinical techniques*. Beverly Hills: Sage Publications.

Murphy, W. (1985, August). Transference and countertransference: Working with anger and violence. Paper presented at the 93rd Annual Convention of the American Psychological Association, Los Angeles, CA.

National District Attorneys Association (1978). *The victim advocate*. Chicago: Author.

Pesner, J. (1985, August). *Psychologist as cop*. Paper presented at the 93rd Annual Convention of the American Psychological Association, Los Angeles, CA.

Pigg, S. (1984, January 13). Statements of three expert witnesses conclude testimony in murder trial. Topeka, Kansas, *The Capital Journal*.

Purdy, F., & Nickle, N. (1981). Practice principles for working with groups of men who batter. *Social Work with Group*, 4, 111–122.

Rosenbaum, A. (1979). Wife abuse: Characteristics of the participants and etiological considerations (Doctoral dissertation). *Dissertation Abstracts International*, 40, 1383–1388.

Rosewater, L.B. (1985). Schizophrenic, borderline or battered. In L.B. Rosewater & L.E. Walker (Eds.), Handbook of feminist therapy: Women's issues in psychotherapy. New York: Springer Publishing.

San Francisco Family Violence Project. (1982). *Domestic violence is a crime*. San Francisco: Author.

Saunders, D. (1982). Counseling the violent husband. In P.A. Keller & L.G. Ritt (Eds.), *Innovations in clinical practice: A source book* (Vol. 1). Sarasota, FL: Professional Resource Exchange.

Schechter, S. (1982). *Women and male violence*. Boston: South End.

Searle, M. (1985). Introduction. In D.J. Sonkin, D. Martin, & L.E.A. Walker, *The male batterer: A treatment approach*. New York: Springer Publishing Co.

Seligman M.E.P. (1975). *Helplessness: On depression, development and death*. San Francisco: W.H. Freeman.

Sonkin, D.J. (1986). Clairvoyance vs. common sense: Therapist's duty to warn and protect. *Violence and Victims*, 1(1), 7–21.

Sonkin, D.J. (1985). *Final report: Domestic violence treatment program*. Oakland, CA: United States Navy, Oak Knoll Hospital.

Sonkin, D., & Durphy, M. (1982). *Learning to live without violence: A handbook for men*. San Francisco: Volcano.

Sonkin, D.J., Martin, D., & Walker, L.E.A. (1985). *The male batterer: A treatment approach*. New York: Springer Publishing Co.

Star, B. (1978). Comparing battered and non-battered women. *Victimology: An International Journal*, 3, 32–44

Stephens, D.W. (1977). Domestic assault: The police response. In M. Roy (Ed.), *Battered women: A psychosocial study of domestic violence*. New York: Van Nostrand Reinhold.

Straus, M.A., Gelles, R.J. & Steinmetz, S.K. (1980). *Behind closed doors: Violence in the American family*. New York: Anchor-Doubleday.

Thyfault, R. (1984). Self-defense: Battered women on trial. *California Law Review*, 20, 480–510.

Walker, L.E.A. (1979). *The battered woman*. New York: Harper & Row.

Walker, L.E.A. (1984). *The battered woman syndrome*. New York: Springer Publishing Co.

Walker, L.E.A. (1985). Feminist forensic psychology. In L.B. Rosewater and L.E.A. Walker (Eds.), *Handbook of feminist therapy: Women's issues in psychotherapy*. New York: Springer Publishing Co.

Epilogue

Justice-Making in the Aftermath of Woman-Battering

Marie M. Fortune

A hundred years ago among the Tlingit people living in what is now southeast Alaska, there was a belief that one should not beat one's wife. If ever a husband deviated from this norm and beat his wife, his clan was required to pay her clan in material goods. The whole community came together for a potlatch to exchange the goods. The whole community knew why they were there. Wife-beating was expensive; wife-beating was shameful. There was very little wife-beating among the Tlingit people a hundred years ago.

Discussions about the legal system and its response to battered women frequently focus on the particulars of intervention (temporary restraining orders, arrest/prosecution/conviction/sentencing of abusers, etc.)and seldom are set in a larger context of their overall purpose. Hence our impressions and assumptions about the legal system are often lost in considerations of its minutiae, and seldom do we have the opportunity to reflect on their reason for being. This chapter will present a process of "justice-making" as a part of our collective discussion of the roles of the legal system, social services, religious institutions, and mental health services as they relate to the needs of battered women. Justice-making will be presented here as an ethical process, but one with clear therapeutic and judicial implications. The opening question will be: What really is the purpose of our interventions to assist battered women? The answer, most fundamentally: To make justice where there has been profound injustice.

Justice will be discussed here as a therapeutic, ethical, judicial, and spiritual process. This discussion will not be an academic exercise, but rather will provide a framework of response for battered women and the men who abuse them. It will also provide a perspective for friends, shelter workers, therapists, pastors, prosecutors, and others who want to assist those who have been victims or victimizers.

A word about vocabulary: Some images, metaphors, and terms used in this chapter arise from Jewish and Christian religious traditions. These images are helpful in illustrating some of the aspects of justice and healing. These are not the only relevant sources but the ones most familiar to the author. These terms should enhance the discussion, not limit it. The term *survivor* is used for a specific purpose (drawing on the insights of the anti-incest movement). There is currently much discussion about terms to describe those persons who have experienced abuse and who are no longer being abused. *Victim* will be used to describe one who has been made powerless by the actions of another and thus harmed in some way. *Survivor* will be used to describe a former victim who is no longer being harmed by an abusive situation but who carries that as part of her history. Some use *formerly battered woman* in a similar way. In addition to being descriptive of the time frame of the abusive experience, however, *survivor* also connotes a condition of healing, empowerment, and, frequently, a proactive stance of choosing to no longer be victimized by the memory of abusive experiences. The term *justice* will not be used to refer to the legal system and its processes per se. Instead, *justice* will be used to describe a context in which persons seek (1) to provide for the needs of one who has been made a victim by an abuser, (2) to empower former victims, (3) to prevent the abuser from continuing to harm others, and (4) to create right relationship. *Reconciliation* will refer to the process of restoring relationship on some level. It refers to a very basic level of restoration of one person to another in a very different context from the earlier one: a context in which the formerly battered woman need not feel fear and the former abuser no longer exercises power over her. It is the establishment of right relationship. *Reconciliation* does not imply intimacy: It does not necessarily mean the survivor's going back to the marriage, nor does it mean her automatically trusting the abuser again.

In order to address the possibilities of justice-making, we begin with an ethical analysis of woman battering; from this analysis we can shape the actions that can make for justice.

✓   Why is the abuse of women in their intimate relationships wrong? This may seem like a superfluous discussion, because it is simply wrong. And yet it is important to maintain clarity about why it is wrong in order to provide an ethical analysis of this injustice that can then help direct our response to it.

Woman battering is wrong because it causes physical and psychological injury to a human being. These injuries render a person powerless in the face of the battering and deny her right to privacy, safety, self-determination, and freedom of movement. It is also wrong because it reflects and reinforces the brokenness of the abuser. His misuse of power to coerce, harm, or otherwise injure his partner comes from his brokenness and causes brokenness in others.

Wife battering is wrong because it fractures relationships. The brokenness of relationship that results from violence and abuse is manifest in betrayal, loss of trust, and loss of intimacy between the victim and abuser, as well as in a diminishing of the possibility of future intimacy in any relationship. The battering also breaks the victim's relationship with the community (friends, employer, co-workers, neighbors, etc.), frequently by cutting her off from it. Friends and family withdraw because of their anxiety and fear. Sometimes her isolation is reinforced by her shame and guilt.

In summary, woman battering violates the right relation that should exist between a woman and her partner, right relation meaning a relationship based on trust, respect, safety, mutuality of power, and protection of those vulnerable due to life circumstance. The violation of right relation is the essence of injustice or, as theologian and priest, Carter Heyward, suggests, evil:

> Where there is no moral act of love, no justice, there is an evil situation. Evil is an act, not a metaphysical principle or a passive absence of good. Evil is the act of unlove or in-justice. It is the doing of moral wrong, specifically of breaking the relational bond between and among ourselves in such a way that one, both, or many parties are disempowered to grow, love, and/or live. (Heyward, 1982)

The injustice of woman battering is the brokenness done to body and spirit and to relationships.

Justice, understood as what is right, fair, and deserved, refers to the healing of the brokenness and assurance of future protection from this violence. Justice is made when the victim feels empowered and whole again, when the situation has been made right or whole again (as much as possible), and when her well-being is assured (as much as possible). Justice is made when the offender has been made whole by being called to account for the damage he has caused, acknowledging his responsibility for it, and changing his behavior so that it is not repeated.

Justice is not a word we use comfortably. Because it is a word that seems to have lost meaning, we seldom use it. The word has always referred to what is fair, right, deserved. Perhaps our hope of achieving what is fair, right, and deserved for those who have historically been denied it has waned and, in our cynicism, we no longer even envision justice as a possibility. Or perhaps we have passed responsibility for justice-making directly to the "justice" system. If it does not happen there (and it frequently does not), it will not happen at all. Yet we long for justice. In our anger at what we see being done to women, in our own experiences of violence, in our frustration in working with a victim who wants to "forgive and forget," in our despair in working with a woman of color who is unwilling to use the legal system because it has never protected her before, in our feelings of powerlessness when we see batterers go from one abusive relationship to the next—in all of these situations, we long for justice. But it is a longing unfulfilled, a vision we have come to accept as impossible.

In the midst of these feelings, I am convinced that we actually long for healing, for restoration, for reconciliation. We use words like *justice* and *forgiveness* in hopes that these are means to accomplish that for which we long. We long for healing from the very depths of our being, not expecting that everything will be fine or just like it was before, but that it will be made right in some way, that the brokenness that resulted from the acts of abuse will somehow be made whole. This is what we long for whether we are victim, friend, helper, or abuser. We long to be made whole again. The approach of this chapter clearly betrays a bias that some experience of justice is necessary in order for healing to take place, in order for a victim to become a survivor, which is our ultimate goal in responding to battered women.

Before we consider the substance of justice-making, it is important to keep in mind what justice-making is not:

- it is not revenge and punishment for the sake of hurting the other person, which often produces bitterness but seldom enables change
- it is not accomplished by encouraging someone to forget about it ("it's probably better to just try not to think about it; he's promised not to do it again")
- it is not accomplished by minimizing the seriousness of the abuse ("he didn't mean to hurt you")
- it is not a collective denial of the reality of the violence by friends, professionals, one's religious community, family members, and others
- it is not accomplished by premature reconciliation, what the prophet Jeremiah called "healing the wound of my people lightly, saying, 'peace, peace' where there is no peace."

There can be no authentic reconciliation without justice. None of these things will suffice when what is needed is justice.

Justice-making begins with truth-telling. A context must be prepared into which the truth is told by a victim. Her story then has broken the silence of her suffering; someone else has heard and believes her experience. The facts may be muddled and confused, but no matter. The truth is the reality that person experienced of being exploited, victimized, and terrorized. That reality needs affirmation and validation from someone else—friend, counselor, police officer, pastor/priest/rabbi, the community. The power of the secret needs to be broken wherever and whenever possible by truth-telling. The abuser should not be protected from the consequences of his violence by privacy or confidentiality. The beginning of justice-making is to hear and believe and to do so in the context of some part of the wider community.

Shelters provide a place of truth-telling in our communities. They are a place where a woman finds, in addition to physical safety, other people who know on a very profound level what she has experienced. Here her experience is confirmed. Community-based support groups provide similar occasions for truth-telling. The presence of both of these help to tell the truth to the community. Because of the presence of shelters, we can no longer pretend not to know that there are battered women among us. Court responses to cases of self-defense where battered women have killed their abusers is another opportunity for truth-telling and justice-making. For a battered woman who killed in self-defense to be heard, believed, and vindicated by the court on behalf of the community is for us to be able to hear the truth of her experience and of her action in the face of it.

Justice-making also means confronting the one responsible for the abuse: The batterer must be called to account for his violence. Rarely is it possible for a victim to accomplish this alone (except indirectly, by leaving and being absent from the home). Alone she is at great risk, and we cannot expect her to be the one to challenge her abuser's violence directly. This is the responsibility of the community and its representatives. One initial confrontation can come from the legal system. This can be an effective way to communicate clearly, forcefully, and unequivocally that the violence is his responsibility and must stop. But the abuser needs to hear this message consistently from various sources: his pastor/priest/rabbi, his lawyer, his peers, his employer, and other family members. The legal system can use prosecution and conviction as leverage to motivate him to change his behavior and thus end his abusive patterns. However, unless this clear message is reiterated by other significant figures in his life, he may continue minimizing or avoiding its importance and implications.

When he is confronted, it is preferable that the abuser admit to his violent behavior, acknowledge the damage it has done, express remorse, and seek repentance. Frequently, an abuser will go through this series of responses but stop with remorse. The remorse may be genuine. But when remorse is accepted by the abuser, victim, or others as adequate to end the abuse, it usually insures that the cycle of battering will be repeated. The abuser who has been arrested for assault and then goes to his pastor with requests for forgiveness and promises of never hitting again too often is convincing in his remorse but unwilling to put forth the effort to change. Without such effort, he will continue to be abusive.

Repentance is the crucial stage of the abuser's response that we must insure. *Repentance* means to turn around, to turn away from past behavior and not repeat it, to change one's way of being in the world on a fundamental level. Genuine repentance offers assurance that the behavior will not recur. This step is seldom possible without some form of rehabilitative intervention and clear monitoring of change. (This is also important in order to assure protection of the survivor(s).) The religious adviser, rather than handing out "cheap grace" or "quick forgiveness" in response to the abuser's remorse, should use her/his authority to hold the abuser accountable and press him into a rehabilitative program. Only this will make his repentance possible.

Restitution is another possible justice-making response by the abuser and can be part of the rehabilitative process. Restitution is a concrete act by which an abuser makes payment for damages done to the victim, e.g., medical expenses, shelter costs, counseling expenses, or repair of property. This is both an immediate, practical need for the victim and her children and a means of making concrete the repentance of the abuser. It serves the needs of both victim and abuser in the process of making justice.

Calling the abuser to account is, for the survivor, a way of taking back control over her life and a way of protecting herself (and her children) from further violence. It empowers her and the community to disallow his violence. For the abuser, it is a way for him to deal with the consequences of his violence, to have the opportunity to be reconciled to right relationship, and to help heal what he has broken.

It is not vengeful to seek justice, to confront the abuser, or to expect repentance. It is not punitive to expect restitution from someone who harmed another and thereby created serious financial as well as physical and emotional difficulties. Yet sometimes victims (and particularly Christian women) and the community as a whole hesitate to confront, to use any system to hold an abuser accountable, because they see this as being vindictive. Victims/survivors may also fear being further ostracized from their faith community if they take action on their own behalf. Rarely do they feel vengeful; they simply want the abuse to stop. Many want their relationship to continue, but without the abuse. They fear that seeking justice will mean losing everything. What they overlook is that seeking justice holds the only possibility of restoration of their relationship.

These acts of justice-making create a potential for healing but do not guarantee its occurrence. Justice-making for a victim breaks through her isolation, affirms for her that what she has experienced is wrong and is not her fault, and affirms this on behalf of the whole community. In this process, we collectively stand with her as well as on her behalf in naming the evil of woman battering and in placing responsibility for it on the abuser. We say that this is not only an evil done against her but an evil done against the community; not only is her intimate relationship broken by the violence, so, too, are her relationships with the community as a whole. Justice-making creates for her an awareness that her pain is heard, believed, and felt by us collectively. She is not alone anymore.

Once these first steps of justice-making have been taken, there is then potential for considering forgiveness as an option, for possibly seeking reconciliation, for healing to take place. But forgiveness cannot take place without justice, and healing cannot begin without forgiveness. A victim cannot become a survivor without healing.

Forgiveness does not pardon the abuse. It is not carried out by the victim in a vacuum as a way of saying that what was done is acceptable and past. The abuse is never acceptable.

Forgiveness does not deny the abuse. It does not serve as a pretense that nothing of significance really occurred.

Forgiveness does not excuse the abuse. It does not offer an explanation or rationalization for what occurred. It does not relieve the abuser of his responsibility.

Forgiveness does not forget the pain of the abuse. "Forgive and forget" is not only bad advice, it is impossible to accomplish. These experiences of violence are unforgettable. They become part of a person's history, always present in memory.

Forgiveness does not deny the anger that was a legitimate response to the abuse. At some point in the healing process, anger is the legitimate, healthy response to being victimized. It can provide the energy needed to act to protect oneself or others from further abuse.

Forgiveness does not supersede confrontation of the abuser. Confronting the abuser as described above is an act of justice and a necessary prerequisite for forgiveness.

Forgiveness does not automatically guarantee reconciliation or trust between the former abuser and the survivor. Trust may be the very last thing that can be rebuilt between these persons. In fact, unearned trust of the abuser may be dangerous for the victim and should be avoided.

Forgiveness is for the well-being of the victim on the way to becoming a survivor. It is letting-go of the immediacy of the wounds and moving beyond the anger and bitterness they caused so that they do not continue to victimize her into the future. It is being unburdened from the experience so as to be able to get on with one's life. Forgiveness happens when the victim is ready, not at the behest of those of us who surround her. It is possible for her when she has experienced some sense of justice. Realistically, she may not receive all of the just responses she deserves, as discussed above. Certainly there is no guarantee of a just response from the abuser. She may only experience the justice of her truth being heard and affirmed. Yet this may be sufficient for her to forgive, to continue her healing process, and to refuse to be further victimized by the memories as she seeks to become whole again. Once she feels empowered, she will no longer feel controlled by the actions of the abuser. Forgiving then means to disallow the power of her abuser in her life.

Once forgiveness is experienced by the survivor, there is possibility for reconciliation. If the preliminary stages of justice-making have been actualized—that is, if there has been truth-telling that has made the victimization public, if the abuser has been called to account and has repented, if the victim/survivor feels ready to forgive—then reconciliation may be approached with great care. Reconciliation at this stage is an attempt to make whole that which was broken, to establish right relationship where there was none. This does not mean that the scars will disappear: it only means that the wounds will heal and the scars will remain.

Reconciliation therefore means that the survivor and former abuser no longer relate to each other as victim and abuser. The survivor is not powerless; the abuser is not overpowering and coercive. The survivor need not be fearful. Battering is no longer an option for the former abuser as he relates to the survivor. In this context, the survivor and former abuser *may* choose to renew an intimate relationship. Many formerly battered women desire to renew their relationships. For them, reconciliation takes this specific form. Others never want to be in intimate relationship with their former abuser again; for them reconciliation may mean clearly ending that relationship while being assured that their former abuser will not continue to pursue and harass them. This is particularly true for women who remain in the same community with their former abuser. To be reconciled is to be finished with that period of their lives. It is the choice of the individual woman to pursue the reconiliation that best meets her needs in becoming whole again. But the reality is that sometimes there can be no reconciliation because of the refusal of the abuser to repent. For this survivor, reconciliation will only be possible with her community.

Reconciliation also applies to the survivor's relationship to her community, a relationship that most likely was fractured by the abuse she experienced. Now that she is no longer a victim, she has the opportunity to renew these relationships, to discard shame or guilt, and to participate actively in the life of the community.

The former abuser who has gone through the process of justice-making now has the opportunity to reconcile his relationship with his community. The community knows of his abuse; it must also see the evidence of his repentance. Then he can begin to rebuild his relationships with peers, employers, his faith community, and so forth as one who has turned away from violence and coercion as a means of interaction with others.

If we begin with these aspects of justice-making as providing a necessary framework for a process of healing from victimization, then we must ask how we can carry out this process. How can we—as lay experts, professionals, friends, the wider community—help make justice? Whatever our particular role in response to a victim of woman battering or to an abuser, whatever institutional setting we occupy, we can help make justice.

The "justice system" itself, to whom the community has traditionally delegated this responsibility, presents us with a profound dilemma:

> To date, there is, unfortunately, only an unjust court system available to validate (1) the fact that a sexual or violent crime against a woman or child has occurred and (2) the role of the victimizer in that transgression. It is still a struggle to get the courts to do that much. While we must be relentless in our efforts to press the courts to deal fairly with all parties prior to conviction, the post-conviction period challenges our creativity. We are challenged to find ways to insure that the court places the victim's needs, the offender's needs, and the community's needs at the center of sentencing decisions. We must assure that justice is not measured by the amount of prison punishment or pain meted out to an offender to the neglect of the victim/survivor. Using an unjust, repressive structure to provide disempowered women with a sense that justice has been done gives power to a system that is set up to protect the status quo, fundamental to which is male violence against women. (Knopp, 1984)

In addition we must also acknowledge the institutional racism and sexism of the "justice system" in dealing with both victims and abusers.

Faced with the paradox that seemingly the only system we have with which to make justice does not in fact serve our interests as women leaves us feeling even more powerless in the face of male violence. Yet by and large as a community we abdicate our role and responsibility to help make justice when we delegate it to the "justice system" that we do not trust to carry out this task.

Given our desire for healing and wholeness and a vision of justice as a means to this end, given a system that is unquestionably racist, sexist, and classist, what strategy best serves our interests as women? It is this question that poses for us the larger context of the issues addressed by this book.

Our strategy must be multifocused. We could not simply abandon or ignore the "justice system" as it now functions, even if we wanted to. The number of battered women prosecuted and often convicted for self-defense makes this abundantly clear. We can work to make the "justice system" do its job: protect the vulnerable from the abuse and exploitation of the powerful. Our efforts in many states have made significant changes in statutes and procedures to respond to battered women, for example, elimination of the marital rape exemptions from sexual assault statutes. We should seek to serve the interests of all women, which means dealing always with issues of race and class, e.g., dealing with the implications of discriminatory mandatory arrest policies when the defendant or victim is of color.

Certainly the legal system has the means at its disposal to help make justice. Appropriately, it has been designated by the community as the primary (but not sole) mechanism by which to protect victims and hold abusers accountable. It has the authority and the mechanism to accomplish these things. Unfortunately, it has too often been inadequate to the task, primarily because it has chosen to overlook the truth of the victim's experience and remain uninvolved in domestic violence. New legislation and increased awareness within this system are changing its approach to woman battering.

But we should also not expect the "justice system" to be the only place where we might make justice. We have the responsibility to utilize other resources and mechanisms in the community to this end.

As discussed earlier, shelters provide a primary place and time for truth-telling for the victim. They also provide that which every woman and child deserves: safety. They communicate to her, on behalf of the community, that what has happened to her is undeserved and inexcusable and that she is no longer alone.

There are other means of providing this portion of justice-making for the victim. Her pastor/priest/rabbi can also provide the opportunity for truth-telling and can connect her to the community resources that can provide for her safety. Her faith community can also provide a safe place in which to tell the truth and receive support: It is a place where the silence can be broken on her behalf and where the abuser can also be called to account. It should not be a place where she is forced to return to a dangerous situation or made to feel obligated to "forgive and forget." Both of these responses deny her experience and suffering, deny the truth, and intentionally or unintentionally support the abuser's violence.

Therapists, counselors, lawyers, police officers, and physicians who encounter the battered woman in their work can also provide a context for truth-telling by giving her permission to share her experience of violence. Then they can assist her in placing that experience in the wider arena of the community by connecting her to the specialized resources that she needs, informing her of her legal options, and so forth.

Friends, family members, co-workers, neighbors, and others can also help make justice by the way in which they respond to victims of battering. Being willing to see and hear what is really going on and being available to the victim breaks through her isolation and supports her in making choices that can protect her from further abuse.

When any of these individuals or systems encounter the abuser, they can also begin the justice-making process. Acknowledging the truth of the abuse, they can immediately hold the abuser accountable, using any source of authority which they may have. They should avoid using their authority to protect the abuser from the consequences of his abusive behavior.

It is critical that the response to the victim or abuser from individuals and from institutions be consistent. This consistency not only makes it clear that the community collectively shares the responsibility for justice-making but also makes it possible to end the violence effectively and bring healing and reconciliation in some form.

Also key to a commitment to justice-making is a willingness to assert that there are not two sides to situations of abuse. It is to assert that someone has been made victim by the abuse of another: Someone is powerless in the face of the misuse of power. Our collective task is to intervene on behalf of the victims. This does not deny that most situations of woman abuse are complicated and confusing. It is not always clear what happened when. There may be two sides to every argument or conflict. The fair and just response to an argument or conflict is to hear both sides and negotiate a solution acceptable to both parties. But if it is clear that violence has been used to settle the argument, we have a situation that requires a different response. There are no longer two sides. There is a victim who needs advocacy and support; there is an abuser who needs to be held accountable. When the community as a whole responds, we are communicating to all involved a norm saying that interpersonal violence within family relationships is unacceptable and will not be tolerated.

Ultimately, justice will only be made in a context that challenges the fundamental arrangements of our social and familial order. Such a change will establish women's and children's status so as to preclude our availability as the most likely victims of violence in the home, as Carol Sparks has pointed out (cited in Knopp, 1984). Thus our "everyday" efforts to make justice for individual victims of woman battering must always take place concurrently with our efforts to make social change that will eventually end violence against women in all its forms.

As we combine our efforts to make justice in both the short and long term, we must remember that all of our efforts are grounded in truth-telling. Adrienne Rich in her superb essay on *Women and Honor* observes:

> Women have been driven mad, "gaslighted" for centuries by the refutation of our experience and our instincts in a culture which validates only male experience. The truth of our bodies and our minds has been mystified to us. We therefore have a primary obligation to each other: not to undermine each other's sense of reality for the sake of expediency; not to gaslight each other.
>
> Women have often felt insane when cleaving to the truth of our experience. Our future depends on the sanity of each of us, and we have a profound stake, beyond the personal, in the project of describing our reality as candidly and fully as we can to each other. (Rich, 1977)

And I would add, we have a profound stake in bearing that reality together as we seek to make justice in the midst of it.

The festering wound must be drained, the secret must be broken, the lie must be shown for what it is—justice must be made manifest—and then the wound can heal deeply and fully, the victim can become a survivor, the abuser can give up violence, we can be reconciled to one another. These are the fruits of justice.

REFERENCES

Heyward, C. (1982). *The redemption of God.* Washington, DC: University Press of America.
Knopp, F.H. (1984, May). *Toward community solutions to sexual violence:Feminist/abolitionist perspectives.* Paper presented to the Conference Toward Community Solutions to Sexual Violence, Toronto, Canada.
Rich, A. (1977). *Women and honor: Some notes on lying.* Pittsburgh: Motheroot Publications.

Index